CATCH ME
IF
YOU
CA

D1516953

KRAIG HANADEL

AVON BOOKS
An Imprint of HarperCollinsPublishers

CATCH ME IF YOU CAN is a journalistic account of the actual investigation and conviction of Dana Ewell for the 1992 murders of Dale, Glee, and Tiffany Ewell in Sacramento, California, written with the full cooperation of the detectives who broke the case. The events recounted in this book are true. Scenes and dialogue have been reconstructed based on formal interviews, law enforcement records, court transcripts, and published news stories. Quoted testimony and other court-related statements from before, during and after trial have been taken verbatim from transcripts.

AVON BOOKS
An Imprint of HarperCollins*Publishers*
10 East 53rd Street
New York, New York 10022-5299

First Avon Books paperback printing: May 2000

WCD   10   9   8   7   6   5   4   3   2   1

to the victims

Acknowledgments

SPECIAL THANKS TO THE FRESNO COUNTY Sheriff's Department and the District Attorney's office. I hope we slight none by singling out a few: Ernie Burk, Mindy Ybarra, Allen Boudreau, Dale Caudle, Richard White, Sheriff Steve Magarian (Ret.), Captain Ken Hoeve (Ret.), all the *Net* team, Ed Hunt, Jim Oppliger, and Jeff Hammerschmidt. "Members of both organizations were the real heroes of this story," said John Souza and Chris Curtice, "as were those with numerous agencies who assisted us without question, the others in the unit who took up the slack when we weren't around, and the superiors who believed in us and allowed us to pursue our ideas."

Also, for their support and assistance in the Ewell murders investigations above and beyond the call of duty, heartfelt gratitude to Sergeant Fred Armstrong (Ret.), Detective Joel Price, LAPD, Santa Clara University Campus Public Safety, the Ewell brothers, Susan Ewell, the late Austin Ewell, those Santa Clara University students who gave freely of vital information (you know who you are), California DMV investigator Jim Bolden, Detective Steve Mack of the Huntington Beach P.D., Helen Martell, Fabrice Allouche, Neil Camenker, Sherry House, Dana Rogers, Branch Meanley, Chuck Colburn, Merv Chapman,

Dave Johnson, Maria Terrell, Roy Bollinger, Cecil Cohenour, and the Ewell jury.

John Souza also wishes to thank "my wife, Sharon, and my sons, Johnny and Michael, for putting up with me during the stressful investigation and giving me the space I needed exactly when I needed it, and Chris, for being such a great partner."

Chris Curtice also wishes to thank "my family: Mom, Alison, Jon, Brian, and Jo, for your understanding during all the missed get-togethers and times when I wasn't around. And John—I can't think of a better partner or friend. You solved this case, no one else. I now have high standards by which to judge future partners. Although you're now retired, we'll have a friendship for the rest of our lives . . . and definitely something to talk about."

Thank you, everyone at Avon Books/Harper-Collins, especially Stephen Power, Bret Witter, Sara Schwager, and Krista Stroever.

For author's assistance, guidance, friendship and more, my gratitude to: Richard Ewell, John and Bobbie Winstead, Richard Moran, Ted "Theodore" Cheney, Glenna Goulet, B. J. Robbins, Billy Mitchell, Bret Bradigan, Maynard Peterson, all the friends who believed in me, and especially, the epiphany prince, Criminalist Mike Giberson, without whom this book would not, *could* not, have been possible.

To my family: siblings Keith, Kathy, Karen, Kim, my sons, and especially Mom and Dad and the lovely Susan, without whom I could not have made it to publication—this book means so much to me because I have all of you.

And finally, to any and all I neglected to mention, thank you.

K. P. H.

PROLOGUE

DALE EWELL, SELF-MADE MILLIONAIRE, TAXIED the twin-engine Beechcraft to a stop at the Watsonville, California, airport. He'd no sooner shut down the airplane and made for the lounge than he received a page from his Fresno office.

The quietly intense, six-foot-three-inch Ewell, his middle thickening with age but his shoulders mountainous, his eyes severe but startlingly blue, located a phone booth and dialed the number of Western Piper Sales, the airplane dealership of which he was sole owner. Bob Pursell answered. He was Ewell's top salesman, and his voice quivered with anger as he complained about his new contract.

Pursell and Ewell had been at odds over the salesman's income and retirement structure. When they'd finally come to terms increasing Pursell's commissions, Pursell had realized, too late, that his retirement benefits had been reduced.

Dale, son of a farmer, did not tolerate people who reneged on agreements—why didn't people nowadays do their homework before they signed, rather than blindly entering into a deal and seeking to back out of it after the fact?

He himself had had the discipline to earn a degree in aeronautical engineering, the fortitude to become an Air Force pilot, and the ambition to get himself off his father's

1

Ohio farm and into an aircraft dealership that would make him a wealthy man.

Ewell told Pursell that business would have to wait. It was Easter weekend, and he looked forward to spending a few quiet moments with his wife Glee, daughter Tiffany, and son Dana. And Dana was bringing his new girlfriend, Monica Zent, a classmate at Santa Clara University, and her parents to meet his family.

Dale eased into the aging Oldsmobile the family stored at the airport. His wife, heiress to an Oklahoma oil fortune, and their tall, blue-eyed daughter were waiting at the Pajaro Dunes beach house when he arrived ten minutes later.

They wandered along the beach and volleyed on the tennis courts. The next day, Dana and his girlfriend Monica arrived as promised.

Glee was trim and vivacious as always, her dark hair cropped short. She warmly welcomed Monica to her vacation home. Monica seemed quite a change from the flashy blondes Dana seemed to favor; she was plain, mousy brown, and maintained a grade-point average at Santa Clara that was nearly as high as Dana's.

Glee and Monica found much to talk about, and it seemed only minutes passed before Monica's parents rang the doorbell. John Zent and Dale Ewell sized each other up. The slim, blond, forty-six-year-old FBI Special Agent and the burly, fifty-nine-year-old ex–Air Force pilot decided they could get along.

At dinner Zent mentioned the glowing newspaper articles he'd seen about Dana. The family must be proud, he said. But Dale only nodded grimly. The rest of the Ewell family seemed to shift in their seats. It was shy Fresno State graduate student Tiffany who broke the awkward silence, asking Monica if she looked forward to law school, and mentioning that her mother was on the Board of Governors of the California Bar.

The topic soon turned to flying. Monica announced that Dana, already an experienced fixed-wing pilot, was very excited about learning to fly helicopters. His father was less enthusiastic. The cost of lessons was outrageous, he said, and the upkeep frightening if one chose to buy one of the contraptions.

The Zents departed Pajaro Dunes at midnight, Dana remaining behind. He and his father had scheduled a tennis game for the next morning. After the game, Dana planned to join the Zents for Easter dinner.

Easter Sunday

He parked the car at the curb and grabbed his gym bag. Looking furtively around the quiet, predawn street, he dragged a car cover out of the backseat, locked up, and quickly concealed his vehicle.

His heart thumped in his chest as he ducked beneath the fruit trees at 5663 East Park Circle Drive. The ground cover smelled dank, like wet mulch. He was inside within seconds. Be cool, he told himself. No mistakes.

The intruder padded through the garage and opened a door, entering the house itself. Immediately, he heard the beeping of the alarm pad. With a gloved finger, he punched in the proper code, whispering each number in sequence. The green light blinked on—the system had been disarmed.

He found the laundry room and put down his gym bag. He spread a plastic sheet over the floor. Crossing into the guest bedroom, the intruder stripped the sheets off the bed, carrying them into the girl's bathroom and spreading them over the floor there.

They're so goddamned rich! he thought. He wanted to be rich, too. Why shouldn't he have an exotic car? Why should he live in some shitty apartment?

Somehow the intruder had assumed that once he got inside it would be easy to strip the place. He'd stolen motorcycles, even cars. But this was different. What does a burglar do? Well, shit! He steals stuff.

Into the girl's room. She had a jewelry box, though most of the contents looked like junk. Nonetheless, he grabbed the box and a case of compact discs and carried these into the bathroom, dumping them on the growing pile of booty. Being careful not to damage anything, he took down her stereo receiver and unscrewed the speaker wires. He wound up the power cord and clipped it to the back of the receiver, stacking the speakers near the system. Checking the time on the pager he wore, he counted the remaining hours.

What if it doesn't work? What if someone sees me leaving this place? What if I screw it up?

The intruder shook off his doubts when he found a string of pearls. They looked expensive. He crammed the pearls into his pocket. Striding into the son's bedroom, he stripped that bed as well, spreading out the sheet in the family room.

He located a couple of rifles and a shotgun in the closet and tossed them on the parents' bed. He yanked open dresser drawers, starting with the top ones, pulling out the contents willy-nilly, occasionally spotting a trinket of jewelry or some loose change, which he carried out and dropped on the sheet on the bathroom floor.

The Browning nine-millimeter Hi-Power pistol and ammunition were in the nightstand, right where they were supposed to be. He sat near the shotgun on the elaborate bed, staring at his shoes and wondering if there really was a God.

At Pajaro Dunes, Dana Ewell said good-bye to his family, climbed into his gold Mercedes, and headed toward the Zents' Morgan Hill home. His father packed up a few minutes later. Dale would fly back to Fresno alone. Fearful of wiping out his entire family at once, he often avoided flying with more than one family member at a time.

When Dale had left, Glee and Tiffany closed up the house and drove off in Glee's Cadillac.

*   *   *

The intruder grew weary of trudging back and forth, piling belongings on the sheet in the hallway. He went into the master bedroom and grabbed a handful of the Winchester nine-millimeter cartridges. The carton, it seemed to him, looked pretty damned old. He let one cartridge fall to the carpet. He left behind the leather case the gun had come in, and the owner's manual. In the laundry room, he loaded his weapon and sat down on the plastic tarp to wait.

The gun felt cold and heavy in his hand. He could smell his own body. The stench of sweat and fear rose up from his shaved armpits. Probably, he told himself, I should have taken a shower yesterday.

The pager on his hip buzzed. He pushed the light button and squinted at the code numbers. It was a go. Soon it would be all over.

He noticed a spiderweb in the corner. He thought about the spider's life: What if no bug ever comes along? Damned spider just sits there and starves to death. Kind of sad when you think about it. The killer stretched out his toe and squashed the spider against the wall.

Glee and Tiffany were nearly home, but Glee was in no particular hurry. Ever since the accident, when Tiffany was just a toddler, Glee had been an exceptionally cautious driver. Tiffany had plowed headfirst into the dash, and she still wore the metal plate doctors had implanted in her skull, the results of which had not left her mentally impaired, but, some said, socially awkward.

They stopped at the Foster's Freeze so Tiffany could grab a cold drink.

The killer had to use the bathroom. Again. He couldn't recall when he'd gone to the bathroom so often in one day.

It would be dark before long. Where were they? He

wiped a drop of oil off the gun. What if they're not coming?

But they were. He'd gotten the code. He wondered what it would feel like to do it. Funny. It didn't seem as though it would feel like anything, really. It would feel pretty good to be a millionaire, though, that he was sure of.

He wished he had brought one of the books to read. He didn't believe he was quite expert enough yet, but he was getting there. Good thing he had a technical mind like his asshole old man.

Another ten minutes ticked by. Where the fuck were they? And then he heard a sound, like the automatic garage door. He froze, listening. It was the garage, wasn't it?

Then a car engine. A car pulling in and idling and shutting off. And voices. He tried to take a deep breath, but his chest felt as if there were a refrigerator on it. Then a bolt of adrenaline shot through him. When he heard a key slip into the lock, he stood up and cocked the gun in his hand.

1992

*". . . three down at
5663 East Park Circle . . ."*

ONE

HOMICIDE DETECTIVE JOHN PHILLIP SOUZA knelt in the dirt. The soil was deep brown, fertile. He lifted a fistful and let it spill through his fingers. Souza had a hunch, an intuitive nagging in the back of his mind, but when he tried to pin it down it vanished like the name of a grade-school crush.

Souza's adversary was wily and destructive. The pest had wreaked havoc with his grape crop, and Souza wouldn't rest until the so-called skeletonizer worm was eradicated. But the detective felt no closer to saving his grapes than he had months before. Most of the tactics he'd employed against the pest had failed; worse, many seemed to have actually strengthened his foe.

"John?"

He turned toward the house. Sharon, his lovely blond wife of twenty-four years, stood in the open doorway.

"It's Dale Caudle on the line."

He nodded and waved to her. Probably not good news, he thought. A call from his superior at the Homicide Unit of the FSO—Fresno County Sheriff's Department— where Souza had spent six years solving the most serious and frightening of crimes, usually meant that somewhere near this California city someone had taken the life of another.

Detective Souza surveyed his ten acres of grapevines and onions, and headed for the house. The hot San Joaquin Valley wind, heavy with grit and scented with sage and fertilizer, tugged at his dark hair as he walked.

The veteran detective was built like a small truck, thick and muscular from a lifetime of manual labor. True, now that he was in his late forties he carried extra weight around the waist, but he could still take down the most street-savvy of punks with his bare hands.

Once inside, as Sharon fixed breakfast in her bare feet, Souza picked up the receiver. He winced and let go a long breath.

She squinted at him through her glasses.

Caudle gave him the address. Souza didn't have to write it down. He'd remember it. Forever, as it turned out.

"I'll be there in half an hour," he said, and hung up the phone. Souza absently brushed his mustache with a thumb and forefinger. He felt Sharon's stare.

"Bad?" she said.

"Very bad," he told her.

Souza's county-owned Ford Galaxy trailed gray dust that drifted and settled over his property. He followed surface streets to the 99 freeway, which carved through the heart of California's San Joaquin Valley. His destination: 5663 East Park Circle Drive, in the Sunnyside neighborhood. Once it was one of Fresno's most affluent areas, but now the neighborhoods surrounding it were in decline and many of its wealthier residents were moving to the newer, north end of town.

It was 9:30 A.M. Traffic was dense. Souza remembered the Fresno he'd known as a child, the sleepy agricultural village, the butt of countless bumpkin jokes, where he and his brother and sister were raised by parents who'd immigrated from the Azores. The Souza children worked the cotton fields and dairy farms when their father fell ill with tuberculosis, and spoke Portuguese before they spoke English.

The valley had been nothing but a vast desert until the heyday of the Southern Pacific Railroad. And though only an hour's drive from the astonishing beauty of Yosemite, Fresno had been shortchanged aesthetically by the Lord, while being blessed with the rich soil upon which a community of over half a million would eventually rise. It was a land of coyotes, vines studded with sweating grapes, sprawling housing developments, aching poverty, and bloody gang warfare.

The compass points of the modern Fresno area each had a distinct flavor: north—shiny, wealthy, in the path of growth; south—lower income, industrial, farming areas; west—much like the south; downtown—older and decayed, crammed with government buildings, beginning a redevelopment phase; and the east, Sunnyside, today the site of a bloody crime that would soon change the homicide detective's life.

A kid in an apple red pickup cut Souza off, then flipped him off. Souza shook his fist at the kid. He loved his life, loved Sharon and the children, but on days like this he longed for slower, more predictable times. Back when, it seemed, everyone worked hard for what they had. When the line between right and wrong was unsmudged, and every family lived and worked together.

And stayed together.

Detective Sergeant Dale Caudle waited outside 5663 East Park Circle Drive, talking with Detective Ernie Burk. Patrol cars were parked all over the place, and uniformed officers milled about. More detectives arrived. It promised to be a high-profile case.

Everybody and their mother-in-law is going to be tromping through here, thought Souza, as a deputy rolled back the banner guard that blocked the end of East Park Circle.

Someone was stringing up more banner guard on the other side of the block. The breeze fluttered it gently. SHERIFF'S LINE. DO NOT CROSS.

The house was nice enough—large, stucco, with a brick facade and a pair of arched windows in front, surrounded by mature trees—but the design was dated. Souza guessed it had been built in the early sixties. The neighborhood was characterized by spacious lots and lush landscaping. Sunnyside was old money, at least by today's standards, but it had an idyllic look that Souza knew would be out of place with the horrors awaiting him inside 5663.

The urbane, sharp-featured Caudle, immaculate as always, imposing by force of personality and extraordinary diplomacy rather than size, nodded toward Souza and came over to meet him as he parked.

"Morning, John," he said, as Souza stepped out of the maroon Galaxy. "At first, we thought it was an FBI agent and his family. That's what came in early."

"But, no?"

"I don't think so. A maid and a neighbor had a look inside this morning and called it in. They say the resident's name is Ewell. A local businessman and his family. We'll see."

"Father, mother, and daughter all got it?"

"Yeah."

"How long ago?"

"Looks like a couple of days. Come on, we'll do a walk-through."

The walkway led to a wrought-iron gate and brick-enclosed porch. A partial shoe track in the flower bed was without sole pattern. The Pizza Hut carton in the bushes would be dusted for prints, but without much expectation.

A thirty-yard driveway led to a twin garage that extended off the house. Another, single garage, built close to the living quarters, lay to the left of the driveway. A Jeep Wagoneer was parked nearby. They walked through the iron gates and the double doors, and entered the gloom of the house.

The smell. It wasn't overpowering, but when Souza blew it out of his nostrils it came back even stronger. Inching carefully along the walls, they padded single file through the main entry hall. The furniture was heavy, ornate oak with velvet fabrics—not as old as the house, but not new either.

As they moved past each doorway, Souza saw drawers and closets spilled in disarray. A deliberate mess?

Was the place ransacked, or had somebody been searching for something? Poking his head into the bathroom, he spotted a sheet, piled with loot but apparently left behind by a burglar who had fled the scene.

"Someone really tossed the place," Caudle said over his shoulder.

The first body, that of a young woman, lay facedown in the kitchen. In order to maintain the integrity of any physical evidence, the detectives as always avoided the area immediate to the victim. She'd probably been shot at relatively close range. Her hands were pinned beneath her stomach, her elbows at right angles to her body, her toes pointed inward. The victim had worn tennis shoes and a blue sport shirt and jeans with a black-leather belt on the day she died. Souza saw nothing to indicate she'd been sexually assaulted.

A blue-cotton jacket, the lining of delicate pink and teal flowers stained with blood, was heaped beneath her right shoulder. She lay in a thirty-inch pool of black blood, hard and cracking at the leading edge.

Souza saw a yellow box of tissues and a cassette tape, both of which the victim had probably been carrying when ambushed. And on the floor near her right shoulder was a Knob Hill Grocery bag, evidently set down seconds before she was killed.

She was dead before she hit the floor, thought Souza. Looks about the age of my oldest boy.

Caudle pointed to the second and third bodies, which lay just beyond the girl—a man, facedown in a hallway directly off the kitchen, and a woman in a small room on the other side of the hall.

Souza and Caudle backed out of the house again.

*   *   *

Detective Mindy Ybarra, tall, striking, with coffee-colored almond eyes, and Detective Christian Curtice, also tall but blond and blue-eyed with the cheekbones and hundred-watt smile of a Calvin Klein model, waited outside. Both could have been prime-time actors, but they were real veteran cops. Detectives Stuart, Huerta, Christian, Flores and Duenes were also on scene.

Identification Bureau personnel—those responsible for collecting evidence—arrived a few minutes later. The processing would be led by a pair of criminologists (a rather dated misnomer for what were now called identification technicians): the huge, jolly Jack Duty and the polished, professorial Jim Tarver. They and technicians Bryan Stones and Bob Brown were briefed by detectives.

The group huddled to plan their approach to the scene. Caudle made the assignments, his criteria detective availability, experience, temperament: Souza would be lead investigator on the triple homicide, Ernie Burk his partner. Mindy Ybarra got the nod as scene coordinator. Chris Curtice, member of the Homicide Unit for two and a half years and currently carrying twelve cases as lead detective, would videotape the scene. Other detectives were sent off to canvass neighbors and determine if anybody had heard or seen anything and would be willing to talk about it.

Souza felt proud Caudle had entrusted him as lead on the case. Still, it was frightening responsibility.

A few years before, he'd been honored as Police Officer of the Year for his work on a bait-shop robbery in which the owner had been shot eleven times by Uzi-wielding gunmen (and somehow survived). Souza put the gunmen in jail, cracking a statewide robbery ring in the process. But he was now responsible for bringing to justice a multiple murderer in what promised to be a well-publicized case, and he would answer to surviving family members who needed closure, a Sheriff's Department under pressure, and a frightened public that would want it solved *now*.

TWO

EVERYONE ON-SITE FELT A BIT OVERWHELMED. The priority, of course, would be to protect evidence, especially that evidence on or near the victims. But one body effectively impeded access to the next, and despite the large size of the house, all the victims had fallen in narrow living areas.

Jack Duty peeked inside the "Woody" style Jeep Wagoneer in the driveway. "Look's like it's unlocked," he said in his cowboy cadence. "And there's a door opener up on the visor."

"Well, hell," Souza said, "let's go ahead and use the damned thing."

Duty, bear-sized, powerful, always quick with a smile, dusted the Jeep's door handle for fingerprints, did the same on the remote door opener, then pressed the remote's button.

The single garage door to the left of the drive creaked open. Duty walked inside and dusted the knob on the door leading into the house. Then he opened the unlocked door. I-Bureau techs entered and began photographing the scene.

Souza eased inside and studied the body at the far end of the hall. A middle-aged man. Mail had scattered as he fell, and four rolled-up newspapers. Between the victim's ankles, a pair of broken sunglasses. What appeared to be fragments of a shattered lens lay scattered near his head, as if his sunglasses had been blasted to pieces by a bullet.

One newspaper was dated the nineteenth. Easter Sunday, thought Souza.

The male victim's ankles had crossed as he fell, and, like his daughter's, his hands were pinned beneath his chest, his elbows sticking out. He wore jeans, tennis shoes, short-sleeved tennis shirt. There was an apparent entrance wound on the back of his neck, an exit wound in his cheek, and a bloody mess on the floor. The man, again like the girl, had probably been shot from behind, and high-velocity blood spatter and brain matter stained the walls.

Jack Duty came in from "processing" the Jeep. Souza pointed out an alarm pad just inside the door from the garage. Duty dusted that, too.

A third and final body lay in the next room, her feet near the head of the male victim. The slim woman of fifty or so had been shot repeatedly.

She had died on her back, her legs and feet canted to her left. Again, jeans and white tennis shoes, but with a sweatshirt that read *Pajaro Dunes*. Her upper right arm covered most of her face, with the back of her hand resting on the floor.

"Car keys," said Caudle, looking at what was clutched in the woman's hand.

"But was she coming in or going out?"

Caudle shrugged.

They backed out of the house and into the front yard for another strategy meeting.

Souza joined Burk, a spindly-legged, full-bellied Babe Ruth of a man with prominent blue eyes, thinning blond hair, and a ready grin. They stepped back at that point and listened to the observations and opinions of fellow detectives. They hoped to see things through the eyes of others, things they might have missed themselves.

It was agreed, now that they had a sense of the floor plan and the particulars of the scene, that their next step would be to reconstruct the event. Then, they'd move on to studying the bodies.

Tall, elegant criminologist Jim Tarver, charged with blueprinting the scene, pointed out that the house faced south and was laid out in three sections: the west wing (bedroom and bath, guest room, master bedroom and bath), main wing (den, kitchen, family room with fireplace, laundry room) and east wing (office and bath, another bedroom, single-car garage).

The investigators would examine the burglary evidence in the west wing.

They stepped in through the front doors again. Souza saw two rolled-up newspapers inside the doors. No signs of forced entry. The detectives moved into the west wing. The first door on the left led into a bathroom and was partially blocked by a stereo, which had been placed on a pink sheet along with cassette tapes, costume jewelry, and a camera.

The undisturbed bathroom led into a bedroom. Drawers in the dresser and nightstand had been pulled out, clothing scattered. The lights were off and the curtains drawn. A sliding glass door appeared locked and undisturbed. Clearly, this had been the young lady's room. Feminine decor, a white Princess phone, a Garfield the cat trash can. Girlish knickknacks.

The guest bedroom had also been rummaged through. The pink fitted sheet on the bed matched the pink sheet laid out near the girl's bathroom.

Into the master bedroom. Dresser and vanity drawers stood open. Piles of clothing lay strewn over the carpet. Large portraits of a pretty blond girl—doubtless the young victim—and a smiling young man hung on one wall. A family portrait included three of the dead.

Seven or eight framed family photos covered the top

of a dresser. A pair of .22 rifles and a shotgun had been dumped on the bed.

Souza saw in the ransacked nightstand two boxes of shotgun shells, a box of .357 Magnum loads, a box of .22 cartridges, and an open box of Winchester nine-millimeter cartridges.

He found a leather handgun case and an open carton on the floor. An owner's manual read: Browning Hi-Power 9mm Parabellum.

Lifting the Browning owner's manual by a single corner, he found no weapon beneath. He spotted a live nine-millimeter cartridge on the carpet and he noted on a steno pad: 9mm cartridge in plain sight. No empty brass apparent in home. Bad guy used Browning, took it?

They moved on to the main wing. Big Jack Duty and Technician Stones followed, snapping photographs and placing yellow number stands near vital evidence.

In the kitchen, Souza found a red-and-white ice chest on the kitchen table near the girl's body. A jacket and purse had been piled on the ice chest as if someone had carried all the items inside together.

A copy of the *Fresno Bee* on the table, dated April 17, featured a lead story about the impending execution of a notorious California murderer: Robert Harris will die.

Kitchen items lay in plain view, as did a Home Federal Bank statement in the names of Dale and Glee Ewell. The statement reflected a recent withdrawal of $100,000.

The family room and den had also been plundered, and another bedsheet, this one striped pink and white, had been spread out in the family room. The laundry room adjacent to the kitchen had an exterior door. Souza found the dead bolt in the locked position.

They entered the east wing, stepping into what appeared to be the son's room: Kemper Securities account statements in the name of Dana Ewell littered the floor. A bookshelf bowed under the weight of dozens of marketing and financial textbooks. Glossy posters of exotic cars papered much of the wall over the disturbed bed. A remaining bedsheet matched the one Souza had seen on the floor in the family room. The bedroom light burned, and all windows appeared secure.

The last room inspected contained the second female victim. Entering the office through a bathroom common to the son's room, they saw a large desk and sofa, between which the woman had died. A closet contained a pair of filing cabinets, a copier, and fur coats. And a bullet hole.

Souza learned that a maid and a neighbor had discovered the scene at nine o'clock that morning. The neighbor called 911. Fire department paramedics arrived first.

They examined the victims and cleared out. A few minutes later sheriff's deputies walked through, secured the scene, and called for homicide detectives.

Father, mother, daughter. All gunned down in cold blood on Easter. Souza had to know why it had happened. And who had done it.

Out in the yard, Caudle pointed out a blond woman who waited on the street. "That's Marlene Reid. She works for a company out at the airport, Western Piper Sales."

Reid said it appeared from the descriptions that the victims were her boss, Dale Ewell, his wife, Glee, and their daughter Tiffany. Dale had flown to the coast to spend the weekend with his family. Before leaving, he'd had a heated phone argument with a client named Lais.

"Do you know the nature of that argument?" Souza asked her. Her features were Teutonic, her bearing dignified.

"Lais has refused to pay the bill for repairs to his plane, an Aerostar. I think we tested one of the engines."

Reid told Souza that Dana, the Ewell's only son and a student at Santa Clara University in San Jose, had called her the previous evening, concerned over the whereabouts of his parents.

Souza said, "And you waited until this morning to drive over?"

"Dana was supposed to call me back."

"But he didn't?"

"Well, not last night. Dana called the office."

"This morning, then?"

"Yes. He said a neighbor came by and saw that Tiffany was injured. Bob Pursell, our sales manager, drove with me. He's right over there, by the mailbox."

"Miss Reid, why didn't you get someone over here last night?"

Souza, knowing that every minute the scene gets colder lengthens the odds of solving the crime, couldn't hide his frustration.

"Dana didn't call back until this morning," Reid said.

Souza and Burk interviewed Bob Pursell. Pursell had last seen Dale on Friday afternoon. When Dale didn't show up on Monday, Pursell grew concerned. When Dale failed to show Tuesday morning, Pursell called the house, but no one answered. Then Dana phoned Western Piper to say there was trouble.

"Dale seemed to have the perfect life," Pursell told Souza and Burk. "He made a ton of money, and the family was awfully close; I don't understand."

Pursell provided the numbers of Dana Ewell and Dana's three uncles, Ben, Dan, and Richard. Souza sensed something was amiss with the man; he would be certain to interview him at length when time permitted.

Souza consulted with scene coordinator Mindy Ybarra, who had been studying the scene with her typical thoroughness. Souza took out a pencil and steno pad and synopsized her comments:

—Paramedics noted head injuries and lividity in all subjects.

—Maid knows of no family enemies, no large amounts of cash on premises, no family difficulties. Ewell son, Dana, in college in San Jose, Santa Clara University.

—No sign of forced entry on outside doors, outside circuit breakers in ON position.

—searched cars: Cadillac (GLEE E personalized plate) luggage, new dishes, new clothing in shopping bag; purse w/Tiffany Ewell California driver's license, makeup, $90.00 currency, shopping bag with clothing, backpack with chocolate Easter bunny.

—Lincoln (2AOU536) keys in ignition; shovel, drain-pipe, other agricultural implements in trunk.

—Thunderbird (TIFFANN)—nothing to note.

—Found shoe tracks in garage, but pattern and size matched shoes found in master-bedroom closet.

—Yard area: metal storage shed, wooden gate and fence separating, woodpile, surrounding wooden fence. Some weeds flattened near shed.

Inside again, Souza frowned at the alarm pad on the wall. He wrote: Alarm? Maid turned it off? Family usually sets it before going out?

In the bathroom, he spotted skylights. Skylights appear to be sealed, he scribbled.

A light-switch was up in the boy's room. "Dust the switch cover," Souza told a technician.

The tech's glance said, No shit, Holmes.

Souza joined Curtice and Ybarra. They examined the bodies and discussed angles of attack—where the killer had been in relation to each victim when he'd murdered them. Curtice mentioned that every time he looked at young Tiffany lying there, he pictured his kid sister.

After Souza had walked the house and checked for broken windowpanes and tool marks on doorjambs, the detectives went outside for air.

"Ain't pretty," Caudle said, toeing the dirt with his shoe. "What do you think, John?"

"I think a lot of the stuff piled on the sheet is just crap. No value to speak of. I mean, cassette tapes? When the real valuables were mostly untouched? And we all know a pro is going to make his haul with pillowcases, not sheets. What is the deal with sheets?"

Rubberneckers were gathering.

Caudle said, "Think it was a stupid burglar?"

"At first, I was thinking it was a fourteen-year-old. But good Lord, what kind of kid handles a multiple homicide with that much style?"

"You think he panicked and bolted without the goods?"

"No sign of forced entry. Victims cut down with precision. A burglary that looks like no break-in job I've ever seen. Did someone really come here to rob the place?"

"Just a smoke screen?"

"Something's out of whack." Souza watched a couple of deputies move the crowd back. "We need to know if they were all shot at the same time."

Souza noticed that the air was redolent with the scents of spring. It was a day that should have held such promise. He thought of his wife and how he loved her laugh.

The men enjoyed the morning air as long as they could before Sergeant Caudle spoke up. "Let's get on with it, then."

Was there more than one shooter? At first, Souza had wondered if the sacking of the house had been engineered by two people. Now he felt, though he himself did not yet understand why, that there had been just one gunman.

Why is this family dead? Souza wished the place wasn't so damned crowded. What were all these people doing here?

Souza, Burk, and Curtice, with assistance from Jack Duty, began to analyze the number and trajectories of bullet holes in the home. Above Dale's body, the investigators found a small nick on a section of ceiling where the height dropped a few inches to accommodate a heating duct, and another scar in the Sheetrock at the end of the hall. Upward trajectory, meaning the shooter might have crouched behind the victim and fired one round. It had gone through Dale Ewell and glanced off the ceiling and hit the wall. Duty studied the wall and concluded the bullet hadn't penetrated.

But there was no slug on the carpet—had the killer "policed up" the expended bullet? And if so, why?

Glee plainly had more than a single wound. And, Curtice pointed out, while the father and daughter probably hadn't known what hit them, it seemed that Glee had been confronted by the shooter and seen her death coming.

Ybarra pointed out evidence of two bullet paths in Glee's office. One hole, a few feet above the floor, was visible in the blue-and-white-striped wallpaper near the closet door. Another had passed through the door itself, punctured a paper bag of clothes atop a file cabinet, and exited the back of the closet. The detectives went outside and found a large bullet hole in the stucco front wall of the house. Mindy Ybarra knelt near the flower bed.

"There it is," she said.

The copper-jacketed bullet lay in plain sight in the dirt. Technician Jack Duty collected, measured, and photographed the bullet, marking the envelope with evidence number JD-15.

Like her father, it seemed Tiffany Ewell had been killed by a single shot to the back of the head. The detectives found a hole high on the kitchen wall, where the bullet that killed her had embedded itself after passing through her skull. What they did not find on the scene, what might or might not have been there in the first place, were empty cartridge casings.

If the killer used a revolver, the empties wouldn't be ejected. But if an automatic had been used, someone had taken the time to police up the brass.

THREE

SOUZA WENT FROM BODY TO BODY, AGAIN AND again. How did you do, it? Where did you hide? Who got it first?

He eyed the ice chest and purse on the kitchen table. And in the next room, Glee's car keys were still in her hand.

So they were slaughtered just as they had come in. It seemed clear the bodies hadn't been moved, yet Dale Ewell lay dead at the end of a hallway that led in from the garage, and if he had gotten hit first, his wife and daughter would have had to step over him to get inside.

So it seemed Dale was the last to die. It occurred to Souza that an assailant might have followed the victims inside.

But, from all appearances, Tiffany had been caught unaware, shot in the kitchen from behind. From the number of wounds and the varied trajectories, Glee had been pursued and shot down. Did she see her daughter get shot? Did she watch as her baby's brains were blown out?

Souza walked it again. How did you do it, you son of a bitch? First, Tiffany.

Perhaps he came out of the laundry room just after Tiffany stepped into the kitchen. One shot, and Tiffany's young life ended. No, that trajectory didn't seem to work.

If he'd been in the laundry, the hole in the wall should

24

have been a few feet west of its location. More likely, he had been in the family room.

Then Glee, apparently hit repeatedly as she ran into the office and finished off with a shot to the face at point-blank range. Her right arm covered her face. Had she struggled to push the gun away with a defensive movement? Tiffany, then Glee.

Where was Dale all this time? In the garage? Did he hear the gunshots and rush in? But the personal items scattered near the body suggested he entered casually. Who runs toward trouble with a newspaper and a few days' mail in his hands?

Souza saw a single sheet of paper near the body. A fax, blood staining one corner. Squinting at the date, he saw: 4.17.92. 4:13 P.M. Friday.

Chris Curtice called Souza's name. He'd just interviewed the maid.

Her name was Rose Avita. She'd noticed as she pulled in that morning a few newspapers piled near the rural-style mailbox. A man approached, wanted to know who she was. The man turned out to be Knapp, the neighbor, and when Avita identified herself he asked if she had a key to the Ewell home.

When she opened the door, two things struck her as odd: the alarm didn't buzz, and the door to the kitchen, "always open," was closed. Further, she could see into Tiffany's room, and it appeared things were in disarray. Knapp opened the kitchen door and saw Tiffany on the floor. He ordered the maid outside and the assistants who'd accompanied her, and called 911 from his home.

But the newspapers were inside, Souza told Curtice. Curtice said Avita stated the neighbor had brought them in when he came over.

The work of Supervising Criminalist Allen Boudreau began at 12:45 P.M. with a call from Sergeant Dale Caudle. Boudreau, the "mad scientist" of the FSO's Forensic Laboratory, was not dispatched to crime scenes as a matter of course.

Typically, Identification Bureau personnel (or "garbage collectors," according to Forensic Laboratory scientists) were dispatched to the scene to gather evidence. But for this extraordinary case, Caudle asked for Forensic Laboratory assistance in the areas of blood collection (if blood other than the victim's was present, it would certainly be vital), spatter interpretation, trace-evidence collection, firearms and ballistics analysis, and other criminalistic services.

Boudreau and Criminalist Andrea Van Der Veer de Bondt arrived at the crime scene at one-thirty. Boudreau glanced at the victims, looked at Souza, and shook his head. Then he got started.

As they worked Glee's office, Duty showed Boudreau the bullet found outside in the flower bed. The bullet was remarkably intact, considering that it had blasted through a thick stucco wall, and Boudreau spent a great deal of time examining it.

Van Der Veer de Bondt studied the blouse of the murdered mother. "Some kind of weird powder traces here," she said.

"Lift 'em," Boudreau told her.

Boudreau identified the bullet as a full-metal jacket handgun ammunition of a size and shape known to experts as "nominal .38 caliber"; that is, any ammunition with bullet diameter of approximately .38, including 9mm, .38 Special, and .357 Magnum. It was consistent with the box of 9mm Winchester ammunition in the master bedroom, and Souza brought Boudreau into the bedroom for a look.

"Sheez," Boudreau said. "Look at the price tag on the carton."

Souza did. "Seven-ninety. Pretty cheap. How old do you think these are?"

"Old. Preinflation old."

"Did the bad guys use the victim's weapon and ammunition?"

"That's the appearance. But who knows?"

"If it wasn't really a burglar—"

"You think it wasn't?" Boudreau said.

Souza looked at him, waiting.

"Because I was thinking," Boudreau said, "it doesn't look right to me. I'm no burglary expert, but it looks spurious. Christ, look at the weapons he left on the bed. They would have brought him some quick cash."

"For the moment, let's say the guy isn't a real burglar. He breaks in, tears the place up, comes in here looking for the victim's weapon."

"You suspect he knew the Browning was here?" Boudreau said.

"That's what I'm saying. And it looks like the women drove in before the father."

"Which means the killer may have waited around with the women's bodies after he killed them? Waited for the man to come home?"

"And," Souza said, "if that's true, no way in hell a burglar, surprised by the women, would have waited around. Unless he came specifically to kill the guy."

"An execution."

"But was it a pro?"

Detective Christian appeared in the doorway. "One couple nearby, the Browns, say they heard strange noises on Sunday. Not gunshots. More like clanging. One noise, then four or five, then a few minutes later another."

Boudreau mumbled something.

"I didn't get you," Souza said.

"I said, 'maybe that explains it.' "

"Explains what?"

Boudreau shook his head. "I can't comment yet."

An hour later word came that the sole surviving member of the Ewell family would soon be arriving at headquarters. Souza and Burk would take a statement from Dana.

Television remote vans lined the curb. Gawkers stared as Sheriff Steve Magarian faced print people and news cameras. To get to his car, Souza would need to cut right through the interview scene, so he and Burk stood at ease near the sidewalk and watched as the six-foot-one-inch, round-faced sheriff fielded questions.

A scrawny young woman, who Souza thought looked like some kind of neohippy in her tiny round glasses and patched jeans, asked Magarian for the victims' identities.

"Investigators believe the victims are members of the Ewell family," he answered. "A son, Dana, is a student, and was out of town at the time. We contacted him, and he is returning to Fresno to be interviewed."

"How were they killed?" asked another reporter.

"I'm not at liberty to disclose that at this time. But they were discovered in two different areas of the house by emergency personnel."

"Do you know when they died?"

"We believe it was more than twenty-four hours ago," Magarian told the questioner. "We have yet to determine a motive, and no arrests have been made. I have every reason to believe we'll solve this promptly, however."

Souza saw people on bicycles, dressed in tights and wearing those ugly bicycle helmets. Neighborhood kids horsed around. There were a few homeless-looking types and a man in a three-piece suit. Where are the elephants and clowns? thought Souza.

Another reporter: "What about the serial burglar who's been working this neighborhood?"

"He's in jail awaiting court proceedings," Magarian said. "So, no. It wasn't the same guy."

Magarian declared the conference over. He said he had work to do. Detectives Souza and Burk hustled to the car, offering only, "No comment," when confronted by eager newspeople.

On the road, Burk said, "Jesus, this is going to be a

high-profile case. We screw anything up, the media are going to roast our gonads on a spit."

"It's a goldfish bowl," Souza said.

The sky was clouding over. A dust devil danced out of a barren field and seemed to follow the car for a while.

FOUR

As it turned out, rumors that an FBI agent's family had been killed had started this way: Special Agent John Zent had taken a frantic call from Dana shortly after 9 A.M. that morning, when Dana said that someone was injured in his Fresno home. Zent, assigned to the Bureau's San Francisco office, called a fellow agent in Fresno, who in turn contacted the FSO and learned that three bodies had been discovered at 5663 East Park Circle. Zent chartered a private plane and flew Dana and Monica to Fresno Air Terminal.

Lieutenant Richard White confirmed to Dana the death of his father, mother, and sister, and was still sitting with Dana when Souza and Burk arrived at the office. The detectives took the opportunity to interview Agent Zent.

It was common practice for the partners that Burk would do most of the actual questioning, with Souza observing. In this manner the Zent interview was conducted.

"Today's date is 4–21–92, the time is 1355 hours," Burk said as the FSO tape recorder ran. (While the FBI had a strict policy against taping interviews, claiming the very presence of a recorder might affect the subject's attitude and veracity, the Sheriff's Department commonly recorded many of their interviews, which were later transcribed to hard copy.)

"This is in reference to case number 92-15285, a PC

30

187 [murder]. This is Detective Burk and Detective Souza. We're presently in Room 156 of the Fresno County Sheriff's Department Law Enforcement Building. This will be an interview with John William Zent, DOB of 4-3-46, of Morgan Hill, California."

The sheriff's building was typical of 1960s bureaucratic design, cinder block and gray paint and chattering fluorescent tubes, made grimmer yet by the toll the years had taken. Room 156 featured a tiny desk and a handful of plastic chairs, a one-way glass for witness identification and mold green carpet that seemed to crawl up the walls, installed that way to improve soundproofing. For the amount of carnage that had been confessed to there over the years, the carpet might as well have been red.

"Mr. Zent, do you, uh, know a young man named Dana Ewell?"

Zent ran his fingers through his short, blond hair as he explained that his daughter, Monica, and Dana were dorm mates and presently dating. Zent said he had met Dana's parents for the first time that previous Saturday.

"What was the attitude like, how were the Ewells—"

"Oh, very pleasant," Zent said, smiling. "We talked about Glee's time with the CIA and Dale in the Air Force and his business. The kids and their relationship. Very normal."

"She was in the CIA?"

The well-dressed Zent nodded. "She was."

Burk said, "Was there any indication that there was any trouble between them?"

"Not presently. We talked about Dale having some kind of flu, which was causing some depression for a short time because he was unable to sleep. Said how proud he was of Dana's GPA."

"And you left that evening, then saw Dana again, when?"

"He was at my house with my daughter when we arrived at seven on Sunday. No. Closer to seven-thirty. He had arrived that afternoon."

"I see. Did you receive a call from Dana this morning?"

"I did," Zent said, pressing his fingertips together. "He'd been worried about his family, since he'd been unable to contact them since Sunday. And when he called the airplane dealership, the secretary said the Bonanza had returned to Fresno but Dale hadn't been seen since. A neighbor went and checked for Dana and said he saw someone down in the Ewell residence. The description matched that of Tiffany Ewell."

"But then Dana called you?"

"Indeed. He was scared, and, yes, he called me. I told him to stay put, and I hired a plane to bring us right down here. I'd learned through your office that his family were probably the victims, so I prepared him to speak to Lieutenant White."

Souza watched quietly. He found Zent a bit pompous, but that was a G-man for you; Zent seemed to fit the stereotype perfectly. But clearly, Zent was a fan of Dana's and hadn't picked up anything from Dana that made the agent suspect Dana was involved in the crime.

"And how was he taking all this information?"

"He was extremely nervous. Dana's, uh, an extremely meticulous person, and he was very nervous, that's why I said I'd handle things, could do some liaison between law enforcement."

Souza broke in, "Does Dana ever fly from San Jose to Fresno, do you know? Fly himself?"

Shaking his head, Zent said, "He doesn't keep a plane up there, to my knowledge."

"Okay," Burk said. "John, anything else you could add here?"

"I think only that, when I told Dana at the airport, Dana seemed very shocked, in disbelief. And when Lieutenant White confirmed it, he seemed to be going into shock. You could tell from the facial appearance, color features, the nervousness, the shaking."

"All right. The time is . . . 1412 hours. At this time we're gonna terminate this interview."

* * *

It was Monica Zent's turn. Souza didn't find her unattractive, merely ordinary, the type that an eyewitness would struggle to pick out of a lineup.

He listened as Burk asked, "Monica, you know Dana Ewell and his family?"

"Yes I do."

"Can you tell us how long you've known Dana?"

"About . . . three months, now. We both live in Casa, the dorm."

"How would you describe the nature of your relationship?"

"Well." A tiny shrug, the left shoulder. "He's my boyfriend."

"Okay," Burk said. "And you and your family had dinner with the Ewells, is that right?"

"Right. On Saturday—"

"The eighteenth."

"Yes, we all had dinner. Both families. At the Pajaro house. My family and I went home that night, and Dana came in the next day." She was very still, her hands folded in her lap.

"What time did you say that was?" said Burk.

"I expected Dana at three. I got worried when he wasn't there by three-fifteen, and I called my mother at my uncle's house. She said not to worry, and Dana showed up at three-thirty and—"

"Did you stay at home?"

"We went out to the Safeway and got some stuff, you know, for dinner. My parents returned at six-thirty for dessert."

"Uh-huh."

Monica Zent chewed her bottom lip. "Dana and I left my parents by nine-thirty and got back to the dorm at ten, ten-fifteen."

Souza took a big swig from a can of Coke. The case was barely under way, and already he felt fatigue gnawing at him. He didn't expect much from Monica.

He asked her, "Did you spend time in his room then?"

"No. I had a lot of studying to do. Dana went back to his room to read and go to sleep."

Burk said, "Did you ever see Dana taking drugs, Monica?"

"Dana? Not at all. There was this rumor I heard before we started going out, but I've been with him, and it just isn't true. He doesn't even drink."

"Okay. All right. How about his family. Did you ever hear about trouble with them?"

"No. I mean . . . no. He had a disagreement over what to do during the summer or something, but no big deal. Dana is a finance major and he's taking over twenty-five units, and he does really good. I thought he and his parents got along great, to tell you the truth."

Monica Zent went on to verify the times and dates that established Dana's alibi. The detectives took her through the drill again and got the same story each time, so Burk terminated the interview. The third discussion was with Dale's brother, Rolland "Dan" Ewell.

"My brother's secretary said there had been some kind of accident at the house, and that Dale and Glee and, uh, Tiffany had been . . . that possibly they'd been killed."

"And what time was this?" said Burk.

"Probably about eleven this morning."

"Okay. Has Dale had any problems in his personal life or even his business life?"

"Not that I'm aware of. But something you should follow up on, um, Marlene Reid said he received a disturbing fax on Friday afternoon, which she left on his desk for him to see when he came back Sunday. Something about an angry attorney."

Dan went on, in a rambling and digressive manner common to those who've suffered grievous loss, to reveal that Dale and his son Dana were very close, that Dale's business was profitable, that Tiffany, a "really quiet gal" who wore a plate in her head from a childhood accident, had no boyfriend to his knowledge.

As for his movements on Easter Sunday, Dan and his family had hosted an Easter egg hunt throughout the day.

Burk asked if he'd heard of any of Dale's airplane customers being involved in drug smuggling.

Dan Ewell's shoulders had slumped. He seemed miles away. "I wouldn't have any idea."

"What about—we understand Glee was in the CIA at one time."

"What? Oh, yes. Glee. Yes, supposedly she was. That was, let's see, I think they were married in 1961, and she got out just before then."

"No mention of any problems?"

"No. I used to kid them about it. But twenty years ago . . . nothing's surfaced since then, at all."

"Okay. The time is 1441 hours, and we're gonna terminate this interview."

Souza sat in his office checking his voice mail when Burk wandered in.

"You in here?" Burk said. Souza's desk was less orderly than his mind.

"What does it look like?"

"Shit, I can't see you behind all the crap. Looks like somebody blew up a stationery store."

"Well, I know where everything is."

Souza spotted Lieutenant White outside the door. White leaned close to the young man at his side. A few words were exchanged. John Zent stood behind them.

White pushed open the door. "Mr. Ewell," he said to the young man, "this is Detective John Souza. He's been assigned to lead the investigation."

Dana was tall, whippet-thin, and very neat, his hair close-cropped and curly. Small eyes set deep in a tight-skinned face.

Souza offered his hand, saying, "I'm very sorry for your loss, sir."

Dana's grip was firm, cool. He nodded.

Souza and Burk led Dana to Room 156. Zent followed. When the detectives and Dana had found chairs, Zent remained standing.

"I think we'll need to talk to Dana alone," Souza said.

"I'll be right outside," Zent said.

Ernie Burk offered his condolences to Dana. "Can we get you anything, Mr. Ewell? Coffee?"

"Nothing, thanks. What happened to my family?"

"There are indications that a burglar had been in the home and was surprised by your family," Burk said. "But we need to know when this happened. We'd like to take a formal statement from you now, if we could."

"Sure. Yeah, okay."

Burk pushed a cassette into the recorder and punched PLAY/REC.

"Today's date is 4-21-92, time is 1500 hours. This is in reference to case number 92-15285, a PC 187. This will be an interview with Dana James Ewell, 1-28-71, 5663 East Par—uh, East Park Circle Drive, Fresno. Dana is a student at Santa Clara University. Dana, you're related to Dale and Glee, correct?"

"That's correct. They're my parents."

"Okay, when was the last time you saw them?"

"Sunday, of last."

"Last Sunday would be the nineteenth?"

"Twentieth, nineteenth," Dana said, his voice soft and controlled.

"Okay."

"At, uh, approximately two-fifteen, two-thirty when I left—"

"Okay."

". . . in my vehicle."

"Okay," Burk said. "Where were you at?"

"Pajaro Dunes, Watsonville, California. We have a beach house there."

"Okay," said Burk. "And you spent that weekend with them?"

"I spent Easter weekend, yeah."

Trying to get a read on Dana, Souza watched and wondered, Is he in shock? Or just unable to show emotion in front of others?

"And what time did your mom and sister Tiffany arrive? Was it Friday or Saturday?"

"No, they got there, uh . . . Thursday." Arms folded, he leaned back in his chair. "They drove over in Mom's gray Cadillac. I came in the evening."

"On Thursday?" Burk asked.

"From school, yeah. After class."

"Okay, and when did your dad arrive?"

"Uh, Friday, I guess it was around four or five, he flew over, and we keep a car at the airport."

"And what was your dad's attitude like?"

Dana hesitated. "Really high spirits, you know, uh, chipper. Typical. Everybody happy to see each other. Mom, too. Very normal, very happy. Nothing unusual."

Somehow, Souza knew he would hear again and again what a happy, loving family the Ewells were. But something sure as hell had gone wrong somewhere.

Burk said, "Did your folks leave together Sunday?"

"Okay, I did not see them leave . . . oh, you're not going to ask about Saturday night? Because we had some people over. Anyway, Sunday I went to my girlfriend's house. I played tennis with Dad, then I left about two, since I was supposed to be in Morgan Hill about three. We all hugged and kissed and said we'd all see each other on my sister's birthday on May 1.

"That's when I left, about two-twenty, went and got gas and Easter cards and went to my girlfriend's house and spent the rest of Sunday there."

"And your parents and sister were supposed to drive right on back to Fresno?"

"Mom and Tiffany. Dad had flown into Watsonville, so he'd fly back." Dana sat very erect in his chair, very still.

"How long a flight, would you say, timewise?"

"It's about ninety minutes with takeoff and landing and all."

Souza broke in, "Do you know which car your Dad would drive back from the airport in Fresno?"

"Which? His own car, a blue Mark VII."

"And the Wagoneer in the driveway . . . is it typically locked?"

Dana chuckled. "Oh, yeah. Should be locked."

"And what time did you arrive at your girlfriend's house?"

"It was, like, twenty after three. Like I said, I got gas and some Easter cards at the Payless, I guess it was, and signed 'em and got there . . . well, three-thirty."

"And who was there?" Burk said.

"Just my girlfriend, Monica Zent," he said, holding Souza's gaze. "Then we went to the store and bought groceries and made dinner."

"She was the only one there."

"Yes, until her parents got there at six-thirty, seven."

"And when did you leave Monica's?"

Dana took a moment. "God I really don't know, losing track of time. Not until nine at night."

"Sunday, did you make an attempt to call your parents?"

"See, in our family I call every weekend on Sunday. We try to make it about six o'clock, have a chat. I used to write letters and stuff. Let's see your question was . . . oh yeah, I let it ring and ring. And I called again and let it ring and ring and ring, and I thought, 'that's odd.' Thought maybe they took a walk and forgot to set the answering machine."

"Uh-huh."

"So anyway, I just went to bed and tried again the next day. And I noticed there was a click in the line when I called, it didn't sound right. I wondered if they put the call forwarding on? Anyway, I wondered what the deal is. But it was the middle of the day, so . . ."

Dana continued on for five minutes or more, detailing the calls home he'd made, trying different lines at the house, and the beach house, getting no answer for days before finally speaking to his grandmother and Marlene Reid. It was an inordinate amount of detail, and Souza didn't know why Dana was going on for so long about phones.

"Dana," Burk said, "has your dad expressed any problems he's been having with business, or along those lines?"

"No, other than lawsuits and stuff, you know," he said, chuckling. "He hates attorneys."

Burk leaned forward in his chair. "It would be helpful to know if your parents usually set their alarm system when they left the Fresno house."

"Absolutely."

"Always, then?" said Burk.

"They were religious about setting that alarm."

"Of course, we want to look at all the possibilities here. Did your father have any enemies?"

"I thought you said it was a burglar," said Dana, suddenly looking perplexed.

"We have reason to suspect that, but we have to turn over every stone. You understand."

"Well, I can't think of any enemies. He's just a real nice, able guy. But the guy Dad bought the company from, Frank Lambetecchio, he's like the biggest criminal in the world."

"Uh-huh."

"And you know," Dana said, laughing softly, "he went to prison once for drug smuggling."

Souza said, "Did your dad have any problems with Lambetecchio, that you know of?"

"Not that I'm aware of. He was something else, but—"

"Has anyone in the last few years been arrested in one of your dad's planes for smuggling?"

"Not that I know of. It was the first thing that came to mind when they said three dead bodies in the house. But

Dad stayed away from those types, guys from Florida and all."

"Did your sister have any boyfriends?"

"Tiffany? No, she was a real quiet girl, never dated much."

"Do you know of any reason why someone would want your family dead?"

Dana paused, staring off at a wall. "Nothing," he said finally, "not offhand, no."

Burk asked, "Have you made any enemies?"

"Me?"

"Yeah."

"Naw." Dana shifted in his seat, turning his body at an angle away from the detectives. "Might if you go back to high school."

"Dana," Souza said, "did you have problems with kids there?"

"Well, nobody would try to hurt me, I think."

"What about kids in the area?"

"There's a real history of troubled people on my block."

Burk wrote down the names of various East Park Circle residents that Dana said had been in trouble with the law in the past, including one young man he claimed was particularly disturbed, Lowell Moril.

"It wasn't long ago my family were talking and said, gee, you know it seems like all the people on our block are just quacks." He laughed. "I mean, the kids have turned out to be monsters."

"Okay," Burk said. "Do you know when your folks put the alarm in the house?"

"We were robbed—"

"Burglarized?"

"Yeah, right. Burglarized. Like five years ago. They put the alarm in, and we haven't had any problems since."

"But they'd always set the thing?"

"Oh, yeah," Dana said. "Unless they were just running to the store or something. Yeah."

He chuckled again.

It doesn't feel right. Souza knew that an investigator should always look to the surviving family member, especially a potential heir like Dana. But there was no way in hell he was going to jump to conclusions. Maybe the jarring laugh was just nervousness.

The kid has lost his whole family, Souza thought. If I focus on him, and I'm wrong, I'd compound the tragedy beyond measure. Maybe the kid just can't show emotion; he's probably just got an odd way that doesn't mean a damn thing.

"Do your parents keep any weapons at home?"

"He had a nine-millimeter auto. We went shooting during Christmas break. And a shotgun, and I think a little .22 he got for Mom. Definitely a niner, though."

"Okay. Did your dad usually carry much cash?"

Dana nodded. "He always carries a lot of hundreds."

"And who's Mrs. Mitchell?"

"That's my grandmother, my mother's mother. I guess she hasn't been told yet."

Souza spoke up. "It's apparently on the news already, so . . ."

"Yeah? Oh."

Lieutenant White stuck his head in the room and said Pimental would be arriving at the scene shortly. Pimental was the Fresno County deputy coroner.

"Okay," Burk said, "the time is, uh, 1532 hours. We're going to terminate this interview."

Dana got to his feet. "Listen, when will you be done with the house? I mean, when can I begin to make funeral arrangements?"

"Um, we'll be done as soon as we can. It may be a day or two yet."

Dana got the door, and Zent let himself in immediately. Zent handed Burk his card.

Burk glanced at it, dropped it unceremoniously on the table.

"Mr. Ewell, where can we reach you personally?"

Dana gave him an uncle's phone number.

"Again, Mr. Ewell, I'm very sorry about your loss."

"Thanks," Dana said. "Anything else?"

"Not right now."

"Thanks," Dana repeated.

FIVE

To Souza's relief, most of the rubberneckers, so quick to gather, as quickly lost interest and left. Early on, deputies had limited automobile traffic coming into East Park Circle to residents and law enforcement. The ranks of reporters had also thinned. Meanwhile, a number of uniformed officers continued to comb the neighborhood for the murder weapon.

At four-thirty, the homicide partners interviewed neighbor Carol Badgley. She described a van—old, white or blue, two doors in back—that she'd seen parked in front of the Ewell home on Sunday morning, or, she said, "it might have been Monday."

Five-forty-five saw the arrival of Deputy Coroner George Pimental and, in another demonstration that this was no ordinary case, county pathologist Stephen Avalos, a heavyset man with thick glasses and a ready smile.

Andrea Van Der Veer de Bondt performed the duties of "chalk fairy," outlining the bodies of victims where they had fallen.

The bespectacled, soft-spoken Pimental compared the ambient room temperatures to liver-probe readings from the victims. Then he collected jewelry and watches from the female corpses, including Glee's diamond rings and Patek Philippe watch. Souza instructed removal-service personnel to carry Dale's body into the garage, where it could be processed further without impeding movements of investigators.

From Dale, Pimental took a wedding band, watch, set of keys, address book, and an empty wallet. Dana had insisted his dad always carried cash—had the killer cleaned out the father's wallet?

The coroner turned the address book over to investigating detectives so that they might contact friends and associates of the dead man.

Deputy Coroner Pimental and pathologist Avalos first went to work on Glee. There is no gracious, truly respectful way of examining the body of a crime victim, and Chris Curtice captured on video all the undressing, probing, and manipulation necessary.

The examiners pointed out the victim's bloody right elbow. One arm covered her face. They lifted a sleeve and displayed an entry wound in her upper arm, then they pulled up her sweatshirt, exposing another wound in her side, apparently made by the bullet that had pierced her arm.

Avalos penetrated the wound with a gloved finger. This surprised Souza, and by their faces, the other detectives. Avalos seemed to be conducting some sort of pseudoautopsy on the spot.

Pimental pulled Glee's sweatshirt up high, exposing her bra. One wound—whether entry or exit wound was yet unclear—was apparent only when her bra was lifted. The victim wore a prosthetic left breast, the top of which had been creased by a bullet. Another hole in her chest was visible just above the prosthetic.

Pimental examined the dead woman's bloody face, her one open eye, the inside of her mouth. The effect of his actions was to mold an expression of horror upon Glee's face. An entry wound was evident on her left cheek. Then the examiners rolled her onto her side.

Souza saw something fall to the floor. He pointed out a bloody blob on the carpet; a bullet had tumbled from her back. It was marked JD-16. For the camera, Pimental indicated two bullet holes in the carpet.

When they pulled up the back of her shirt, the examiners found a pair of gunshot wounds and evidence of lividity on the skin. Finally, the coroner dug through Glee's sticky hair until he found an exit wound at the back of her head. The camera motor whined as the lens moved for a close-up. The examiners believed Glee Ewell had been hit four times.

Tiffany lay in an enormous blackened pool. It was a struggle to roll the young victim over—she was virtually glued to the floor with her own clotted blood. One examiner had to jam his hand inside her belt and yank her from the spot where she'd perished. Her head swung limply. A plastic headband fell to the floor. While much of the blood had dried, some remained damp under her body. A flattened plastic drink cup was stuck to the tile, where it had been crushed beneath her as she'd fallen.

They unbuttoned her shirt, lifted her bra to be certain she had no chest wounds. Her eyes were closed, the lids black from decomposition, and possibly the effects of the initial impact of the bullet. It took considerable work to clear her hair from the buttonhole-shaped exit wound in her forehead, and even more effort, when she had been turned facedown once again, to isolate the entrance wound in the back of her skull.

Dale now lay in a plastic body bag behind his wife's Cadillac in the garage. Much like his daughter, Dale had been struck from behind by a single bullet.

Mindy Ybarra noticed his darkened skin and a stronger odor of putrefaction, and said, "Why does this victim appear to be decaying so much faster than the others, providing they died the same afternoon?"

"Well," said Pimental as he examined the victim's wound, "could be that the hallway was generally warmer than the rooms."

The bodies were bagged by removal personnel and hauled out to the coroner's vans. Souza was angry at the human destruction—always was, no matter how many homicide scenes he'd viewed. And this time he was frightened by the obvious skill and sangfroid of the shooter.

Soon more I-Bureau technicians appeared on the scene. Guy Patterson and Sherry Creager began to process for prints. Souza searched for Boudreau and found him in the master bedroom, once again pondering the carton of nine-millimeter cartridges.

"You're thinking those were the bullets used?" Souza asked the criminalist.

"Can't be sure until we get back to the lab, but I wouldn't be very surprised."

Meanwhile, Souza had received a message from Robert Pursell. Pursell needed to talk to detectives, and as soon as possible.

The drive was a welcome relief from the crime scene. The evening air felt cool and cleansing.

His face waxen, the odor of alcohol evident on his breath, Pursell showed Souza and Burk into his home. He told them he had serious concerns about Western Piper shop foreman Jack Whitman.

Pursell said Whitman was an abusive drunkard. Dale and Jack had argued Friday when Jack was asked to work on what was supposed to have been a day off.

When questioned by Burk, Pursell said he couldn't be certain what the men had argued about, but Pursell felt it had something to do with an Aerostar aircraft and a disputed repair bill with the attorney owner.

Most incriminating, Pursell said, his voice rising, was Jack's comment to Marlene Reid that the family had been killed as they returned home. Jack had access to the business on weekends, said Pursell, and it wasn't unusual for Jack to be there on Sundays—and, of course, Dale had visited the office on Sunday.

"Talk to Marlene," Pursell offered. "I don't like to point fingers, but I believe Jack Whitman is quite capable of killing someone, especially the way he and Dale have been arguing over the last few years."

During the trip back to the crime scene, Souza said, "For somebody who doesn't like to point fingers, Pursell sure has a talent for it."

Souza wouldn't have been be shocked to find that Pursell had been attempting to deflect attention away from himself.

After the interview, the detectives remained on the scene until nearly midnight, when Caudle instructed them and I-Bureau technicians to call it a night. Investigators held a brief brainstorming session; questions were more plentiful than answers. The scene secured, two deputies took up positions to guard the muted home until seven the next morning.

Souza's farm belonged to another world.

He parked in front of the house, the light from the windows soft and friendly, like candlelight. From atop a telephone wire, a barn owl watched him impassively.

There'll be at least one less rodent around here by dawn, he thought.

He stubbed his toe on a Tonka dump truck, left behind by one of Sharon's day-care children. By the time he reached the porch steps, Sharon was coming through the front door.

"Hey," she said.

"Hey, yourself."

She bussed his cheek. "You okay?"

"Sure. Why?"

"No reason."

"Do I have that look tonight?"

They leaned against the porch railing and stared out at the dim fields.

"The murders are all over the news," Sharon told him.

"I'll bet. Something tells me they will be for a long time."

"Do you mean it'll take a long time to solve?"

"I wouldn't be surprised. We don't have much. But who knows? Most of these type of jobs get solved when we get a tip. Maybe we'll get lucky."

"Time was, you meant something completely different when you mentioned 'getting lucky.' "

He put his arms around her waist, hooked his fingers in the belt loops of her jeans. "Yes, but I'm s-ooo old now."

"Hey, you're not useless yet. Want some dinner?"

"You betcha. Forgot to eat today."

She led him into the house. "Then after, maybe you will get lucky."

The next morning, Lieutenant Richard White, head of the detectives section, met with Souza, Burk, Curtice, Ybarra, and Supervising Criminalist Boudreau in the detective's briefing room. White stretched his legs out beneath the table.

"Okeydokey. Let's summarize around the horn. John?"

"Guy didn't know squat about robbing a house. Opened the drawers from top to bottom. Well, most of them, anyway. Sometimes I think two people were there, but then I waffle. Whatever, most of the valuables were left behind, apparently."

"And?"

Souza sipped acidic coffee from a Styrofoam cup. Daylight filtered in through dingy windows.

"I don't know. Why didn't the alarm go off if someone got in there? Okay, maybe the alarm wasn't set, but the kid, Dana, said it always was. Why weren't there any signs of forced entry? We all wondered if the crook waited and followed the victims in. But from the way they were shot, I just don't think that happened."

"Chris?"

Curtice, ever organized, checked his notes. "It would appear that the shooter killed the women and then waited around to kill the guy." He frowned. "Why? Why didn't he just get the hell out of there? So, either Dale was the target, or they all were."

When White gestured toward him, the compact Allen Boudreau cleared his throat. "We have no empty brass. And from the bullet I got a look at yesterday, a nine-millimeter, it wasn't a revolver. Which then means there were ejected casings."

Souza chimed in, "You've got to ask yourself: Why bother to police up the brass?"

Mindy Ybarra, carving the air with her hand, said, "I'm concerned with what we don't have. No witnesses. Apparently no prints. No murder weapon. Was it a hit? If someone hired a hit man, and we can't get the shooter in here and talking, we may never have anything. Never, ever."

"Revenge or greed?" Souza said. He stood up and rolled his neck around his shoulders, like a boxer before a bout. His bad knee felt tight.

"We're starting to get a picture of Dale Ewell that may suggest he had enemies. We'll see if they were angry enough to eliminate most of his family.

"But . . . this kid Dana. Maybe he was in shock, or something, but I've seen a lot of surviving family members, too damn many, and his reactions were unlike any I've ever witnessed. We can't count him out yet, but it looks like he was having dinner with a goddamned FBI agent when the family was killed, so . . ."

White announced, "First we run down anyone else who could have or would have liked to kill off Dale and his brood. Then, if we find no one else, we can see what makes this Dana tick."

White dismissed everyone. He had to report to the sheriff. The pressure was already on, he said, to solve this case fast. Three victims—wealthy people, connected people. The sheriff, White said, planned to keep up on this one personally. Souza knew that meant he'd get resources when he needed them. And it meant he'd be under a microscope from here on out. He felt his stomach tighten.

SIX

THE PROCESSING OF THE SCENE, BIG JACK DUTY estimated, would take days. At least.

During the second day, Jim Tarver continued to diagram the scene. Paper items were bagged and tagged. The guns found at the scene, like other evidentiary items, were gathered and transported downtown. Ybarra would be attending the autopsies, scheduled to continue until the next day. At times, tempers flared and detectives and I-Bureau techs bickered.

Souza and Caudle and Burk reviewed the evidence inventory with I-Bureau personnel, then Souza went off by himself to get away from the crowd and think.

Did you want to kill them all? Did you plan to kill the women or did they just walk in at the wrong time? Maybe Dale was the only intended target.

Maybe if Dale had come home first the assassin would have just shot him and slipped away. The women would have found Dale dead. They'd be traumatized for life, but alive.

First, motive. Greed? Who'd profit from the deaths. Dana? Probably.

Revenge? Did Dale merit that kind of enemy? And why kill the women, then? Again, unless they were just in the wrong place at the wrong time. Or the killer was the kind of sociopath who would as soon do three as one. Was it love turned to jealousy and rage? Did one of the Ewells have a lover? One capable of this?

Souza slumped into a sofa. He felt sticky, soiled. And remarkably tired.

What manner of madman had come to this house? Souza couldn't know until he knew why the killer had come.

I-Bureau technicians continued to lift fingerprints around the home. Any prints found would be compared to elimination prints from family, housekeepers, friends. Duty located a series of footprints in the den. One set appeared to have been made by shoes with a horizontal line pattern, the other might have been made by bare feet. Duty illuminated the area with an Alternate Light Source (a very bright light with a narrow-band pass filter, used as an inexpensive alternative to a laser) and photographed the prints.

The ALS also brought out palm prints on the wall (determined by technicians to have been made before the wall was painted) and shoe tracks on vertical surfaces inside the skylights (obviously made before the skylights had been installed, unless, as Souza said, "Spider-Man did it").

Souza was disappointed. So far, they had turned up little of substantial investigative value, and no fingerprints had been found on items obviously touched by the intruder—which meant the crook had worn gloves. As for the footprints on the carpet, they could have been there for weeks and were probably useless.

One best chance still remained: the extant murder bullets. Three others had been recovered thus far. The first, outside the home. The second had fallen from Glee's back when her body was turned. A third was found when I-Bureau techs cut out the carpeting where Glee had died, locating a flattened bullet, number JD-17, the copper jacket severely compromised from the impact with the home's concrete slab.

Allen Boudreau seemed extraordinarily interested in all three bullets.

"What, what?" Souza said impatiently.

Boudreau grunted. Then he suggested Duty recover the bullet in the office. "Let's see what else we find."

Duty used a keyhole saw to carve a large rectangle out of the wall.

"Hey, Jack," Souza said. "The power's live, and you have a couple of wires in there from the light switch."

"I got it handled," Duty said, grinning and sawing away. Then, *zap*, the wall sparked and smoked. Souza and Duty jumped. The overhead light went black.

"Shit, Jack! We've had enough corpses in here already."

Duty had exposed a two-by-four stud—with a hole in it. The investigators assumed they would have another damaged bullet on their hands—after all, it had passed through a human body, the wallboard, and burrowed into a solid piece of lumber. But they were lucky.

Duty extracted a remarkably intact specimen, one which could have been reloaded and refired. He marked it as evidentiary item JD-18. Boudreau went to the window for better light, examining the bullet that had probably brought Glee down before she was finished off at point-blank range.

The bullet that had killed Tiffany wasn't in sight when Duty used the keyhole saw to remove a square of wallboard from high on the kitchen wall. Duty peered down into the hole, then climbed down and cut another at floor level. He reached in and retracted the copper-jacketed projectile. Number JD-19.

Again, Boudreau studied the damaged slug. He shook his head. "Let's take a walk," he said to Souza and Burk.

The detectives and the criminalist slipped into the mobile command post parked on the street. Boudreau found a seat and kneaded his temples with his fingertips.

"What's up?" Souza asked him.

"You guys are going to think I'm out of my tree."

Souza and Burk exchanged glances.

"There are strange striations—scratches—on the slugs. The bearing surfaces are all hacked up."

"All of them?"

"So far."

"You've seen those types of markings on the sides of bullets before?" said Souza.

"No."

"But you have some sense of what they are."

"Sense?" Boudreau chuckled without humor. "Sense might be the wrong word here."

"Sorry, you're losing me."

"My fault. I needed to think this through. But I'm fairly sure the shooter used a suppressor."

"Oh, man," said Burk, shaking his head.

Upon closer examination of the bullets, Boudreau had noted two things: First, the rifling characteristics of the projectiles—marks left on the bullets by a series of "lands and grooves," machined into the gun barrel at the time of manufacture. (After the barrel is hollowed out, a special tool is pulled through the bore, carving out a series of grooves. These grooves are twisted either right or left, and impart spin on the bullet that stabilizes it and allows it to fly straight, much like a football tossed with a spiral.)

In this case, it appeared the gun barrel of the murder weapon was manufactured as a "six right"; that is, the barrel had six lands and grooves with a right-hand twist, and quite common.

But what shocked Boudreau, and what he alerted detectives to, was the bizarre series of scratches (called coarse stria) covering the land-and-groove impressions on the bullets; he'd not seen anything like them before.

Boudreau would later note in his report: I believed these stria were present on the bullets because the murder weapon was equipped with a silencer, flash suppressor, muzzle break, or some other device or barrel attachment.

Later, Sergeant Caudle told me that neighbors reported

hearing unusual noises that were not perceived as gun-shots.

A total of five of the uniquely marked bullets were found at the scene:

JD-15, found in the flower bed.
JD-16, found under the shoulder of Glee Ewell.
JD-17, found under the head of Glee Ewell.
JD-18, recovered from the office wall.
JD-19, recovered from the kitchen wall.

It was clear to investigators that seven shots had been fired. One, investigators learned that day, had been located in the body of Glee Ewell. But the bullet that had killed Dale Ewell was not found.

Boudreau would write: A total of six bullets were recovered. A total of seven shots were accounted for at the scene. Given that one fired bullet and seven expended cases were missing, it was apparent that the murderer(s) had picked up these items . . . a rare event within all the accumulated experience of investigators present.

"That clanking sound Christian said the neighbors heard," Boudreau said to the detectives as they huddled in the mobile command post. "A silencer would sure as hell explain it. People think a suppressor silences a weapon, but more accurately it changes the way the report sounds. Right?"

After going out for lunch, Souza returned to the scene and pulled his car off onto the sandy shoulder at East Park Circle. Dana, his uncle Richard, and John Zent had been going up the walk toward the house. Dana looked over his shoulder, didn't turn around, but waited in the afternoon heat. Zent stuffed his hands deep into his pockets.

Zent, Lieutenant White learned, had traveled to his home in Morgan Hill, searched the trash at Dana's request, and dug out a pair of receipts for Dana's April 19 purchase of Easter cards and groceries. Zent had yet to hand the receipts over to investigators.

Souza and Burk stepped over candy wrappers and Coke cans left behind by spectators and caught up with Dana. They would walk Dana through the house and ask him to describe any items that had been stolen, so that investigators could get a description of the goods out on the teletype.

Souza took a moment to admonish Dana. "I have to ask that you not touch anything. If there is any need at all, please check with me. We'll go through the house single file, room by room."

Souza led the way inside, first walking Dana through the western, nonevent side of the home, in a "controlled walk-through."

SEVEN

IT WAS COOL INSIDE. SOMEONE HAD LOWERED the thermostat. In the master bedroom, Dana glanced into the dresser. He kept his hands by his side.

"The nine-millimeter must have been stolen, all right."

He saw a container in the shape of a coconut and said his mother usually hid her pearls in there. Then, as investigators had done the day before, the group went back out the front door and entered again through the garage. At the end of the hall, they edged around the spot upon which Dale had died. The carpet had been cut out by criminalists.

Souza watched Dana for a reaction to the killing house, but none came. No breakdown at setting foot where his family had perished so suddenly, no wave of nausea that often accompanied proximity to the carnage.

They moved into Glee's office. Here, too, a large section of carpeting had been removed.

"I need to get to the files," Dana said.

Souza blinked. "In here?"

"Yeah. Right there, right in her closet."

"Well, you can't go in there until we release the scene, Dana."

"I need to get some papers."

"Sorry."

Dana looked pleadingly to Agent Zent, but Zent only shrugged and shook his head. His face, Souza felt, registered disgust at the attitude of the local rube cops.

"Can you at least check the answering machine?"

It was dim in the office, and Burk said, "I can't really see the buttons."

"Well, turn on the lights!"

"The lights aren't working."

"What happened?" Dana said.

"The criminalists accidentally cut the wires when they took out a piece of wallboard," Souza said. He wanted to add, "Digging out one of the bullets that killed your momma," but didn't.

Dana, his gaze ticking back and forth between Souza and the hole in the wall, one fist knotted at his side, pointed at the hole. "Is someone going to pay for this?"

For a foggy moment, Souza told himself the kid couldn't have had anything to do with the crime. For God's sake, wouldn't he at least act like he was grieving? "I think there's a form—"

"Forget it," Dana said, with a wave of his hand.

Burk hovered over the answering device. "How do you retrieve the messages?"

Dana instructed Burk, but despite repeated tries, Burk could get nothing out of the machine.

"This button right here," Dana said, moving closer, stepping on the spot where his mother had died.

He punched a button, and Tiffany's quiet voice came on, asking callers to please leave a message. Dana rewound and tried again, shaking his head in frustration.

Son of bitch, Souza thought. This guy's an ice cube.

Outside again, Dana watched IB personnel load boxes into cars.

"Where are they going with all that?" he said.

"It's dishes, things like that," Souza said. "They'll take it all down to the lab to gas for fingerprints."

"Well," said Dana, "I want an itemized list of items taken from my house."

*   *   *

At 2:42 Souza and Burk interviewed Dale's brother Richard. Unfailingly polite and nearly as towering as his late brother had been, Richard told the detectives he'd lived in the San Francisco area for twenty-five years, before moving to Fresno in 1990. He'd retired from the phone company and come to work with his brother Dan.

Yes, Richard said when they'd settled into chairs, he knew the layout of Dale and Glee's home, but no, he had no key nor did he know the security alarm code. He and Dale had talked mostly about family, Richard said, and their only shared financial interest was the beach house, which the brothers had bought together years before.

Burk asked about Dale's relationship with his immediate family.

"It was a beautiful family," Richard said sadly. "If I were asked to give an example of a model family, it would certainly be that family. As a matter of fact, as recently as a few months ago I told Dale it was strange he was the only one of the brothers who ended up with a real nice family that stayed together. That's . . . that's just what makes this more tragic. I don't know how Dana's holding up under this, his dad was so proud of him. Dana really loved his father, because they did a lot together. Of course, Tiffany is the same way."

Richard went on to say that Dale and his children had no more than the "normal" family problems. He'd heard of no drug use by Dana, and, as for Tiffany, she had been reserved and extremely well behaved. His eyes sparked as he talked about her, but the sorrow soon returned to his face.

Burk and Souza pressed Richard for any information that might hint at Dale's involvement with drug smugglers, or anyone else who could have proved dangerous if crossed. But Richard insisted he'd heard nothing of the kind until Dale's death.

The detectives asked about any insurance policies on Dale's life. They brought up Glee's time with the CIA.

Richard said no motive in any of that came to mind. It all just made no sense.

"That's why we're talking to the family," Burk told Richard. "Basically this crime doesn't make a whole lot of sense."

Burk finished the warm-up for the second meeting with Dana.

"This will be in reference to case number 92-15285, the second interview with Dana James Ewell, DOB of 1-28-71. It's 1430 hours." Burk said, "Dana, could you go back to Sunday, from the beginning?"

"Oh, from the beginning? Okay, Dad and I played tennis at ten in the morning, then we came back and took showers, ate lunch. Then we did Easter presents and went for a walk on the beach at about twelve-thirty. I had to get to Monica's by three, so we packed up and started to close up the house. I think I took off at about . . . two-fifteen, and then I stopped for gas, cleaned the windshield. When I was driving to Monica's, I said, 'Oh, I better get some Easter cards.' I bought cards, three of 'em, at the Payless."

"Okay," said Souza. "Then you had dinner and her folks came?"

"Yeah, that's right."

"What kind of food did you eat?"

"Uh, chicken, some breaded chicken thing, and zucchini she heated up. I guess her parents came about six, and we played with Monica's sister, she's like ten, Old Maid and stuff." Dana snickered.

"And you left when?" Burk said.

He sat straight in his chair. "Nine. After nine."

"I see. And getting back to your dad. He flew home on Sunday?"

"Right," Dana said. "As far as I know. I mean, he would have, and the Bonanza was there."

"Have you ever flown out of Watsonville? Over to Fresno?"

"Watsonville?" Dana nodded. "Of course."

"When was the last time?"

"The last time?"

"Yeah," Burk said. "When was the last time you flew?"

Souza watched Dana's eyes. Nothing.

"That'd have to be . . . Christmastime. Have to check my log."

"Sure. What kind of business relationship does your dad have with his brothers?"

"Not much. They all bought the beach house years ago, before they were wealthy. But since then, Dad kind of did his thing with the airplanes."

"Does your dad have anything to do with the Brighton Crest development?"

Dana shook his head. "No, not at all."

" 'Cause we were hearing there was a policy on your dad, with the money going to the corporation of theirs."

"That's a wonderful fabrication, then." Dana smiled.

"Okay. See, we don't know . . ."

"Yeah, I know. Sure."

"People are calling us with this information," Burk said.

"That's wild."

"Who is the Ewell Company?"

"That's, that's the license plate on my car."

"Okay," Burk said.

"That's just the license plate I started."

"Started? A license plate?"

"I mean, created."

"Oh. Okay. How much is your dad worth, do you know?"

Dana puffed out his cheeks and let go a breath. "I think when I typed it [the family net worth statement] last time it was around seven mil, somewhere around there. It's in the office, like I said."

"And your mom?"

"The cover said 'Dale and Glee Ewell,' so it was both of them. That's it."

Souza asked, "Dana, is there anyone you know, other

than the obvious person—yourself—who would gain by their death?"

Dana took his time here. "I don't know how the corporation works. But, Bob Pursell, over at Western Piper? I guess he might become president now. He wants to sue everyone who touches him, and he's lied to my dad in the past. Otherwise, I don't know."

"Anyone else at the business he's had a problem with?"

Chuckling, Dana said, "Most of them are really screwed up. Our head mechanic, Jack Whitman, is a drunk and divorced and fighting with his kids, and Bob Pursell is a loose cannon on the ship. Stuff like that."

"And you mentioned Frank Lambetecchio the other day."

"He's a drug dealer."

"But so far as you know, your dad has never received any death threats?"

Shrugging, Dana said, "Not that I know of. Something tells me he has before, though."

"And how about you and your folks, you ever have any disagreements—"

"No. I mean, Dad wanted me to go to school in London, but I was bored with school, I aced my classes, and I felt I wasn't being challenged enough. I've been working on job offers in New York. That's where the action is. I have pictures of the Stock Exchange on my wall. You know, I got real interested in doing that stuff when I was young."

"So," Burk said, "how much do they give you to live on?"

"Okay," Dana said, straightening up, "they don't give me so much per month. They give me a couple of credit cards, and when I need stuff, books and stuff, I call 'em up and ask them to put some in the checking account."

"Who, um . . . is there anyone you know that would want your parents dead?"

"Dead? I don't know of any specific people. Tiffany is the most harmless creature in the world, but my mother's on the State Bar. Dad's usually pretty calm, but once in a while he gets upset or gets in a lawsuit. Or, like once we're trying to get a rack of lamb? He's driving all over Fresno, hitting all those stupid Fresno traffic lights, and he's kinda obsessed about this meat, and he's going nuts. I told him to calm down it was no big deal, but he's just trying to find this meat, but to answer your question—"

"I have a question. Did you have anything to do with your parents' death?"

Dana looked down at his lap. Took a quick breath, looked up again.

"No." Firm, without anger.

But, to Souza, who had witnessed hundreds of responses to that very question, Dana's answer rang as hollow as the metallic ping of a silenced weapon being fired.

"Okay," Burk said. His voice had gone flat. "As we said, we get a lot of people that like to throw dirt. Do you know if Bob Pursell is part owner of the corporation?"

"I don't know if he owns any shares or not."

"Okay. The time is 1515 hours. We're going to terminate this interview."

Souza and Burk also interviewed the maid, Rose Avita, and most of her family; after all, she had a key and knew the alarm code to the Ewell home. Souza had seen more than one instance of a housekeeper's relative stealing a key and burglarizing an employer's home.

Avita family members allowed I-Bureau to take elimination fingerprints, but nothing the detectives had seen or heard led them to suspect any of them.

A detective who had canvassed the neighborhood mentioned the name of Lowell Moril to Souza, the same person Dana had claimed was a local troublemaker. Milo was a strange one indeed, the detective said, and neighbors reported that he'd once blown a hole in his room wall with a shotgun blast.

Souza took particular note of Milo; maybe he was simply the neighborhood nutcase, maybe he was someone more sinister, but he certainly would be checked out.

Later, Souza and Ybarra found the number of the alarm company on a small sign on the front lawn. *Armed Response*. The alarm representative arrived within twenty minutes and froze in his tracks at the sight of the bloody kitchen floor.

"Just try not to look," Ybarra said, knowing she was wasting her breath. "And don't touch anything unless I give you specific permission, okay?"

The alarm guy licked his lips. "Whatever you say."

Led around by the detectives, the alarm-company technician inspected the alarm box in the hall closet near the entryway. He then inspected and tested the motion detectors and sound monitors. Finally, he activated the alarm at the keypad near the garage, opened the door, and waited. Forty-five seconds later the alarm wailed. He shut it down and telephoned the monitoring office.

"They got the activation alert," he told Souza, hanging up the phone. "It's all in perfect working order." He dragged a forearm across his brow.

"You're saying it wasn't set," Ybarra said.

"Well, maybe the, ah . . . dead people turned it off when they came in."

"But what if there was someone in here before they got home?"

"Waiting? Is that what you think happened?"

"An intruder would have obviously tripped the alarm, right? Unless it hadn't been set when the occupants left the house?"

"Sure. Yeah."

"What if he got in through someplace that wasn't wired to the alarm?"

"Well, it's pretty much all wired. They got a goddamn good system here. Pricey."

"Come here," said Souza.

He led the way into the bathroom.

"What about the skylights?"

The alarm technician stared upward, creasing the sunburned layer of fat on the back of his neck. "Nope. But they're sealed off, ain't they?"

"That's what it looked like to me."

Outside, the alarm rep said, "Looks like they forgot to set it." He walked toward his truck, then stopped and turned back. "Unless the guy that done it knew the code. But, hey, how could he?"

Souza had wondered about that, too.

Souza found a message on his machine when he stopped at his office late that afternoon. He returned a call to a young man named Peter Tapia, who claimed his brother Mario had gone to school with Dana. Dana, Peter said, was fascinated with Joe Hunt, convicted murderer and founder of the infamous Billionaire Boy's Club. Dana had gone so far as to write Hunt in prison, and Hunt had written back until he discovered that the "Dana" in this case was not a woman.

At the scene that evening, the end of the second day of processing, Souza learned that the I-Bureau had lifted twenty-two latent fingerprints. But there was a sense among investigators, as no prints had been found on items moved by the killer, that those lifts would prove useless.

"What are we missing here?" Souza asked Caudle and Burk, as I-Bureau packed up.

What they had was an amateurish burglary, yet a precision shooting. Dale and Tiffany's entry wounds had been nearly identical in location, and the detectives knew well how difficult it was to attain that kind of accuracy under stress. In situations of officer-related shootings, police rarely hit fifty percent of their targets, and most officers spend time on the shooting range.

This hadn't been the shooting range. The shooter would have been pumped with adrenaline, his targets in motion.

The investigators agreed: While the burglary looked

like it had been pulled by a fifteen-year-old kid, the shooting had the mark of a cool, steely-eyed professional. One who would not have left fingerprints.

And with Boudreau's growing certainty that a suppressor—a silencer attached to the gun barrel—was involved, the likelihood of some kind of contract killer seemed a lock.

They also felt the women had been hit half an hour before the father came in. So somebody wanted—or needed—Dale dead. But why?

Was it a grudge killing, perhaps ordered by this Lambetecchio character, ownership of whose airplane dealership Dale Ewell had assumed after Lambetecchio's imprisonment? Or some unnamed drug runner? Were the Aerostar owners perturbed enough about a repair bill to kill the Ewells? Was it a crazy neighbor, like Lowell Moril?

The investigators called it a night, without finding answers. But of one thing Souza felt certain: The Ewell murders had not been the result of a botched burglary.

At ten o'clock on Thursday morning, Marlene Reid, whom Souza had interviewed on the street the morning of the murders, appeared at the FSO so the detectives could talk with her at length.

She said she'd been Dale's assistant for eighteen years, and Dale "always" stopped in at his office on Sundays when returning from Pajaro. When last she'd seen him on Friday, Dale remained upset about the phone conversation with the Aerostar owner.

Dale had even raised his voice, though he hadn't cursed. She had never heard him curse.

This Aerostar owner agreed to pay only two-fifty of the two-thousand-dollar repair bill. The dispute was taking up a great deal of company time, Reid claimed, and seemed to have angered Dale as a matter of principle. She went on to detail her fears of mechanic Jack Whitman, whom she claimed drank to excess and had an ungovernable temper.

"He frightens me," Reid said.

And when she called him to tell him about the murders, Whitman had asked, "Were they killed when they were coming home?" How would he know that? she asked.

Finally, Reid talked about salesman Robert Pursell, a "devil-may-care kind of guy."

"How did Dale and Pursell get along?" asked Ernie Burk. "Pretty good, or was it an up-and-down kind of relationship?"

"Oh, they had their disagreements, but Bob would never have the nerve to do anything violent."

After Reid's comments, echoing the opinion of Robert Pursell that Jack Whitman was hotheaded and seemed to have some knowledge of how the Ewells died, Souza called Whitman and set an appointment for an interview later that day.

Reid was no sooner out the door than Souza got a call from the Fresno Air Terminal Police. It seemed a private plane in the care of Western Piper (located in a fenced industrial park bordering the tarmac of Fresno Air Terminal) had been stolen from the airport moments before.

Burk and Souza rushed out to FAT and met with airport police. The detectives learned that Robert Pursell had called and claimed, inexplicably, that the murderers of the Ewell family had just stolen a plane.

It took just a few minutes to learn that in fact the man who'd flown off was one of the owners of the disputed Aerostar. He'd come in on a commercial carrier, seen his plane chained up near the runway, and simply removed the chain from the prop and taken off.

Where Pursell got off claiming the "murderers" of the Ewells were in the plane, Souza had no clue. Before he got into the car, he kicked the door a few times. The goddamn case was moving backward. Worse, he had a sense it might never be solved.

EIGHT

SHORTLY AFTER THE VISIT TO FRESNO AIR TERminal, Chris Curtice advised Souza that he'd taken a call from a Fresno physician who claimed to be friends with Ewell mechanic Whitman. The caller relayed that Whitman had also overheard the "heated" call between Dale Ewell and an owner of the Aerostar. Whitman told the caller that Dale had a "look of fear on his face" that Whitman had never seen before.

The caller also invoked the name of Frank Lambetecchio, whom he said blamed Dale Ewell for the loss of his business. Souza and Burk took a drive to Whitman's house.

Sure, Jack Whitman told Souza and Burk, he'd argued with Dale at times, and Reid and Pursell; it was a small company and people clashed occasionally. That's all. But he'd managed to remain as Dale's service manager since 1973.

Didn't know the family well, he said, except that Dana was a "good kid," and Tiffany, "a beautiful girl."

Burk asked about the rumors that Dale had smuggled drugs.

"No," the aging, leather-skinned mechanic said, "I don't believe that at all."

Whitman told the detectives that accused drug dealers

had once attempted to foist blame on Dale to save their own hides, but Dale was always clean.

On Friday, Whitman said, he'd taken the call from one of the Aerostar's owners. The attorney threatened to sue, so Whitman passed the call to Dale, and Dale had been beet-faced when he emerged from his office after the conversation.

Dale, Whitman claimed, was the only person who had ever really stood by him. Dale had even given him a key to the Ewell cabin at Shaver Lake, to make up for calling him in to work on Friday. Whitman had been considering retirement, but on Saturday he telephoned Dale at the beach house.

"I want you to know," Whitman told Dale, "I love you and your family, and I'm gonna stick by you for the duration."

"Okay," Burk said, "and you didn't go to the airport or anything and see him on Sunday?"

"No, not at all."

"Well, what did you do Sunday?"

Put a sprinkler system in his yard, Whitman said. All day. Wife was there, too.

He claimed no knowledge of the Ewell home or security system, or the way they had died, though he felt it might have something to do with the Aerostar dispute, or perhaps a number of property lawsuits.

"Listen," Burk said, "before we close, due to the fact that you've been in Dale's car, we'd like permission to take you downstairs for elimination prints, since we're dusting—"

"No problem."

". . . We're dusting the cars now. We want to make sure to eliminate those prints."

"No, it's no problem," Whitman said.

Souza wanted to know whether Whitman had been in the armed services. Whitman admitted he'd been an Air Force mechanic.

"Do you . . . are you a hunter or fisherman?" Souza said.

"No."

"You're not into that at all? Have any weapons in your residence?"

"I have a pellet pistol and I have a pellet gun."

"Okay. No shotgun or other—"

"No shotgun, no pistols, no."

"Okay, so I take it you don't do any target shooting or anything like that?"

"No."

"Trapshooting?"

"No."

"Okay, that's it."

A Bank of America branch manager called Detective Christian at the FSO that same day. The manager said she had been approached a few years earlier by a Ewell employee named Robert, who had inquired about receiving bank financing to purchase Dale's dealership.

But when she'd contacted Dale, Dale had told her the business wasn't for sale. When she told Robert this, he became "livid to the point that he was shaking and trembling."

And just a few weeks ago she had run into Robert: when asked how Dale was doing, Robert snorted, "He's still getting rich."

The caller said Pursell was awfully angry with Ewell, and she felt the police ought to know.

Later that evening, Dana Ewell was again granted access to the crime scene. Mindy Ybarra walked Dana through so he could pick out burial clothes for his family. While sorting through Dale's closet, Dana pointed out to Ybarra a Ruger .357 revolver, in its case, which had been stored on the top shelf of the closet.

While no one had linked the .357 to the crime, the department was collectively red-faced that they'd missed the handgun during their search. Mistakes like that could come back to haunt you, especially in a courtroom.

NINE

Souza and Burk now pieced together a history of the Ewell family:

Dale Alan Ewell was a bright young man who grew up with a remarkable fascination for airplanes, in a time when the nation knew breadlines and a world war. Son of Ohio farmer Austin Bert Ewell and his schoolteacher wife Mary Rebecca Thompson (a graduate of Kent State) Dale was the firstborn son. He and his older sister and three brothers learned to toil from sunup to sundown on the 250-acre property their father had bought in 1937, his mortgage thirty dollars a month for the life of the seller (who would live to be nearly a hundred). To the Ewells, life was milking cattle on frosty mornings and tending fields of grain under a punishing sun.

Few farmboys of that era made it to college, but Dale went off to Miami University (Ohio) and in 1954 graduated with a degree in aeronautical engineering. More enamored than ever with flight, he signed on with the Air Force and learned how to fly. Dale pulled elite duty in the service, ferrying Air Force brass around in a King Air turboprop.

When assigned to Phoenix in 1957 Dale met Glee Ethel Mitchell at a party. She was taken with the towering Air Force pilot with the dry wit and driving ambition, as was he with the vivacious, apple-cheeked college girl who seemed to attract friends with uncommon ease.

71

Glee had known privileges unfamiliar to the Ewells of Ohio. Born in Chicago on January 13, 1935, her mother, "Big Glee," inherited substantial oil holdings from her father, physician G.E. Irvin, though Glee's father was an instructor at the Chicago Squash Club and not a man of means.

Glee excelled in school, spent summers with relatives in Oklahoma, shone in social circles. There was little doubt she would continue her formal education after high school. She enrolled at the University of Arizona. She earned an undergraduate degree in Inter-American studies, and was elected to Phi Beta Kappa. She continued at the university with postgraduate studies, while Dale, his hitch in the service complete, accepted a job with Douglas Aircraft in Long Beach, California.

Despite the geographical distance between them, Dale Ewell and Glee Mitchell knew they would share a promising future. But their paths to that future took unexpected twists: Dale found he wasn't happy at Douglas Aircraft. He wanted to be outside, flying planes, building a future based upon his own substantial wit and uncompromising work ethic. In 1959 he left Douglas, moving north to the agricultural village of Fresno and accepting a job selling private aircraft.

That year, Glee, too, made an unusual career move—she joined the Central Intelligence Agency. Sent to Argentina, she reportedly worked as a "company" translator. After two years with the CIA, Glee returned to the US, and to Dale Ewell. They were married on December 28, 1961.

Dale made bucketloads of money selling aircraft. He'd barnstorm unannounced into a farmer's field, show off his shiny, powerful machine, and proclaim that he would personally teach the farmer how to fly if they could make a deal that day.

In 1965, Dale went to work for Frank Lambe Aviation, where he continued to rack up hefty commissions and build his net worth. But in 1971, Lambe (sometimes Lambetecchio) was arrested for drug smuggling, his dealership shuttered. When Lambe was sentenced to prison, Piper Aircraft offered Dale a chance to buy the dealership; Dale grabbed it.

He also bought a nine-millimeter Browning Hi-Power handgun and two boxes of ammunition—just in case Lambe or one of his cronies decided they didn't appreciate Dale's business decisions.

Western Piper Sales was soon far more successful than had been the Lambe enterprise. These were great years for the private aircraft industry. Dale sold everything he could get his hands on. Though Lambe claimed Dale was "the most hated aircraft dealer in the world," Bob Follett, manager at a nearby flying service, said Dale wasn't hated but he "wasn't out there to be the most lovable. He was a no-nonsense kind of guy."

Glee threw herself into public service work and charities. She was as gregarious and likable as Dale was private and tough; a longtime friend said of her, "You could talk to one hundred people in Fresno and they'd tell you she was their best friend."

Dale poured his money into investments and real estate, intending to pass on a legacy of wealth to his two young children, Tiffany Ann, born May 1, 1967, and Dana James, who entered this world on January 28, 1971. Dale swore his children would never need to slave under the hot sun as he had.

Tiffany, perhaps affected psychologically by her childhood head injury, was described by friends as, "very sweet, very shy, very lovely. A wonderful personality, but you had to really draw her out in a conversation." Before Tiffany went on to graduate accounting courses at Fresno State, she attended Fresno's San Joaquin Memorial High School, then a small Oregon college, where she was voted the shyest member of the class.

Dana, conversely, came to be known as a hot-tempered

"Mr. Wall Street," who was "very competitive," and "always in a hurry," walking what he called his New York walk. Dana's parents, friends claimed, were quick to cover for Dana when he wrecked his car or got into trouble for minor vandalism. With his Mercedes and substantial allowance, Dana was voted Most Likely to Succeed by high-school classmates, though many were to later claim that Dana would stop at nothing to achieve that success.

TEN

On April 24, Souza drove out to the Fresno Air Terminal and learned from the FAA that Dale's airplane had landed at 3:23 on the afternoon of the murders. Souza also interviewed Jack Whitman's wife at their home. She confirmed that Jack had been at home on Easter. Friends and family had been in and out when he was there. It was a solid alibi; despite the implication of Whitman by Dana and Pursell, Souza had no reason to believe Whitman was involved in the murders.

The same afternoon, Sheriff Magarian ordered his investigators to complete their crime-scene work and turn 5663 East Park Circle over to Dana Ewell. Technicians packed up and Ybarra spread newspapers over bloodstains and released the scene to Dana at 10:30 Friday evening. She later reported to Souza that she'd recommended a cleaning service (police do not clean up crime scenes). Deputies maintained security while a locksmith changed the house locks.

During the walk-through of the yard areas, Ybarra said, Dana removed a key from beneath the tool-shed awning, and he seemed rather stealthy about it. When she told Dana that I-Bureau personnel had cut the latch off the backyard gate, Dana, raising his voice, repeated his demand for a list of items collected by investigators.

As she was leaving Dana apologized for losing his temper. Ybarra assured him she understood, and a few minutes later left him alone at the home where his family had been massacred.

Shortly after Dana and his relatives buried their dead in Belmont Memorial Park, the Fresno First Congregational Church on Van Ness Boulevard was filling to capacity. Souza waited until most of the four hundred people made their way inside the fortresslike old church for the Saturday, April 25 memorial service. He stood at the rear, hands clasped before him. Ernie Burk took a seat in a pew across the aisle.

The extended Ewell family filled up the first five rows of the church as the subdued strains of classical music filled the air. Dana and his girlfriend moved among family members, shaking hands, nodding, whispering. The preacher approached his pulpit. Souza shifted his weight from foot to foot.

"What happened in the house?" asked the Reverend Frank Baldwin. "Was it senseless urban violence or bizarre, twisting killings?"

He called Glee, "the ultimate giver." Dale was "a gentle giant." And Tiffany, "a delicate flower just ready to bloom," and prayed that God give the detectives the strength and wisdom to track down those responsible.

After the echo of the preacher's words had faded, Dale and Glee and Tiffany were eulogized by family and friends, including the Chief Justice of the California Supreme Court. Then the crowd filed outside.

Dana accepted the condolences of mourners. Under clouds the color of steel wool, it all appeared unremarkable until Marlene Reid approached Dana. Dana stepped closer, complimenting her on her outfit. Then he took her hand.

"Man!" he said. "What a rock!"

Before that, Souza had witnessed but one notable display of emotion from Dana: anger over the blown light fixture in the house. Now, he was giddy over the sight of a diamond.

"Listen," Souza said to Burk as they drove downtown, "kids just don't have the whole family whacked."

"Happens all the time, John," Burk said, "and you know it. The son stinks. I don't know why you're hesitant."

Souza thought about Dana's demand for a list of items seized by the department. He considered the rumors that Dana had claimed that the police cleaned out his father's wallet.

"I sure as hell have never seen anyone like Dana, but it doesn't mean he killed them. Shit, he wasn't even around."

"Whatever."

"So we'll get going with a background check. See what turns up."

On Sunday, April 26, exactly one week after the murders, Souza and Burk returned to the Ewell neighborhood.

They lingered in the car, taking the neighborhood's pulse. Kids playing, people walking dogs or jogging along the sandy shoulder of East Park Circle. The detectives wanted to get a feel for who might have been around on the previous Sunday.

They knocked on doors. A few neighbors, including one who hadn't been interviewed during the first canvass, claimed to have heard strange noises on Easter. One woman described the sound as a metallic clank, like something being whacked with a shovel. Another said a white van had been in the area, but it was probably a gardener's truck.

Souza and Burk found Lowell Moril, the supposed headcase who'd discharged a shotgun in his bedroom. Lowell was clean-cut, looked a bit like fifties' actor Sal Mineo, and patiently explained that he'd only fired his shotgun because a pack of Ninjas had attacked him during dinner.

Souza and Burk looked at each other—how strange could this case get?

But, Lowell insisted, on Easter Sunday he'd been at his aunt's house. Hey, ask her, okay?

Monday, April 27. Boudreau took custody of the bullets found at the scene; the following day, he received the bullet recovered during the autopsy of Glee. Each bullet had been placed in a coin envelope, then sealed in a Sheriff's Department evidence envelope.

First, Boudreau initialed and photographed the autopsy bullet, then he weighed and examined it to learn if it matched the other recovered bullets; it did. Next he compared the bullets under the Forensic Comparison Microscope and concluded that all six bullets had been fired by the same weapon.

So that he might rule out completely that the bullets had been fired from a revolver (which would explain the lack of expended cartridges at the scene) Boudreau conducted a series of test-firings comparing a Browning Hi-Power, similar to the missing Ewell weapon, a Smith & Wesson Model 59 pistol, and a Walther P-38 pistol to a number of .38 caliber revolvers. Ultimately, the lack of "skid marks" on the murder bullets led Boudreau to believe an autoloading weapon, not a revolver, had probably been used in the killings.

(So-called skid marks are characteristic evidence that a bullet has been fired from a revolver. Unlike cartridges in an autoloading pistol, revolver cartridges are chambered in a cylinder behind the barrel; when fired, the yet-unspinning bullets enter the rear of the bore at high speed before engaging the lands and grooves within the bore. The bullets skitter, or "skid," momentarily before passing into the bore. When an examiner studies a bullet that has been fired from a semiautomatic pistol, the land impression width is usually constant from front to back, while a revolver bullet will have land impressions somewhat wider toward the front of the bullet.)

The rifling characteristics left on the murder bullets were fundamentally similar to the Browning's rifling; that is, the Browning also had six lands and grooves and a right twist. Still, differences in the width of the lands and grooves led Boudreau further to conclude that the Browning had not been the murder weapon.

Finally, Boudreau made enlargements of the murder-bullet photos and prepared a cover letter for the inquiry he would send to forty-four forensic experts:

Dear Firearms Examiner,

The Fresno County Sheriff's Department, Forensic Laboratory, is seeking assistance in the investigation of a homicide. A number of bullets were recovered in this case. All demonstrate continuous markings around their circumference. These markings are shown in the enclosed photograph.

Boudreau went on to describe in detail the bullets and the stria. In closing, he wrote:

If you have encountered bullets having this type of markings I would deeply appreciate learning what brand or type of firearm produced them. A short note would be adequate, or you may telephone me or Det. John Souza. Due to the nature of this investigation this letter and the enclosed photograph should be considered confidential.

Boudreau continued to puzzle over his own experiments as he awaited replies.

ELEVEN

JOHN SOUZA HADN'T VISITED EVERY COLLEGE campus in California, but it seemed most of them looked an awful lot alike. The kids with backpacks, the expanse of lawn. And not a single open parking space within two hundred yards of the place. The breeze whipped fast-food wrappers through the university parking lot. Jets from nearby San Jose Airport screamed across the sky. Souza and Mindy Ybarra had driven nearly two and a half hours to Santa Clara, a prosperous, nearly treeless city south of San Francisco Bay.

The professor Souza and Ybarra interviewed didn't look like the tweedy professors of Souza's day. This one, friendly but obviously very bright, looked like an artist with a hefty appetite for cheeseburgers. Dr. William Prior met them in the Public Safety office. He sipped his Snapple and tapped his feet nervously as he sat and talked.

"I teach in the philosophy department and head the honors program. I knew right away where Dana had plagiarized his paper. It was a professional work."

"What class was this?" said Souza.

"Business Ethics."

"He plagiarized a paper for ethics class?"

Souza hadn't meant to blurt it out that way.

"Ironic, no? When I confronted Dana about it, he didn't seem particularly concerned about the morality question. When Dr. Heckman flunked him, Dana tried to obtain a late drop from the class so he could avoid an F, but nobody fell for it. This was typical of how Dana would attempt to manipulate the system to his own end."

Ybarra said, "How did he take it?"

"After he was suspended from the honors program, he took it quite hard. And then he wrote me that letter."

"Letter?"

"Oh, Dana sent me a long letter. Frankly, I found the contents frightening."

"Did he threaten you?"

"Not directly, but it was a disturbing correspondence. I referred it to a colleague of mine, a practicing psychologist who works with violent offenders, and he stated the person who wrote the letter was in dire need of counseling."

"Have you seen Dana since?"

"Oh yeah. As a matter of fact, Dana came to me and said he'd been accepted at Princeton. He asked me to return the letter. I told him I'd misplaced the original and handed him a photocopy." Prior finished off his drink and let the bottle clunk into a steel wastebasket.

Souza said, "Was Dana actually accepted at Princeton?"

"Not that I know of. But I can't say for certain one way or the other."

"Can we get a copy of that letter?"

"I anticipated that request. I'm consulting with our legal department about the possibility of releasing it to law enforcement. I'll let you know as soon as I can."

"We appreciate that, Dr. Prior. Anything else you can tell us that might assist us?"

"Only that Dana appears very driven. He seems to need to be seen as flawless. When you couple those traits with an inflated opinion of himself and an apparent bent for manipulating others to his own benefit—well, in my view, Dana believes he's brighter than he actually is, and he feels it's fine to cheat." Prior grinned. "As long as you don't get caught."

"And others share your view?"

"I can't speak for others. However, I think Dana's quite transparent. People aren't as stupid as he assumes them to be."

"And his family. Did he ever mention his family?"

"Not that I recall. I'm afraid all I know about them is that they were murdered. Sad to say. Look, I don't want to add to Dana's problems, but since I received that letter, and especially after his family was killed, I've been concerned. Understandably, I think."

"If you can get that letter to us ASAP, we'd be grateful."

"I'll do my best. Believe me."

On the twenty-eighth, while Souza and Ybarra continued to roam the Santa Clara campus, Ernie Burk phoned Dana Ewell and asked for permission to search the Shaver Lake cabin and the Pajaro house, so detectives could be certain the missing Browning Hi-Power nine-millimeter was not at either of those locations.

Dana consented, and Burk went through the Shaver cabin. When he found nothing of import, he called Souza on the cell phone and said Dana would meet Souza and Ybarra at the beach house.

"Afternoon, Dana," Souza said, as Dana showed them in.

Dana was polite, though not talkative. He unlocked the home and waited, never far away, as the detectives searched. Souza looked around the plush, five-bedroom home, with its open floor plan, walls of glass, and views of sand dunes and creaming surf, admiring a world he would never know on a cop's salary.

Mindy asked Dana if he'd found a key by the shed at Circle Park East the day she'd turned the home over to him.

Yes, Dana said, he'd picked up a key. The locks had been changed, so who needed it? Dana grabbed his father's briefcase and produced a letter.

"Look at this. It's supposedly a letter to Bob Pursell

from my dad. Here, you can take this copy."

He handed Souza the letter. "No way my dad wrote that thing. I think Pursell faked it."

The letter, dated April 12, 1992, was addressed to "Bob," and argued that the addressee should not leave his employment at Western Piper. "It's possible that a salary equal to my own current salary and a negotiated bonus structure based on profits could be worked out," the letter read.

Souza couldn't know for sure who had written the letter, but if Pursell had authored it after Dale's murder, the sales manager was someone to keep an eye on.

The detectives did not find the Browning. Dana saw them to the door and stayed behind.

Outside, Souza peered at Glee's Cadillac.

"Mindy, look at this."

She frowned when she spotted the black powder—fingerprint dust—on Glee's car.

"He didn't even bother to wash it," she said.

"He may not have anything to do with the homicides," Souza said, "but he's a creepy son of a bitch."

On the way out of the secure complex, Souza and Ybarra stopped at the gate and asked the guard whether security personnel maintained a logbook of vehicles coming in and out of the area.

The guard said no such records existed. He did mention that the houses were checked daily, and his log showed the Ewell home had been empty by 3:00 P.M. on Easter Sunday.

Later, Souza tracked down the name of a classmate who Dr. Prior had said was friendly with Dana. Her name was Alicia, and she had a round face and a fleshy build that bordered on fat, but wasn't.

Souza found her quite attractive, saw a spark of intelligence and optimism in her oval green eyes. He badged her.

"Wow," Alicia said, staring at the gold star. "I heard about his P's getting killed. Very nasty."

"Can we sit over here?" He motioned toward a bench near a stand of trees. They sat.

"Are you after the guys who did it?" she asked.

"We'd sure like to catch the kind of person that would kill three people like that."

"So, you asked about Dana? Pretty smart. Had a 180 IQ."

"How did you know that?"

"Huh! Guess he told me!" She laughed. "Gets good grades, though. Dresses expensive, Armani suits. Got a new Benz. He's into the money thing, made a few million already."

"Uh-huh," Souza said. Then her comment hit home. "You say he made a few million? Himself?"

"Oh, yeah. It was in all the papers. How he sold airplanes and made a shit . . . a truckload of cash in the stock market."

Souza made a note of that development.

"He have many friends?"

Alicia gathered up her long locks and let them swing free, flaxen hair reflecting sunlight.

"I wouldn't say it was a lot. But he had a girlfriend, uh, Monica. And his buddy, Joel. God knows what he and Joel had in common. Dana in his business suits, and Joel in ripped up T-shirts."

"What's Joel's last name?"

"It's a mouthful. Radovcich." She spelled it twice. Then she said, "Joel got busted for breaking into the dorm. That was a real kick in the ass. Excuse my French."

Souza took a sharp breath and cocked his head. "This Joel guy was arrested?"

"Yeah, him and some other schmuck stole stuff out of one of the dorms. I'm telling you, Joel's a real piece of work."

*   *   *

Before returning to Fresno, Souza and Ybarra stopped at the Pajaro gas station where Dana had filled up before his trip to Monica's on the day of the murder. Souza realized that, had Dana lingered there, he might have seen his family on their way home. If he'd hired a hit man, Souza pondered, how would he let the killer know precisely when the family members would arrive home? It was pure conjecture, of course, but Souza found it reasonable that Dana could have waited until the family cars passed, and then phoned the Ewell residence to let the hired gun know that his targets were on their way.

The detectives also visited local airports, inquiring whether Dana Ewell had rented any type of aircraft on Easter Sunday. There were no records to indicate that he had. But so what?

Dana had a history, Souza had learned from speaking with Dana's former classmates, of hiring others to do his dirty work, even in junior high school. He certainly didn't seem the type to soil his hands. So if the road continued to lead to Dana, Souza had to find the hit man and maybe the hit man would bring down Dana.

After his return to Fresno, Souza joined his wife for dinner at the farm. They discussed the Rodney King riots that had just rocked Los Angeles, and the filing of the Ewell wills.

"You look a year older than you did last week," Sharon told Souza as she served up a potato and cheese dish.

He spooned some fresh tomatoes onto his plate. "Well, I feel ten years older. I wonder if I wouldn't have been better off sticking to baling hay and milking cows."

"Hey, we're doing pretty good after all these years," Sharon reminded him.

They'd met in high school, not kept in touch while Souza spent time in college and attended National Guard basic training, then stumbled into each other at a friend's wedding. She was bowled over by his big, smiling brown eyes and his muscles; he thought she was a knockout, and probably the cheeriest person he'd ever met. They began dating.

After some ups and downs, they were married on August 30, 1968. Two sons, Johnny and Michael, arrived a few years later.

Souza worked at a number of unimaginative jobs before he entered law enforcement. And then it took years to reach his ultimate goal, the Homicide Unit. He trudged his way up from reservist to deputy constable (where he worked his first homicide, a shootout at a bar), to Fresno County Sheriff's deputy, to burglary detective, before finally making homicide detective.

All the while, Sharon had been supportive, understanding, more so than he felt he deserved. Souza knew plenty of peace officers whose wives, unable to stomach the long hours alone and the stress of anticipating that knock on the door that would tell her she was now a widow, just packed up and left.

He looked at her. They had done pretty well, he thought. Especially me.

Meanwhile, Boudreau had received departmental permission to conduct a series of experiments with a nine-millimeter pistol that had been seized by deputies and stored at FSO. Working primarily on his own time on nights and weekends, Boudreau attempted to replicate the murder bullet markings, but without success.

He was working backwards, from bullet to gun, and was still uncertain what type of device had scarred the murder bullets. The progress was glacial, but Boudreau kept his eye on the prize.

Monday morning. Souza, Burk and Ybarra briefed their superiors, sharing information gleaned from the interviews at SCU. Souza and Burk sat down afterward and picked each other's brains.

Burk said he was convinced Dana was involved. Souza agreed that Dana was a suspect, but stubbornly insisted that he was just one of many at this juncture.

And then Burk mentioned another concern; he had recently been awarded custody of his children, and the demands of the case were already compromising his role as a single parent. He wondered if he'd be able to hold on until the case was put to bed.

That same day, the 5150's—the headcases—began crawling out of the sewers, as they did in most cases that were media events.

Souza cradled the receiver against his shoulder, his eyes closed. "But why were you driving by, ma'am?"

"Oh!" she said. "Oh! I . . . think I was just out driving."

"A Sunday drive."

"Yes, that's it."

"What did this man look like?"

"Well, he was dressed all in black. Like a Mafia assassin."

"Like Mafia?"

"Uh-huh. And he had a gun in his hand. And he was running, pointing the gun straight up. So I knew something was wrong."

Hoo, boy, thought Souza.

"And there was smoke coming out of the barrel," the caller said.

Souza pinched his mouth in his fingers. The smoking gun. He wasn't sure if he should laugh or cry. He wanted this case solved, he wanted the person who had shot a twenty-four-year-old girl and her parents to feel the weight of the justice system, crushing him like an insect. But he knew there would be more calls like this, and he'd have to take time with every damn one of them.

"Oh! I almost forgot. I'm also a psychic."

"Wow."

"Yeah. And in a trance I saw a dark-complected man, Italian maybe, boarding a plane with a suitcase full of drug money."

"Ma'am, why don't you give me your name and phone number and we'll be sure to be in touch if we need you."

She said, "Can I give you the number at a phone booth?"

Another call came in the next morning from a Las Vegas newspaper reporter. The nature of the reporter's information was the kind Souza wanted no part of.

"I've been tracking a money-laundering operation involving President Marcos."

Batting a fly away from his desk, Souza said, "The Philippine dictator?"

"That's the guy. I have evidence that the Feds—who, you understand, were this guy's buddy until he got tossed out—set up a money-laundering deal over here for him. All kinds of nasty shit. You know that this Mrs. Ewell used to be with the CIA?"

"Something I heard."

"You got it. And Dale Ewell's brothers are in a development deal in Fresno. Uh, Brighton Crest. A Chinese Tong Family gets the cash from Marcos, brings it over here through Tong connections. They invest it in gold and real estate. Of course, the real estate is bought through front men, like the Mob used to do here in Vegas when they bought casinos."

"But about the Ewells—"

"I'm getting to that." Souza heard the caller take a big pull off a cigarette, sucking air between his teeth as he drew smoke into his lungs.

Souza was impatient. "Uh—"

"You got Mrs. Ewell and her Langley connections," the guy said, exhaling into the receiver. "And Dale Ewell's brothers are in on the deal, see? The whole thing's got the tacit okay of the CIA, and a network of Feds and shit."

I wish this guy would just shut up. It was all too wild. Even if it were true, Souza didn't wish to stumble into a pack of Tong killers and CIA operatives. But he had to ask.

"Even if Dale's brothers were involved, what's this to do with Dale? Or Glee?"

"Well, probably just peripheral. But what if they wanted to send a message to the brothers?"

"By killing Dale and his family? Seems kind of circuitous to me."

"Well, maybe. But I thought you should know about this Marcos-Fed connection. When a family's practically wiped out, I thought you should know about these things, that's all."

"I'll keep it in mind."

"Hey! What if these guys meant to kill one of the brothers' families but got the wrong address?"

Souza got rid of the receiver like it was an angry cobra. But that wasn't enough. The reporter faxed in the names of judges and retired Federal agents supposedly involved in the Marcos scheme and its cover-up. Souza yanked the pages off the fax, and filed them.

As it was, Glee's CIA background had generated talk around the FSO: "What if?" What if Souza was poking his ignorant nose into covert Federal operations? The folks from Langley could disappear him in the blink of an eye.

The CIA, money laundering, fallen dictators. That was all he needed.

That night, Souza sorted through reprints of newspaper and magazine articles from the year before. The stories seemed a bizarre composite of snippets of Dale's life and lies made up out of whole cloth by Dana.

From *Career World, Focus on Entrepreneurs:*

DANA EWELL AND COMPANY

When Donald Trump spoke at the *Wall Street Journal* Seminar, he probably did not realize that one of the participants would soon turn out to be a competitor. Dana Ewell, then a high-school student at San Joaquin Memorial High School in Fresno, California, was sitting in one of those seats, noting the style and substance of the flamboyant entrepreneur he had read so much about.

By the time Ewell had graduated from high school, he was owner of a profitable aircraft distributorship and the proud owner of a Porsche 928 S4. He was also a sophisticated stock trader.

Now a 20-year-old sophomore at Santa Clara University, Ewell started Dana Ewell and Company in 1987. While his primary income came from selling airplanes—a trade he learned from his father—he also diversified into transporting electronics in his own planes from the Silicon Valley to computer-hungry Los Angeles. With the money from these enterprises and extra cash pooled from other investors, he was able to sink a significant amount of money into stocks on Wall Street. The company's gross income topped $2.7 million in 1988 and $4.1 million in 1989.

In the *San Jose Mercury News:*

MILLIONAIRE LEADS QUIET DORM LIFE ON SCU CAMPUS

It's easy to pick Dana Ewell out of a crowd.

. . . at age 19, Ewell is a self-made millionaire who amassed his fortune playing the stock market, running two companies and selling mutual funds.

The tall tales had first surfaced in the Santa Clara University student paper and later picked up by the *Mercury News* and other publications. In every account, Dana was described as a teenage, self-made millionaire, his fortune amassed through savvy stock-market plays and his masterful management of an airplane dealership.

That last claim troubled Souza the most.

While the other whoppers seemed the work of an inveterate liar, an apologist could argue they were nothing more than the rantings of ambitious youth. But the appropriation of Dale's life, even before his death, seemed to hint at some deep and frightening psychological problem in Dana. Still, Dana claimed in the article that his ideals had little to do with wealth.

"Some people are obsessed with money," Dana told the reporter. "I'm more obsessed with achievement."

TWELVE

A MAY 3 *FRESNO BEE* LEAD STORY DELVED INTO the business dealings and reputation of Dale Ewell. The article stopped short—just short—of branding Dale a ruthless operator. Souza felt the story bordered on character assassination—this guy was a victim, not a crook!

Souza unwrapped his sub sandwich and took a bite. A dollop of mayonnaise plopped into the middle of the paper. He wiped it with a napkin, mostly just smearing ink around the page. Cursing, he tossed the napkin into the wastebasket.

Souza read accounts of Dale's penchant for angering others as he built his airplane dealership and acquired farms and investment real estate. The tone of the article suggested there were plenty of people who would not lose sleep over Dale's demise.

The story mentioned that Dana had been interviewed twice by detectives. This was the first time the *Bee* had hinted at Dana's possible involvement.

Chewing his sandwich, Souza wished he had some idea where to go from here. When the phone rang Souza dumped the soggy wrapper in the trash.

"Sir," the caller said, "this is Sean Shelby."

It took a moment to place the name: A school friend of Dana's, Shelby had talked to detectives at the crime scene, suggesting that Dana, "the most materialistic person I'd ever met," might have been behind the crime.

"Yes, Sean?"

"I saw Dana a couple of days ago."

"Oh?"

"I just felt you should know he acted very strange. He told me the cops bugged his house. It was as if he were bragging or something. Said he couldn't talk inside his place."

"Okay."

"We met for lunch, and he goes on with this bizarre lecture, saying I should leave a paper trail to prove where I was, in case anything like this ever happens to me."

"That's what he said? Leave a paper trail?"

"Exact words."

Souza grabbed his steno pad, scratching away with a pencil. "Okay, Sean. Anything else?"

"Hell, yes. When we left the restaurant, he started to touch me, pat me down. When I asked him what he was doing he said he was checking to see if I wore a wire. He's really into this whole bad-boy routine."

"Okay. Now, you were his best friend in high school?"

"Middle school. And we spent time hanging out, doing crazy stuff."

"What do you mean by crazy stuff?"

"Oh, one time we tee-peed this house. But Dana went and damaged the people's car and stuff."

"Did you ever see Dana doing drugs?"

"No. Said he did some coke, but I never saw it."

Shelby said Dana was always scheming, planning stock frauds and other quick-money scams. The former friend thought this fit what he'd heard about the crime: the airtight alibi with an FBI agent, then calling a neighbor and ostensibly hearing for the first time about the murders, "so you don't get to see his initial reaction."

"So I could see Dana giving someone a copy of a key to his house, they get in, and then his parents come home."

"Do you think he'd use someone from school?"

"Sure, he could just say, 'look, my parents are loaded.'

You know, just dust 'em and wait for the inheritance. Oh, and Dana had a few things to say about you and your partner . . . what's his name?"

"Ernie Burk."

"Burk, that's it. Dana says the both of you are too dumb to solve anything. Said Burk couldn't find a gun in a gun store."

"I see."

"Listen, I have to run, but you might be interested in a story about Dana that went around school for a while. Dana was on the lawn with friends, discussing, you know, how they might get rich. Everybody was offering up boneheaded ideas and all, but Dana finally says, 'I know the fastest way to get rich. Kill your parents.' "

Souza thanked Shelby and hung up, then rummaged the files and read the synopsis of Shelby's April statement. Shelby said that Dana had once asked him to burglarize the Ewell place.

"Dana likes being called a crook," Shelby had stated. "He's the most materialistic kid I ever met. Everything had a price tag, you know? He would always tell you how much his clothes cost."

Further confirmation of Dana's greed, the detective felt, and further confirmation that Dana hired others to do his dirty work.

Souza did a record check on Lowell Moril, and learned authorities had seized a nine-millimeter carbine with a laser sight from Lowell some months before. He found the address of Lowell's aunt and stopped by unannounced. When no one answered his knock, he stuck a business card in the door.

The next day, Souza found in his morning mail a copy of Dana's letter to Dr. Prior at Santa Clara:

Dear Mr. Prior:

I am writing this letter to you because I want you, the philosophy department and the honors committee to know the pain I have and am still going through. If I had to say anything to anybody, I would say that I am guilty—guilty of the hardest crime, according to the law community, to prove— "intentional infliction of emotional distress." Right now, Dr. Prior, I am standing, psychologically, about 2 feet tall. I have spent numerous sleepless nights lying awake thinking about what has happened. Now I know what it means when people say that the feeling of guilt is more stressful and harder to overcome than the inhibition of committing some type of wrongdoing in the first place. My anger at myself has caused me to do several things. I have experienced all sorts of thoughts and feelings about my life. At times, I become religious. At other times, I get so enraged that I jump on a bike in 105 degree Fresno weather and peddle [sic] a bike for several miles, or jog until complete exhaustion. I have worked out until I can't lift another pound of weights, and then I look at my distressed face in the mirror for a long time and ask myself, "Who am I?" You, Dr. Prior, are a student and graduate of philosophy. Perhaps, you can understand what I am telling you and make something of it . . .

During my freshman and sophomore years in high school, my obsessive personality and strong desire to succeed caused me to stay up all night to study for a test, even though I had been studying all week. I wanted to do as close to perfect on those six-page legal sheet tests as possible. I wanted the highest grade. I wanted to do things that no one else had done for that Christian brother. I wanted these things, and after putting my nose to the grind-

stone for hours on end, I got them. On occasion, I would get very nervous the morning before a test when I had studied all night. I would eat some breakfast, but my generally "weak stomach," when it comes to eating, couldn't take it. I often vomited right before I took the test. I went to a doctor and he said that my "obsessive" behavior was exceeded by my physical limitations. Regardless of my then physical conditions or limitations, I succeeded in high school very well with that behavior. My perfect grades and good test scores are what got me into Princeton and the honors program at Santa Clara . . . Convinced I could run my businesses and attend school at the same time a lot easier in Santa Clara, I made the choice I did.

I know [sic] ask myself why did I just give you "my life story" in the paragraph above? I really don't know why, I just want to talk with somebody about this. Just as my stomach gave out in high school, my body just can't take any more of this psychologically induced stress and pain, worrying about what I did at Santa Clara. Frankly, I am just on the virge [sic] of snapping . . . As a philosophy teacher, I am sure that you know how powerful, impressive and all-might [sic] the human will is. There is nothing stronger than an extremely motivated man. Such a man can start wars, kill millions, save millions, or permanently change the earth. I have felt some of what human adrenaline can do. It is the most powerful weapon man has. In my fits of anger, I have taken my body beyond what physical limitations I thought existed before . . .

From what I have said so far, can you understand what kind of life I am currently leading? I have all sorts of strange thoughts lately, Dr. Prior. I see movies about serial killers, people committing suicide, highly immoral men, and what psychologically stressed people do. It is a bit frightening at times. I don't want to do anything else wrong!!!!! This whole thing is just ripping my sanity apart. I always need to have a serious goal in front of me to stay focused. I have always loved structure, cleanliness and excellence. Putting my nose to the grindstone is what I do best. Just as I sit her [sic] sweating and typing this letter, I long for someone to bring out the best in me . . .

It was [statistics professor] Dr. Feinstein who said to me on the first day, in his exact words, "You guys are terrible. What do you think you are doing? This is going to be the hardest class you will ever take at Santa Clara, and if it isn't, come tell me and I will make it harder." It is a genius like that that [sic] will elevate the capability of Dana James Ewell to perform to new levels unsurpassed before. You know what I mean when I say that the classes where all you have to do is read, memorize, and spit back data are the easiest in the world. That's why, I think, there are programs like the honors program— to go beyond wasting all that time. I came to believe during Freshman year that a class without Dr. Feinstein's sentiment was really a class not for me. You can look at my record and see where I thrive. Getting the highest grades in Honors Econ 1 and 2 is what I live for because it proves that I mastered the material. Is that so wrong? Can't I stay up all night just for the personal satisfaction of knowing that I will get that one extra question correct? Sure I can. I guess one would call this behavior as that of a perfectionist. The papers I wrote in Econ, Religion, English, Computer Science, etc., show how Dana J. Ewell can perform. That's what I am proud of, not my infantile, retarded, disgusting actions last quarter. I wish you would slam my head against a window and crack a few pieces of my skull, then

*yell at me and tell me how immature and ridiculous
I am—a poor excuse for a human being. That's
what I long for. I've done it to myself a thousand
times this summer . . .*

I wronged myself.

*I think of myself at 40 years of age saying, "Yes,
I too was once stupid, just as every man is at one
time or another." Just like Ted Kennedy got in trouble by cheating on a Spanish exam at Harvard, or
Congressman [sic] Joe Biden plagiarized a speech,
etc., etc. etc—just like Dana Ewell messed up once
at Santa Clara. I look at Ted Kennedy and other
successful figures for comparison . . . I look at them
and see that they turned out successful even after
their monumental failures in good [sic] judgement.
Can I do the same? I think I can . . . I need to prove
myself a man to you, my teachers, and to Santa
Clara, and to myself. It is time to get up from this.
I have been living in a personal hell all summer
and I can't wait to get beyond it . . . I got an F in
Ethics in Business, which means I need to take it
again in order to graduate. This time, no one will
be disappointed . . .*

*I've hurt a lot of people, friends, family, teachers,
and myself. This is not to mention the original author, Mr. Brady . . . I am going to call Mr. Brady
tonight and explain again to him how I feel about
the lack of deference I showed him last quarter. Our
society doesn't like it when one man does so much
damage. That's why the majority of America supports the death penalty. I have tried to reverse roles
and ask what I would do if I were a teacher and a
student broke this moral code. Well, of course I
would give him a huge, fat, "F" just like I have
received. Then I would batter his head against the
wall until the part of his brain that made him do it
is shaken loose forever. I would belittle that student
to the point of mental breakdown. In my case, I have*

been doing most of the belittling. Then I would ask that student if he or she intends to ever be a person worthy of living with any kind of decency, self-respect, and consciousness. If that student has endured and understood these concepts, such as I have, I would considered [sic] the notion that the best way to get rid of a cold is to sweat it out. I am going to come back to school in a week and am going to put my nose to the grindstone like I have never done before. I am not just talking about spinning my wheels. But looking at what maximum drive and potential Dana J. Ewell has done before, I think even I will be impressed with my work. I have realized just how much greatness I can truly achieve when I put my mind to it. It is time to leave this tangent that I got into last quarter and back on track-living like a true American. I, as always, thank you for your valuable time. I should be extremely grateful after what I have done if anyone even gives me the time of day. I'm glad I wrote this letter. I learn something new every time I think about it. See you at school, Doctor . . .

Dana J. Ewell

Dr. Prior had found the letter overtly threatening; Souza disagreed. His perception of Dana here was that Ewell was incapable of realizing that some of his remarks were grossly inappropriate. To Souza this reinforced his belief that Dana lacked a fundamental sense of right and wrong, and thus Souza found the letter more frightening than a run-of-the-mill threat.

THIRTEEN

SOUZA AND BURK, MORE CONCERNED THEN EVER that something was fundamentally wrong with Dana, showed the Prior letter to Dale Caudle. Caudle, an adjunct professor of criminal science at Fresno State University, phoned a psychologist with whom he worked at the college.

The psychologist examined the writings and pronounced Dana seriously troubled, possibly a classic sociopath who would view other human beings as mere objects. But one characteristic did not fit Dana: the psychologist said Dana would have chosen to commit the murders himself.

Another question came up: Why had no one at the university bothered to follow up and help such an obviously disturbed student?

Filing the Prior letter, Souza again considered the position of Bob Pursell; Pursell had wanted to buy Western Piper. Dale wouldn't sell. What if Pursell had had Dale taken out of the picture?

Souza drove out to the airport to interview Pursell once more.

Pursell insisted he had nothing to gain by Dale's death, and said he still believed the Mob and Lambetecchio, or maybe those Aerostar owners, were behind it all.

Souza and Burk concluded that Pursell had been at

home with his wife when the Ewells died. Souza had no evidence to link Pursell to the crime, and Pursell's viability as a suspect was fading.

Still, Souza didn't appreciate that Pursell had been bad-mouthing Dale to the press, depicting his dead boss as money-hoarding and abusive. Dale was unable to defend himself, and Pursell was proving to be less than reliable. Souza had come to agree with Dana that the letter to Pursell purportedly written by Dale had probably been penned by Pursell himself—and what kind of man seeks financial gain from another man's murder?

On May 7, Souza and Burk drove south to Santa Ana, an ugly, sprawling, heavily commercial area near Disneyland. It was time to get to the bottom of the Western Piper/Aerostar billing controversy.

Family attorney Ronald Lais, who co-owned the Aerostar with partner James Glidwell and had piloted the plane out of Fresno after the killings, told the detectives the tale was relatively simple: His business manager, Wayne Wendell, had been flying the Aerostar when one engine malfunctioned. Wendell landed in Fresno and Western Piper stored the plane. But the attorneys felt they'd been gouged on the billing.

Yes, Lais said, they'd begun court proceedings on April 20, but when he had a chance to take the plane himself on the twenty-second he did so.

"And in case you're interested," Lais added, "I spent Easter with my parents in Palm Desert."

After the interview, the detectives felt the whole affair was nothing more than Lais had portrayed it, and the notion that the attorneys had had the Ewell family murdered over a seventeen-hundred-dollar repair was a bit of a stretch. Another possible suspect was scratched off.

On the crowded highway out of town, Souza picked up his cell phone and dialed the West Hills, California, number of Joel Radovcich's mother, which Burk had found.

"Why are you calling me?" said Radovcich, after his younger brother, Daniel, had handed him the phone.

"I'm a homicide investigator, Mr. Radovcich. We're looking into the deaths of members of the Ewell family."

"Who?"

"Dana Ewell. I understand he's a good friend of yours."

"Well, just casual friends. I don't know Dana that well, and I don't know what happened to his family."

"Nevertheless, sir, we'd like to come talk to you, if we may."

"Hang on," Radovcich said.

Souza slipped his palm over the mouthpiece. "He's a bit hesitant," he said to Burk.

"Sorry," said Radovcich, back on the line. "Um, now why did you want to talk to me?"

"We're doing a standard background check on the Ewells, Mr. Radovcich. Even the smallest detail might help. We can meet you there tomorrow."

"Not at my mother's. Anyway, I don't know anything."

"That's what most people think," Souza said. "But we really need to talk to you. How about in the morning?"

"Why?" Radovcich said, his voice higher. "Are you going to arrest me?"

It didn't sound mocking, didn't sound sarcastic.

Maybe Radovcich knew something. But if so, Souza had the same problem with Radovcich he'd had with Dana: difficulty reconciling an intricately planned execution with the unreasoned responses offered up under questioning. To Souza, their answers seemed too stupid to come from a couple of guys bright enough to have planned the crime.

"We're not going to arrest you. We simply need some background information. Okay?"

"I guess."

"We'll be down there in the morning, Mr. Radovcich. How about we see you at 10 A.M.?"

"Look, I don't want you guys coming by and rattling my mother."

"We've got a motel booked nearby. We'll meet you there. Okay?" Souza gave Radovcich the motel name and address.

"Not ten. I'll come by at twelve."

"That's fine, Mr. Radovcich. We'll be in the lobby." Souza just sat there, listening to the dial tone.

"John?"

Souza punched the END button, leaned back, crossed his arms over his belly, and told Burk what he'd just heard.

Burk's gaze went back and forth from the road to Souza. "No shit. He said that? 'Are you gonna arrest me?' "

"Ah, hell. Probably just a wise-ass kid."

FOURTEEN

AFTER HEARING THE SANTA CLARA STUDENT'S description of Joel Radovcich, Souza had formed an image of the kid in his mind. One that, as it happened, wasn't particularly accurate.

Radovcich wasn't a fashion plate, but neither was he a troll. He was a solid, good-looking young man, if a bit slack-jawed. Full lips, hooded eyelids. Brown and brown. Wearing jeans and a green long-sleeved golf shirt.

He pulled off his black ball cap and ran his fingers through his dark hair. Souza and Burk introduced themselves in the bland lobby of the Holiday Inn, and Burk tapped the elevator call button.

"I can't believe I asked if you were going to arrest me," Radovcich said. His smile was fleeting.

Souza cocked his head. "No?"

"I just get nervous."

The elevator doors opened hesitantly. The detectives held their tongues as all three stepped inside.

An obviously tense Radovcich rattled on, "I kind of got into trouble once at college. Me and a buddy borrowed some furniture from the dorm lounge. Just a prank, but everyone got bent out of shape. We were arrested."

Souza had learned years before that disinformation, often rehearsed diligently, tended to come out as a clumsy proffer. This desperation to plant misleading material in the mind of detectives was often as telling as a suspect's attempt to withhold information that might be incriminating.

"I thought maybe you were the Santa Clara campus police tricking me or something." Joel laughed.

"Oh."

Souza listened to the Muzak, wondering where the kid fit into the case. Someone had scratched the word PUSSY into the elevator wall.

Once they'd unlocked their room, Souza sat on the bed and Burk and Radovcich each found a chair.

Burk said, "We've got a little recorder here."

"A tape recorder?" Radovcich said.

"It's for your protection, too. Know what I mean?"

"Oh. Yeah."

Souza studied Radovcich, the kid's face harshly lit in the sunlight that streamed in through the window.

Didn't sleep last night.

Was he up pacing, worrying about the statement he'd made over the phone? Did he rehearse and practice until he heard the noise of cars cranking up and people shuffling off to work?

Burk walked him through the warm-up—name, address, age. Souza's attention flagged for a moment, but he gently brought it back as Burk continued.

"Joel, are you aware that we are police officers from Fresno?"

"Yes sir."

"We understand that you went to school with Dana Ewell."

"He was on one of my floors at Casa, the dorm."

"I see. Would you tell us how long you knew him, how good of friends you were, et cetera."

"Okay. Let me see, I guess I have something I can write down here." Joel produced a pen and scribbled on a hotel notepad. "I'm trying to think. It wasn't a year ago . . . Okay, 1992, '91. I have to think about this. I graduated in last year so it'd be fall I was in the Casa dorm. Yeah, '90, I met him."

Joel was animated, his voice rising and falling as he spoke, unlike Dana's stiff-posture and monotonic delivery.

"The same dorm."

"Right, but I got kicked out in January. Uh, we were friends. I mean, not real tight, but we like to kick it together. Other than school we weren't communicating."

Joel was relaxing somewhat. If he was involved, the kid was acting impressively cool, reasonable, coherent. Of course, it would have taken a cool-headed person to lie in wait and assassinate three people.

"Have you ever been in Fresno?" said Burk.

"Yes, I have."

"To visit Dana or . . . ?"

"Yeah, We, I, we picked up one of his cars, switched his Mercedes for a Jeep."

"When was that?"

"When? Hmm." Joel repeated the question, mumbling to himself, furrowing his brow in concentration. "Let me think. Hmm. Spring of '92, 90 . . . spring of '91, I guess."

"When was the last time you went to Dana's house?"

"Spring '91."

"That was the only time?"

"Yes."

Souza thought, Pretty much only gives the information he's asked, not more.

"Did you go in?"

"Uh, yes I did."

"Did you meet his parents?"

"Um, we said hi, then we had to go. We dumped off his car, went inside. I said hi to the mom and I don't know if his dad was there, don't remember . . . yeah, he was there."

"And you went back and you picked up his car?"

"No, no, no. We just, he picked up his car. I didn't go back."

"Okay. Had you ever seen his parents before then?"

"Let's see." Again, he frowned, mumbling, pursing his

lips, lost in thought. "Yes, yes I did. Uh, we went to the beach house, I can't remember if it was before. I spent a weekend with them. I believe it was before."

"At school, where did Dana like to go hang out at night, maybe have a drink?"

"Well, Dana, he's not the hanging-out type," Radovcich said with a flash of a grin. "Anyway, he wasn't twenty-one yet."

Animated, but somehow distant. Detached.

"Any other friends you can name?"

"Of Dana's?" He cocked his head. "Let me think . . . friends. Hm. There was one guy. Long hair. Skateboard dude. I don't really remember his name."

"Joel," Burk said, "you're going to have to speak up. If your voice drops below the noise level of the tape, it won't pick it up."

"You don't have to be real close," Souza told Joel, "it's just you tend to go up and down with your voice."

"Okay."

"This friend, white male?" asked Burk.

"Yeah, white male."

"Okay. Was Dana the type of person who had a lot of friends?"

"I would say he was very social. He was close, he was good to hang with, you know."

"Did Dana throw around a lot of money?"

"Oh, no. Very conservative, extremely conservative. Very."

"Did you know if he had money?"

Burk took a few moments to form his next question. "And when you're with Dana. What do you guys talk about? Anything in particular?"

"We had Finance together. And, you know, what we were going to do . . . uh, anything in particular I can help you out with?"

"He ever talk about his family?"

"Yeah, he talked about his family."

"What was he saying?"

Shrugging, Joel said, "He liked his family, far as I could tell, but I wasn't that nosy."

"He mention any problems with his family?"

"No."

"Okay," said Burk. He shot Souza a glance, and asked, "Joel, when's the last time you had contact with Dana?"

"Last year. Last fall."

"You call him since then?"

"No," he said without hesitation. He shuffled his feet on the floor.

"And you haven't been to Fresno since then?"

"No."

"You've only been to Fresno that one time?"

"Yes."

"Would you know how to get to his house?"

"If I had the address."

Good answer, thought Souza. He hoped, in a way, this guy wasn't in on the Ewell crime. Joel would not be an easy nut to crack. But his vocal style—was it merely acting?

"So you just finished up school in December?" asked Burk.

"Yeah," Joel said, crossing his ankle over his thigh. "I took thirty-one credits the last semester, just so I could get it over with."

"He ever say his folks were wealthy?"

"Hm. No, can't remember that particularly. I just assumed. I mean, he had all the niceties."

"Okay. Have you ever seen Dana with a gun?"

"No, definitely not."

"I got one question. We . . . we've been doing this investigation since Easter, so we've learned a lot. Did Dana ever talk about having someone kill his parents?"

"Definitely not."

"Never, he never—"

"No." Very firm.

"Did you see the articles about Dana in the Santa Clara newspaper."

"Sure," Joel said, smiling now.

"And you thought that bunch of baloney was true?"

"I thought the article was pretty neat."

Radovcich was leaning back in his chair, one foot bouncing. Souza watched quietly.

Something's not right with Joel.

"You're saying it was an accurate reflection of his life?"

"Well, no but—"

"That's a big deal, to lie like that."

"Look, I wasn't going to . . . I mean if you're a friend I'm not going to—"

"Sure."

"You know."

"Sure. Was he that kind of person?"

"Oh, no."

"That's a big deal, to talk to a reporter like that and have the majority of it be such a bunch of baloney."

"Mm. So ask me a question, ask me a question, ask me a question."

"What I'm asking is this the type of character Dana is? Was it for his ego?"

"No, it was more of a political maneuver."

"Why?"

"To open doors and stuff."

"You're in school! What kinda doors is it going to open?"

Squirming, Joel said, "I mean if you can prove you're something, it may be a little BS, but if I'm going to you for a job, say a sales-manager job, when I bring this PR stuff. You know, it's more of a PR thing. I read the article and thought it was funny."

"Dana ever mentioned belonging to any club?"

"Uh, Honors Club—"

"Has he ever mentioned the BBC?" said Souza.

"BBC? The television station?"

"Billionaire Boy's Club?"

"Oh! Billionaire Boy's Club! It doesn't jump out."

"Did he have goals of being wealthy?"

"I think more to be well-off, it was just succeed, in Dana's world, not a question of mega-power."

"Okay, this situation you got yourself into at the dorms. Dana have anything to do with that?"

"No." Joel shook his head emphatically.

Souza leaned his hands on the Easter-egg bedspread. The room smelled of cigar ash and Lysol, and something else: fear perhaps, a few molecules of evaporated sweat that had risen up from Joel's armpits. But he sure as hell didn't look fearful.

"A couple of questions that we ask anybody we've been talking to. Uh, Easter Sunday. What did you do?"

"Easter Sunday? Hm, Easter, huh? Oh, I was at Hamrick's, an auto body here in town."

"How do you spell that?"

"H-A-M-R-I-C-K-S. I was washing, moving cars."

"Did you spend all day there?"

"I got there probably about eleven or twelve."

"Until?"

"Left at eleven."

"P.M.? You didn't spend Easter with your folks?"

"I don't get along with my dad. He's an engineer, travels. When he comes I sort . . . of leave."

"Okay," Burk said. "Another question, since we've recovered some prints that are unidentified, would you be willing to give us a set of prints so we could eliminate—"

"I'm on file, you know. The dorm thing, they printed me maximum."

"Okay. Did you have anything to do with the Ewell deaths?"

"No."

"When were you aware that they were killed?"

"Yesterday."

Souza thought, Only yesterday? Didn't he already know when I called?

"That was the first time?"

"That was the first time."

"Weren't you a little surprised?"

"Yes, I was surprised. I was shocked, but I didn't take it seriously at first. I didn't hear about it in the papers and stuff with the Rodney King riots going on just a half hour away."

"Well, it was before the riots, but still. You have three family members killed and one survivor who tends to benefit. See where I'm coming from?"

"Yes, I do," Joel said.

"And you don't know anything about it?"

"No, I don't."

"Okay. At this time I'm terminating the interview."

Joel glanced out the window. "If I think of anything else, I can let you know."

"Thanks, Joel. John?"

On the bed, Souza showed his palms. "That's about it. We'll walk you down."

Joel was on his feet. They followed Radovcich out into the parking lot, where he unlocked a black Honda CRX. Souza memorized the license number, last three digits 911. Radovcich didn't bother to wave as he roared off.

"What do you think?"

"Most of his answers were good, and he was pretty cool, but sometimes I got the feeling he was acting. Know what I mean?"

Burk nodded. "And he tried way too hard to talk his way out of the 'are you going to arrest me' thing. So what now?"

"Background. And follow-up. But probably, another blind alley."

Souza wondered whether the department would authorize the funds to set up a rolling surveillance on Radovcich.

Burk phoned a female classmate from Dana's high-school days. She said (as had just about everyone else the detectives had spoken with) that Dana was single-minded in his pursuit of wealth.

"Every Friday afternoon Dana had a limo pick him up after school."

She also named a Michael Poindexter as Dana's school buddy, and said Poindexter was in college near Salt Lake City, Utah.

Back at his Fresno farm the next evening, Souza found himself on edge, haunted by a feeling that an entire generation—an age group that included his own sons—had grown up devoid of the kind of moral certainty that had been instilled in people of his generation.

He trod his fields. The onions showed signs of mildew. Skeletonizer pupae were stripping the grapevines of leaves, leaves that sweetened the grapes and provided shade from the harsh sun.

It was a damn mess.

Of course, things weren't going well with the case, either. He wanted it solved, and the mucky-mucks at the FSO certainly wanted it solved. But a solution seemed light-years away.

Souza decided to learn more about Dana, where he was, what he was doing. And with whom he was spending time.

FIFTEEN

THE EWELL BROTHERS FILED INTO THE FSO ON May 18. Dan, Ben, Richard, brothers to the late Dale, uncles to Dana. Souza led the silent trio into a conference room, where they could stretch out and relax as best they could under the circumstances.

"We're very concerned," Dan, the smallest of the brothers, told Souza.

Richard nodded. The polished, sharp-featured Ben stared at his shoes.

"And of course, we're torn. We don't want to implicate Dana without cause. We've all had enough hurt, and if Dana had nothing to do with this, God help him and us for coming here."

"For whatever it's worth," Souza said, "I feel you did the right thing. Listen, we'll take your concerns seriously, but we won't use them as an excuse to persecute the boy. Okay?"

Dan had phoned the day before, requesting the meeting, the sadness evident in his voice. Souza waited, pencil poised above notepad.

Dan glanced around, brushed back his thick hair, seeking support from his siblings. Ben never lifted his gaze from the floor. Souza sensed Ben was holding back, as though acknowledging his fears would make them come true.

"At first, we just thought Dana was in shock," Dan said.

"You know, closed down. We figured he'd just come apart one of these days. You were at the service. He was unaffected. Until he saw a diamond ring. And the next day, he and his buddies went out boating!"

"We've been trying to understand," Richard said. "But for me, I just can't."

Dan again: "Everything revolves around money with this kid. He pestered the hell out of Ben here. He's an attorney, you know."

Souza nodded.

"He pestered Ben to read the will. My God, the kid could've at least shown a degree of subtlety! He threw a fit when he found out he wouldn't get all of it right away. He said, 'How could Dad do this to me?' Just like that! As if Dale got himself shot to death just to spite Dana.

"Then we got into it with him about cremation. He wanted his whole family cremated. Save money. We told him we couldn't stop him from doing that to Glee and Tiffany, but we sure as hell could stop it when it came to our own brother. As if that wasn't enough, when the funeral director showed him the caskets, Dana pointed to a cheap model, and says, 'that's good enough for Tiffany.' "

Dan turned away, obviously disgusted at the words that he'd had to repeat. Richard, the warmest of the three, spoke up again.

"Look, Detective," he said softly. "We can't be certain that Dana was involved, but his actions tell us that he didn't care much about his own family. For me, the straw came when the mortician told Dana he could have a little flowerpot placed on Dale's headstone at a cost of thirty-five dollars."

Souza felt he should ask, make it easier for Richard.

"And what did Dana say, Mr. Ewell?"

"He said, 'I'm not spending thirty-five dollars on that, I won't be seeing it anyway'!"

Souza heard himself take a sharp breath.

The quote seemed to finally rouse something in Ben. "Thirty-five dollars," Ben said. His face came up. He held

Souza's look. "Wouldn't spend thirty-five dollars on his own daddy."

Souza had been calling Dana on a regular basis, but Dana never picked up the home phone and didn't return Souza's answering-machine messages. The visit from the Ewell brothers solidified Souza's suspicions about Dana, even though the brothers themselves stood to gain financially if Dana was disinherited.

He tried Dana's number again.

"Dana, I need your help," he said after the machine beeped. "It's important that you phone me so we can get this investigation moving along. Please call me anytime."

Dana's lack of responsiveness, his lack of inquiry about the status of the case, and his refusal to be of any assistance to investigators would become instrumental in Souza's getting approval from his superiors for a surveillance operation.

He settled down to catch up on his report writing. It was dreary work, and his mind kept clicking: Even if Dana is the type to want his parents dead, where would a college kid find a professional hit man?

Hoping Dana's movements might provide an answer, Souza went to Lieutenant White and requested that members of the Narcotics Enforcement Team, detectives highly experienced in undercover work, organize a surveillance detail on Dana Ewell and the family home. The brass agreed, and NET began to plan their impending operation.

Lowell Moril's aunt phoned Souza. She said she'd found his card in her door. Was it about Lowell?

Souza asked why she thought he would inquire about her nephew.

Well, he's unstable, the aunt said. She'd been trying to get him to a doctor, but Lowell never showed up for his appointments. Still, he's no murderer. She insisted that

Lowell had been at her house on Easter Sunday. He'd come by about noon.

Souza wanted to know where Lowell had been earlier that day. The aunt suggested Souza contact Lowell's brother, Roger.

On Easter Sunday, Roger said by telephone, Lowell got up around two in the afternoon, left the house for a while, returned at three-thirty. And Lowell didn't own any guns, Roger claimed, not since the police had seized all his weapons.

What was Lowell's demeanor like on Easter? Souza asked.

Fine, Roger said. For Lowell.

Possible suspects were quickly dropping off the radar: Whitman, Pursell, Lowell Moril—all, it seemed were in the clear. Another one, Frank Lambetecchio, was not . . . but he was quickly fading into the background.

While Lambetecchio clearly had no love for Dale Ewell, the man who'd assumed ownership of his airplane dealership, Souza and Burk found it a stretch to believe Lambetecchio would wait twenty years to taste the cold dish of revenge—and would also murder Dale's wife and daughter.

Lambetecchio had been convicted on narcotics charges, and might or might not have Mob connections, but nobody suggested he had a propensity for murder.

This was underscored by a former sheriff's deputy who had turned to working as a kind of hired muscle for Lambetecchio. Souza had worked with George Krotter, and he believed Krotter when the former lawman stated that neither he nor Lambetecchio were involved—hell, there wasn't even anything in it for them!

Indeed, Souza learned that both had alibis for April 19.

The same week, the county agent bent over for a closer look at Souza's vines. The skeletonizer egg larvae were evident on the back of the leaves.

Everyone in the area had been frustrated by the pest; no one seemed to have come up with the right combination of chemicals to kill the worm. The agent recommended a kryosite solution—whether this was the correct stage of incubation, or whether the solution would work, was only a guess.

Souza and his sons, Johnny and Michael, set up the booms and adjusted the nozzles on the spray rig, and went to work.

Souza and Burk flew to Utah in late May. During the drive to the Logan police station the sun was white-hot in the sky, the road undulating in the heat waves that rose from its surface.

The detectives interviewed clean-cut Michael Poindexter, Dana's friend from high school. Poindexter spoke of greed, the Billionaire Boy's Club, and how Dana had idolized convicted swindler and killer Joe Hunt.

Burk, sickened by this adulation of crooks and killers, asked Dana's friend how they could worship such amoral people, but an angry Poindexter was unapologetic; he was unsure if he would turn in Dana even if Dana admitted to having the Ewell family murdered.

The detectives escorted Poindexter to fingerprinting, where an elimination set was taken, then they sent him on his way. Burk, for one, was glad to be rid of Poindexter. Gave him the creeps.

Since the murders, shrill rumors had swept through Fresno. Tales of Mafia revenge and Marcos's killers and CIA involvement had surfaced, despite the best efforts of the FSO to keep a lid on both information and innuendo.

But particularly disturbing to the Sheriff's Department were the lurid whispers that the Ewell women had been sexually molested on that Easter Sunday, or that family members had been mutilated by their assassins and left as a grisly warning to others who might get out of line.

And so on June 18, 1992, FSO information officer Sergeant Margaret Mims issued a press release. The release recounted the particulars of the crime and noted the continuing investigation and the standing $25,000 reward. Additionally it stated:

The investigation reveals that none of the victims were molested, nor did they receive any injuries other the gunshot wounds that killed them. Sheriff's detectives wish to dispel these rumors as being totally false.

Eventually, Allen Boudreau received eight responses to his inquiry for assistance in identifying the oddly marked murder bullets. Some suggested rust in the bore might have produced the stria, but Boudreau had already considered this and deemed it highly unlikely: as shots are fired through a rusty barrel, bits of rust and metal tend to get blown out of the barrel with each discharge, slightly altering the markings on successive bullets. Here, the Ewell bullets were virtually identical.

Other experts offered that the bullets had been fired from a Glock-style polygonal barrel. Unlike a standard weapon, polygonal barrels don't have sharp land-and-groove impressions cut into the bore. Rather, the bore is a spiraled hexagon with slightly curved sides, and at a glance reminiscent of old-style, smooth-bore weapons. Hence, most poly barrels don't reproduce their markings well and are difficult to identify by rifling impressions.

Again, Boudreau had pondered this possibility, but based upon his experience he didn't expect a match. A series of test-firings through pistols of a polygonal barrel construction confirmed his belief.

It was Carlos Rosati, with the ATF Special Testing Laboratory in Maryland, who seemed to be leaning toward the same conclusion as Boudreau. Rosati, in a June 4, 1992 phone conversation with Boudreau, asked if all the bullets were identical.

"Like they came out of a Xerox machine," Boudreau told him.

They discussed the rusty barrel and polygonal barrel theories, but Rosati stated flatly that Boudreau was dealing with a sound-suppressed barrel in this case. He advised that

Boudreau begin to experiment with silencers, explaining that an ATF permit would be required for the FSO to build a suppressor. In the US, even law-enforcement agencies are forbidden from building silencers.

Rosati walked Boudreau through the permit process, and Boudreau agreed to keep Rosati informed of his experiments.

The Narcotics Enforcement Team, after a five-day surveillance operation, reported that they'd seen Dana—and Joel Radovcich—engaged in some interesting activities and one unanticipated encounter which became a favorite anecdote of Souza's: Detective Chris Osborn, a pilot, was using a small plane to track Dana's movements from Western Piper. At one point, alerted that Dana was heading for his car, Osborn hustled from the offices he was holed up in near Western Piper—and ran right into Dana. "Hey," Dana said to the detective. "You going flying?" Osborn replied, "Sure am!" Osborn then hopped into his plane and followed Dana's Mercedes out of the airport.

Souza, hoping any successes would help the sheriff open up the county purse and continue surveillances on Dana, reviewed reports from the rolling surveillance that had staked out 5663 East Park Circle:

```
SURVEILLANCE
FSO 92-15285


ASSISTING OFFICERS:
Sergeant Hollis              FSO/FCNET/METRO
Detective Moore
Detective Rein
Detective Kelly
Detective Osborn
Detective DeCamp
Detective Lyons
Detective Lee                FSO/FCNET/METRO
Detective Johnson
Detective Martinez
```

Beginning June 25, 1992, The Fresno County Narcotics Enforcement Team assisted the Fresno County Sheriff's Department Crimes Against Persons Division in the surveillance of 5663 East Park Circle Drive.

The surveillance was conducted on subject Dana Ewell, described as approximately 21 years old, 6'1", 160 pounds, short sandy blond hair. The following observations were noted.

0910 hours: Team observes a Mercedes, CA LIC # 3AIX366, leave the residence with two occupants, driver Dana Ewell and a passenger, white male, 22–25 years, short dark hair, wearing baseball cap and sunglasses.

0920 hours: Team observes the Mercedes to drive in a counter-surveillance manner, going in and out of driveways and making several U-turns.

1236 hours: Both subjects leave United Security Bank with subject Ewell carrying a briefcase.

1240 hours: Team observes the Mercedes to drive in a counter-surveillance manner. Subjects park and view real estate lot with "For Sale" sign.

1259 hours: Team observes subject Ewell and partner viewing a helicopter near Corporate Air.

1346 hours: The vehicle arrives at 5663 East Park Circle Drive, whereupon both occupants enter the residence.

June 26, 1992

1112 hours: Team observes a 1989 black Honda CRX, CA LIC# 2MGN911, exit garage

(registered owner Radovcich, Joel Patrick, West Hills.)

1121 hours: Team loses vehicle in area
of McKinley and Gateway.

1320 hours: Team observes Honda to arrive back at subject address. Ewell arrives in Mercedes. Subject and Radovcich
exit driveway in 1991 gray Cadillac, Lic #
GLEE E, registered to vic Dale Ewell.

1445 hours: Cadillac arrives attorney's
offices, 6051 N. Fresno St.

1541 hours: Team observes Cadillac to
arrive at Union Bank, Fig Garden. Ewell
exits, passenger Radovcich remains in vehicle.

1544 hours: Ewell returns to Cadillac.
Ewell is running and laughing, waving what
appears to be a check in his right hand.

June 27, 1992

1052 hours: Subject Ewell and second-
ary, Radovcich, enter Jeep Wagoneer and
arrive at Corporate Air. Both followed to
Shaver Lake area. Arrive at cabin on north
side of lake.

June 28, 1992

1605 hours: Team observes open garage
door at subject residence. Inside is tan
Mercedes and black Honda CRX. Tiffany's
car is parked outside, apparently so Radovcich can park the CRX.

June 29, 1992

1329 hours: Advised Ewell arrived at
Home Fed Bank, East King's Canyon.

1340 hours: Subject arrives Bank of America, East Kings Canyon.

1603 hours: Observed subject arrived Western Financial Savings, West Shaw Ave.

Banks, banks, banks, thought Souza. And the Shaver Lake cabin that had belonged to Dale and Glee. Souza checked the ownership of the lot: also Dale Ewell. He flipped through the pages again.

. . . Ewell is running and laughing, waving what appears to be a check in his right hand.

Practically clicked his heels in joy over what . . . his first big check from the estate? Surveying his domain. And doing it with Joel Radovcich.

What about Joel's statement that, "we haven't seen each other since college?"

Souza's head throbbed. He'd dropped the ball about Radovcich. Joel had claimed an alibi during his interview, said he'd been working at Hamrick's Auto Body on Easter and the boss had been there.

But neither Souza nor Burk followed up and interviewed the shop owner; somehow that task slipped through the cracks after a few calls to Hamrick's when Nick Johns hadn't been on-site. Now, little arrows were pointing at Joel Radovcich. And where was Dana's buddy now?

As it turned out, Radovcich's alibi was no alibi at all, as Souza found out when he and Burk showed up Hamrick's Body Shop on July 1.

A kid in the corner of the shop was drilling holes in the fender of a foreign car, a make Souza didn't recognize. The smell of metal filings reminded him of high-school shop. Nick, the owner, had a phone in one callused hand. He'd excused himself to the detectives to take a customer call. When he put the phone down, Nick said, "Where was I?"

"Trying to remember when Joel called you about Easter."

"Oh, yeah. Not exactly sure, but it wasn't long ago that he called me. A week? Anyway, he tells me that I should remember that he was around on Sunday."

"And do you?" Souza said.

"No, I didn't see him here. He said I saw him here, but I don't think so. He says, 'Gee, Nick. You remember talking to me, right? All you need to do is tell the cops what you saw.' "

Burk, taking notes, made a crash-and-burn sound, a little whistle like a plane diving and exploding into the tarmac.

Souza said, "We appreciate your help, Nick. Let me ask you one more thing. Did you get the feeling that Joel was trying to plant his story in your mind?"

Nick looked off into the distance. "I hate to admit it, but that's what it seemed like."

"We won't take up any more of your day. Any idea where Joel is today?"

"No clue. His brother Peter is around."

"Here?"

"Next door." Nick hooked a thumb over his shoulder. "The plumbing place. Sketchly-Mason."

The two detectives wandered next door and asked a young lady at a cash register where Peter could be found. She directed them out into the yard. The southland was sticky, and Souza wanted to peel off his jacket. At times FSO detectives wore khakis and polo shirts, but Souza noticed people tended to stare at his weapon when he was casually dressed. He found the attention a bit embarrassing and preferred to wear a jacket.

In the young man in the yard, Souza could see some resemblance to Joel, but this Radovcich was taller, more rawboned. Thinning dark hair cut to stand straight up and spiky.

"Peter Radovcich?"

"Yo. How can I help you gentlemen?"

Peter was crouched near a stack of sewer pipe, rummaging through a carton of galvanized fittings. Souza identified Burk and himself. "We're investigating the murders of the Ewell family."

Peter seemed unfazed. "Can't imagine how I can help."

"Actually, we were wondering if you knew where we can find Joel."

"I don't know. I usually just page him."

"Would you mind paging him for us?"

He looked up from the box. Souza could read no concern in Peter's face. "When I get a minute, sure."

"Peter, did you spend Easter with Joel?"

"Nope."

"He didn't come visit you?"

"Nope. He does sometime when our dad is in town, but my wife and I were at Knott's Berry Farm that weekend."

"Where does Joel live now?" Souza said.

"Last I heard, he was staying with friends."

"Here in Los Angeles?"

"That's right."

Burk asked, "Has he gone to Fresno lately, do you know?"

"I know he went a while ago to pick up a light for my grandparent's anniversary. That was a few months ago."

"Does he have a girlfriend we can call?"

"No, no girlfriend."

"Okay," Souza said. "Peter, is Joel into firearms at all?"

"He's into computer and boats. He doesn't own any weapons that I know of."

"Peter, do you think your brother is capable of killing someone?"

"Jesus, what a question. I don't think so. He talks mean at times, but . . . listen he's my brother, but I don't really know him all that well."

Souza took out a card and wrote his hotel phone number on it. Peter glanced at the card and stuck it in his top pocket.

"Hey," Souza said, "in case we don't hear from him, you have his pager number?"

"I'm not much for remembering numbers. I can spell it out for you though."

"Okay."

Burk waited, pen and pad in hand.

"It's 818 K-I-L-L-A-J-R."

Burk read it back, "K-I-L-L-A. Killa . . ." Burk turned to Souza. "Jesus Christ. Killa J.R.?"

SIXTEEN

THE DETECTIVES DIDN'T GET A CALL FROM JOEL Radovcich. They paged him themselves, but nothing. Souza phoned Peter at his apartment and asked if he would try Joel again, but again the cell phone never rang. From the car, they placed a second call to Peter, who said he'd finally reached his brother and had given him the message to call the detectives.

When they grew tired of waiting, Souza and Burk headed for home. Two calls came in on the cellular phone as they traveled north on the freeway. Both times, the caller hung up when Souza answered.

But Joel would remain much on the detective's mind.

July was almost gone, August just around the corner. Fresno had been dry and scorching, the mercury climbing above one hundred degrees, the air quality pitiful. Souza stared at a desk littered with reports and interview transcripts, and around him the stacks of Ewell case files were growing, closing in around him. Sheriff Magarian, as he'd done nearly every morning, had already stuck his head in the door and asked Souza if he needed any help on the case. It was a show of support, certainly, but it also had the effect of ratcheting up the artery-bursting pressure that Souza felt from the moment he blinked open his eyes each morning.

When his phone rang, Souza grabbed it on the second

ring. The caller identified himself as Richard Berman, attorney-at-law. Former District Attorney Berman, now a criminal defense lawyer.

"I'm representing Mr. Dana Ewell."

"I see."

"Just so we're on the record about that."

"Okay, sir."

"And anything you have for Mr. Ewell must come to me first."

"I'm sorry?"

"Detective Souza, I believe I've made myself clear."

Screw you and the horse you rode in on. "You want me to ask permission before I speak to Dana?"

"Specifically, I'm informing you that all future contact must go through my office."

"I'm afraid I can't do that, Mr. Berman."

"Detective, why are you making this more difficult than it need be?"

"I have the right to talk to Dana when I want to."

"As I've told you, all contact regarding Mr. Ewell is to be referred to this office right away."

Being spoken to like he was some kind of office assistant wasn't the best way to approach Souza. "As they say, sir, you have your job, and I have mine. It's up to Dana to say if we wishes to talk to me or not."

"Yes. Right. And as his attorney, I now speak for Mr. Ewell."

"And I say I can talk to him when I damn well please, Counselor."

"No. No you can't."

"Mr. Berman," Souza said, "this discussion isn't going anywhere. What do you legal types call it, a circular argument?"

"I agree we're wasting time here, Detective. You've been informed of our position, and a letter to that effect will follow in a few days. That is, once again, you're to refer all questions regarding the Ewell case and Dana Ewell to me in the future."

"Are those your words or his, Mr. Berman?"

"His words."

"Fine."

"Thank you, Detective," Berman said, the words fading as he hung up.

Souza sighed. He never liked it when the good guys decided to work for the bad guys. He plucked the transcript of the Radovcich interview from his desk and looked at it, but the words on the page made no sense, and his head felt as if it were stuffed with cotton.

During the dog days of August Souza and Burk wrote an incredible twenty-two search warrants seeking the financial records of Dale, Dana, Glee, and Tiffany Ewell. When the records came in, they also included the accounts of "Big" Glee Mitchell, as her daughter had been trustee of the Mitchell accounts. Happenstance perhaps, but within the rows of figures lay a clue that would one day help bind together the fates of Joel Radovcich and Dana Ewell.

Dana was now trustee of his grandmother's money, and it appeared he was using Grandma's money to pay his monthly VISA credit card bills. But most notable were two withdrawals in the amount of $5,660.00 each. Now what in God's name were those for?

The young hostess sat Souza and Burk at a table in the corner, which was fine by Souza. DiCicco's was crowded, and he wanted to hear himself think. They looked over the menus. Souza's had a spatter of red sauce inside. He didn't allow the crime scene to enter his mind.

After ordering, Burk, bread in his mouth, said, "Johnny, I got the feeling we are going to be on this case too long."

"Time we got."

"Been up to the houseboat lately?"

Souza shook his head.

"And with all the money you sink into that thing."

"Don't remind me."

Burk flashed his big toothy grin. "You of all people."

Souza considered himself frugal, but a few friends told him he was a tight-ass, said George Washington would be blinded by the light if Souza ever cracked his wallet. But at least he got out and did things, didn't spend every Sunday in front of the television.

The waiter brought their soup. Souza was starved; he immediately dipped a spoon into the minestrone and burned his tongue tasting it. A cube from the ice water helped.

"The crops any better?" said Burk, dragging another chunk of bread out of the basket.

"The grapes are going to hell. County agent came out, but nobody seems to be able to get a handle on this skeletonizer bug."

"Are you going to get cleaned out this harvest?"

Souza shrugged.

Sometimes he wondered what he was doing with a farm, anyhow. Wasn't it enough that he'd spent most of his childhood slogging through cotton fields?

Souza realized that Burk was speaking to him.

"What?"

"I said—"

The waiter slid their dinner plates in front of them, not bothering to bus the empty soup bowls. Souza noted happily that they hadn't chintzed on the size of his steak.

"I said, I'm concerned, Johnny. I been worried sick about the kids. I'm away so much. And I feel like you're carrying me here."

"Nah. Forget about it."

Burk was silent a moment, then he said, "Wish I could."

Later that week, Souza and his family picked their grapes, but the skeletonizer had taken its toll. The sugar content barely made the minimum necessary for sale to the raisin co-op, the yield was meager, and work on the onion field would begin almost immediately.

*   *   *

Souza and Burk drove to estate attorney Michael Dowling's north Fresno office and sat and listened as he ticked off the assets that comprised the Ewell estate. Dowling, his hair gray or blond or both, was beefy, but not fat. Souza figured the lawyer was in his early fifties.

"Of course," said Dowling, pacing the floor, "there's the airplane concern, then you have millions in cash in various institutions, the Shaver cabin, and the Pajaro Dunes beach house. The farms, of course, which produce a big income. Other interests here and there."

"Over seven million dollars?" Souza said.

"Around that. What are you guys looking for?" Clearly, Dowling was under considerable stress in dealing with the estate.

"If I may, Mr. Dowling, what are your responsibilities?"

Dowling sipped from a coffee cup. He nodded toward the cup, his eyes on the detectives.

"No, thanks," said Burk.

"With an estate of this magnitude, I'm pretty busy. I have to keep the business enterprises—Western Piper and the farms—up and running without Dale's stewardship. I'll begin to liquidate assets as I see fit and work with a CPA on the tax returns for the estate. Of course, I work with the heir as he receives his inheritance."

"But it's our understanding he doesn't get all of it immediately."

Souza could see that Dowling was surprised by the comment, but the attorney didn't bother asking how Souza had known.

"That's correct," the attorney said, taking a seat behind his desk.

Shifting buttocks in his chair, Souza said, "Look, can you tell us when he gets what?"

Dowling took a moment, glanced over some legal documents on his desk. Being deliberate.

"Dana Ewell, through an account set up in his name as

well as another in Tiffany's, will soon receive almost half a million dollars."

Ernie Burk cleared his throat.

"But the bulk of the estate," continued Dowling, "will be paid out in increments. At the age of twenty-five, Dana will inherit the accumulated interest on the assets. At thirty, he'll receive half the total assets. At thirty-five, it's the whole sheebang."

The image of Dana having a temper tantrum at the reading of the will, "How could my dad do this to me!" played through Souza's mind. So Dana had expected to come into seven million or so within a very short time, only to find he'd have to wait for the big money. Clearly, Dale had never told his son exactly what was in the will. It must have been a nasty surprise. (Had Dale, Souza wondered, known his son better than others might suspect?)

"Look," Dowling was saying. He got to his feet once more, pacing behind his desk. "Detectives, is there something you want to tell me?"

"The investigation is ongoing," Souza said.

Dowling snorted. "Spoken like an attorney."

Watch who you're calling a lawyer, pal, thought Souza. He said, "Obviously, in a situation like this it's important that we know who stands to benefit from the deaths."

"Are you saying Dana is a suspect in the deaths of his family?"

"We haven't eliminated anyone yet."

"As you know, if an heir is involved in a homicide that precipitates his receiving his inheritance, he's not entitled to that inheritance."

Souza and Burk nodded.

"So you see my fiduciary responsibility includes decisions on disbursements . . . gentlemen, is Dana Ewell a suspect in this case?"

The detectives got to their feet.

"When we have more, we'll let you know immediately, Counselor," Souza told Dowling.

"Sooner's better than later," Dowling said.

Dowling mentioned that he'd felt sorry for Dana and let the young man use his office, even given Dana a key. But Dowling discouraged him from coming in after Dana racked up huge phone bills and balked at paying. Dana explained that he had no money yet. Besides, many of the calls were made by his buddy, Joel.

When they left the attorney's, Souza decided to again go looking for the elusive Joel Radovcich.

"I told you last time, I don't know where Joel is." Her small, narrow face at the open door.

The West Hills area, an upper-middle-class suburb in Los Angeles's San Fernando Valley, was nearly as hot as Fresno had been. The fronds on the neighborhood palm trees looked baked and brittle, the hillsides leeched to a biscuit color by the sun.

"Mrs. Radovcich, may we come in?" Souza said. They'd driven nearly three hours from home, some of it in gridlock traffic, and they had no intention of quietly going away.

Burk added, "We're worried about your son, Judy. We need your help."

Souza had called Judy Radovcich two or three times, but each time she'd claimed she hadn't seen Joel. Today, the nervousness was evident in Judy Radovcich's labored breathing, and in her hands, as if she didn't know what to do with them.

Judy let them into the house. They took a seat in the den. She said, "I don't know where he is."

Souza didn't believe Judy. And he wasn't in any mood to sweet-talk her. "Listen to me, Judy. Wouldn't you feel better if we find him?"

"I don't know what you mean."

"I mean he might be in danger. Or worse."

She blanched. "Stop scaring me."

"This is serious stuff, here, ma'am. I think you should report him as a missing person."

"I won't do that."

Which meant she knew he wasn't missing.

Souza looked out the back door into the yard. The empty swimming pool was dusty. Scattered leaves swirled around the pool's edge.

Souza said, "Do you know where we can get Joel's dental charts? In case someone turns up?"

"That's not fair! Why are you doing this? Why are you picking on Joel? That boy never had a chance in life!"

Her response told Souza two things: something was wrong with Joel, as he'd guessed, probably some type of personality disorder, and Judy's maternal instincts would lead her to protect the wounded puppy of the litter.

"Judy," Burk said, "we're not here to pick on your son. We're concerned for his safety. And we need to talk to him as soon as we can."

"What is Joel living on, Mrs. Radovcich?" said Souza. "Does he have a job or any means of support?"

"I don't know what he's living on. And I don't think he has a job yet. He hasn't been using his checking account or VISA card."

"Can we see his financials? That might help us out."

She stared at the floor. "I don't know."

"It could be a big help to us. And wouldn't you feel better if we knew he was okay?"

Without a word, she got up and left the room.

"She hates us," Burk said.

"She's joining a big club."

Judy returned with a fistful of paper. She sat and thumbed through the stack. "See? He hasn't written a check since June 3." Thrusting a page toward the detectives, she added, "Three dollars."

Souza wrote down the check number, date and amount, and the payee—Downey Muni Court, citation number RU55602.

He knew what the three-dollar charge was; a teletype fee for the "abstract of clearance" the DMV requires as proof an offender has attended traffic school. Souza jotted down Joel's VISA number and bank-account numbers.

"Can you contact Joel?" Burk said. "Ask him to call us?"

"I'm telling you I have no way to contact him. He used to carry a pager, but now when you call it just makes a funny noise. And that was my only source of communication with him."

"Okay, Mrs. Radovcich," Souza said, getting up. "We've given you a chance. I only hope he's unharmed, that's all. I suggest that if you talk to your son, you have him contact us immediately."

She saw them to the door. Her face was etched with pain, and Souza looked away. So often the parents were the indirect victims of their children's actions.

"Fine," she told the detectives. She closed the door behind them.

"Yep," Burk said, as they walked to the car. "She hates us."

On October 23, Souza called Nick Radovcich, Joel's Ph.D., engineer father, who worked in the aerospace industry in Atlanta. Dr. Radovcich immediately asked the detectives what they had said to Joel during their interview. Souza answered that the discussion had involved a homicide case.

"Well, I don't know what you did to him," Radovcich said, "but whatever it was, he hasn't been the same since."

And then, shortly thereafter, Souza got an anonymous phone tip that Dana had traveled to Switzerland. Was he gone for good?

SEVENTEEN

A FOLLOW-UP REVEALED THAT DANA HAD PUR-chased a round-trip ticket. He returned a week later. Souza wondered if Dana had taken money out of the country, cramming it into fabled Swiss bank accounts.

But then a call came into the FSO from a New York private investigator. The PI said he worked for an attorney in the employ of an expatriate named Marc Rich. The name rang a bell; Rich was an infamous eighties financier who had fled the country on federal tax-evasion charges, and remained a fugitive in Switzerland.

Dana had flown to Zurich, Souza was told, to apply for a position with Rich's company. But when the private eye did a background search his eyes had popped out of his head. A possible suspect in a triple homicide?

"That's Dana," said Souza. "Wanna give him a job?"

That evening Souza found himself snapping at Sharon without provocation. She stuck a cold beer in his hand.

"Here," she said, showing him the back door. "Go out to your hot tub and come back in when you're human."

He did as he was told, returning an hour, and three beers, later.

Sharon looked up from her newspaper. "Better?"

Souza apologized.

"Forget it," she said. "It's all part of the job, isn't it?"

135

"All part of the job," he said, cracking open another beer.

In the briefing room the next morning, Souza, White, Burk, and Curtice sat for one of their regular strategy sessions on the conundrum that was case #92-15285, murder. Dale, Glee, and Tiffany Ewell, victims.

Burk: "We've got Marcos money and the CIA, and the CIA again with Glee, and we got possible drug smuggling and, I don't know . . . goddamn space aliens, probably. But nothing's come of it."

Lieutenant White was leaning forward in his chair, knees bouncing. "And you have the kid."

"And we have the kid. Stands to collect millions, acting pretty damn gleeful . . . sorry, pretty giddy for a grieving son. Something's up with him, I am telling you."

Souza: "This dude is by all accounts obsessed with money. Obsessed with the Billionaire Boy's Club, as if killers are someone to worship. Brazen and conniving enough to let the newspapers print a bunch of crap about him being a self-made millionaire. His own uncles are concerned that he might be involved. Shit, he just isn't acting right for a situation like this."

Burk: "You know, usually when we talk to someone whose friend or relative is a killer, I mean the proof is there, these people go, 'No way he could do such a thing!' But with Dana, we keep interviewing people who say something like, 'Dana? Yeah, I could see him planning this.' "

Souza: "And his buddy Radovcich, KILLA J.R. If Dana was involved, he sure wasn't the trigger man. There's no cracking his alibi. But if he used a stooge—"

White: "If he did, you make Radovcich for the stooge?"

Souza: "Not yet, exactly. But he sure as hell is at the top of the list. His alibi was a bluff. And then we had the Radovcich kid more or less living with Dana, in the house where the murders happened!"

White: "But you haven't talked to him again?"

Souza: "He's avoiding us. It seems he's canceled his KILLA J.R. pager, too."

Curtice: "We need to look for some financial links with these two. See if Dana is paying this guy, like he was hired to do a job."

Souza: "Radovcich was cool, maybe cool enough to do the Ewell job, but I think he's a weaker link than Dana. I mean, without a credible alibi. Of course, Dana has the perfect alibi, with Zent being an FBI agent."

White: "We need something to prove one of these guys had a nine-millimeter. What has the mad scientist come up with?"

Souza: "Boudreau? I'll find out."

Souza found the "mad scientist" in an appropriate place— the laboratory. Boudreau had a loupe to his eye, squinting at a close-up photograph of a bullet.

"These murder bullets are identical," he told Souza. "Like they came out of a copier. One murder weapon."

Souza examined the photo. He could discern the remnants of the land-and-groove pattern—but most striking were the stria, the odd scratches that were etched into the bearing surfaces of the projectile.

"The evidentiary possibilities here are remarkable," Boudreau said. "At the very least, I have to replicate these striations. But it'll take the right combination of weapon and silencer. It's still a needle in a haystack."

Boudreau told Souza about the inquiry responses from firearms experts.

"Big national expert with the ATF asks if I have more than one bullet. I say yes. He asks if they're identical, I say yes. He asks if the gun barrel might have been corroded, but we agreed that if that were the case the bullets wouldn't be identical because each discharge would alter the pattern."

The suppressor theory had always made Souza cringe. The specter of a silencer gave what was already a strange case a nudge toward the bizarre. He said to Boudreau, "So now what?"

"As I said, if we can't produce the murder weapon, I've got to attempt to replicate the murder bullets somehow. I'm experimenting with a nine-millimeter from Property."

He went back to studying his photos. "I'll let you know."

Souza wrote a search warrant seeking information from the Sunnyvale company that provided Joel's pager service. When the warrant was signed by a judge the very helpful staff at Page One pulled their records and gave Souza an account history:

Joel Radovcich had originally ordered service in October 1991, with a 415 (northern California) area code. A few months later he switched to an 818 (San Fernando Valley) service—the KILLA J.R. number.

On July 1, 1992, some three months after the murders, Radovcich called and canceled service. By mid-month they received the unit in the mail, and in August they refunded the security deposit of two hundred dollars.

Souza asked if he could get a copy of the canceled check. No problem, he was told, we'll even send you copies of our records.

The check copy arrived via fax. Two names were signed on the back.

Joel Radovcich and Dana Ewell.

With this solid financial link between their two suspects, Souza and Burk returned to Santa Clara University for a second background check on Dana. Burk talked to the dean and was given the name of a friend of Joel's, a graduate named Tom Duong. Meanwhile, Souza located a student who had lived in the same dorm as Dana.

"One funny thing," the student said. "Dana was always coming over to use my phone. Had a phone in his own damn room, but a lot of the time he said he needed mine. Never really explained why."

Richard Berman, Dana's criminal attorney, released a copy of a letter he'd sent earlier to Sheriff Magarian in which he threatened legal action for libel against Dana. Berman's letter appeared in a November 1 lead story in the *Bee*, the contents of which hinted at Dana's being a suspect and questioned Dana's integrity, quoting from the bogus articles about Dana's "self-made" status. The article also named, for the first time, Joel Radovcich as an individual wanted by detectives for questioning.

Berman accused investigators of defaming Dana. *"Dana feels that he is being scapegoated because the investigators have been completely ineffective in finding and prosecuting those responsible. If in fact, the Sheriff's Office is not intending to spread these rumors, then they should make it clear on the record that Dana is not a suspect."*

Around that time, Souza also learned how Dana had come to administer the trust set up by Glee Ewell to provide for her mother, Glee Mitchell. The former administrator, Ruth Lind, said Dana had had no interest at first in the Mitchell Trust—until he saw that some $400,000 was involved. Then he summarily fired Lind and set himself up as trustee.

Richard Berman soon contacted investigators, asking that he and Dana be allowed to inventory jewelry still in police possession and pick up Dale's Ruger .357 Magnum revolver. Souza called Berman on November 10 and told him to bring in his client.

Upon their arrival Ernie Burk hurried off, ostensibly to find Sergeant Caudle, who was hiding in the captain's office, then returned and told Dana the Ruger would have to wait until Caudle returned the next day.

Souza had dreamed up this delaying tactic in the hopes that Dana, unwilling to pay Berman to accompany him for a second visit, would show up alone the following day at the Sheriff's office.

Souza led them into the briefing room. The conference

table was stacked with evidence envelopes. Souza knew which envelopes contained jewelry, but . . .

Slowly, deliberately, carefully, he unsealed each envelope, allowed Dana to view the contents, resealed each, and then jotted his initials on the evidence cards. It was taking some time.

Dana began a slow burn. He squirmed in his seat and glared at Souza, who hummed merrily along, seemingly oblivious to any time considerations. Berman, too, appeared content. He was, after all, billing Dana by the hour.

Dana finally said to Berman, "Is there any way to move this along? I have things to do today."

"Detective," Berman said evenly, "how much longer?"

"You know I have to follow procedures, Counselor."

"Noted. But how much longer?"

"Tell you what I'll do," Souza said. He produced a form that had been drawn up by the DA's Office.

"Mr. Berman, if you'll sign this, which as you can see waives the chain-of-evidence procedures, I can just hand the whole batch over to you in about two minutes."

"Dana?" Berman said without lifting his gaze from the form. "Leave us alone for a while."

Dana mumbled something that sounded like, "Gladly," and he was gone.

"Detective," Berman said with a smile. "You don't really expect me to sign this do you?"

Souza cleared his throat. "You're the lawyer."

"It isn't going to happen."

"Richard," Souza said. "I'm very concerned. And I know you look out for your client's welfare."

"What are you so concerned about, Detective?"

"This Joel Radovcich kid. He's spooky. Dana could very well be in danger from Joel."

"Yeah," Berman said, heading for the door.

Dana showed up the next day at 11:25 A.M. His business suit looked brand-new. Burk and Souza took Dana into the interview room, where they asked him to sign an evidence card releasing the Ruger .357 Magnum revolver, Model GP150, serial #171-54871.

Then Burk said, "Dana, has any other property turned up missing at your folks' house?"

"Oh, yeah," Dana said. "You want to take a report or anything?"

"We certainly want to get the word out on anything that might have been stolen from the house."

Dana claimed he'd been unable to locate the following items:

one pearl necklace, value $4500.00.
one pearl-and-bead necklace, value $4500.
one pearl bracelet, value UK.
one diamond bracelet, value $2500.
one woman's emerald-and-diamond ring, value $4000.00.

"Okay, we'll put out the word on these items," Souza told Dana. "While you're here, do you know anything about your dad being a witness in a Federal drug case last year?"

The drug case meant little—it involved a plane Dale had rented to a customer, nothing more—but Souza wanted to get Dana talking.

"I heard he was going to Sacramento to testify."

"Okay. Do you know who he was to testify against?"

"The guy's name was Nick Latansio."

"Did your dad tell you that?" Souza asked.

"No, he never said anything about it. The estate attorney, Mike Dowling, told me. I don't know where he heard it."

"Hey, Dana?" said Burk. "You know, we're very concerned about Joel Radovcich."

Dana stiffened. "You what?"

"Joel. Could you tell us about him? Might help us out."

Dana was on his feet. "I'm out of here. I got what I want."

"Dana, we need your cooperation here."

But Dana, the bagged Ruger in hand, was going for the door, his face tight.

"You've been getting it," Dana said over his shoulder. He rushed through the interview room door and was gone.

"Goddamn it!" Souza said, incredulous.

Burk shook his head. "This guy blows my mind."

Souza hurried into the hall. No sign of Dana. He approached the receptionist who checked visitors in and out of the lobby area.

"Doris, did a tall kid just come by here, short dark hair? The Ewell boy?"

"Are you kidding? He stormed into the lobby and threw his visitor's pass down on the counter. I passed his ID back through the glass and he ran the hell out of here."

"Ran?"

"Almost. Looked pretty ticked off."

Souza went outside as Dana's Mercedes shot away from the curb.

On a brisk day in late November, Souza took a call from a man named Hewitt. Hewitt said he was the boyfriend of a neighbor of the Ewells, and he remembered now that he'd heard noises in the wee hours of the night before Easter. He'd had a few cocktails while awaiting his girlfriend's return. About 3 A.M. he noticed that an outside light at the Ewell's—generally burning—was not lighted that night. A shed door appeared open. And, Hewitt claimed, he heard whispering. Two people, one of them a bossy guy with a soft voice, were up to something out there.

When interviewed shortly after the crime, Hewitt had insisted he'd heard nothing. Now, after the murders had gotten so much press, he claimed to have witnessed much more. And he was drinking at the time.

Still, Souza found the account intriguing—two male voices. What if Dana had let Joel into the Ewell home the night before the murders?

EIGHTEEN

CHRIS CURTICE LOOKED AS IF HE'D JUST SNIFFED a plate of bad fish. He stood in Souza's office doorway, a newspaper in hand. Another detective peeked inside, then hurried away.

"Uh, John? You see the paper this morning?"

"Haven't got to it yet. Why?" Souza sifted through notes he'd made while meeting with Allen Boudreau.

Curtice said, "I think you better. The Letters to the Editor."

Souza glanced up. "What's in it?"

"A little love letter to the Sheriff's Department. From John Zent."

Curtice clicked his tongue and walked off. Souza found the Letters section in the November 25 issue of the *Bee* and nearly fell out of his chair.

In response to your recent article concerning Dana Ewell, my family believes that both the Fresno Bee *and the Sheriff's office have without validity tried to link Dana with the death of his family. It is well-known to the Sheriff's office that Dana was with our daughter having dinner in our Morgan Hill home when this crime occurred. Evidence along with witness statements including my own fully support Dana's whereabouts. The concept that Dana hired someone to do this crime is really grasping for* straws. Perhaps it isn't apparent but Dana is a victim, he has lost in one crime all of his immediate family.

During that Easter weekend on Saturday, my family spent a long and enjoyable dinner with Dale, Glee, Tiffany and Dana at their Pajaro Beach home ... Dana's love for his family, his respect for his parents, was mirrored in their love for him—that pride parents have in realizing their children are doing well.

I've been in Federal law enforcement working complex, criminal investigations for over 21 years. In my opinion there have been a number of improper procedures coupled with a lack of professionalism and objectivity within this case ...

Some have taken note that Dana has a nice car, clothes, and goes to an expensive college. Having spoken with Dale and Glee, I know they very happily provided the best for both Dana and Tiffany. The fact that the Ewells had significant financial resources, simply made it easier for them to give the best to their children. This is an action any parent would do if money wasn't the issue.

Without question Dana has suffered a great loss compounded by those who would link him to this crime without any factual basis. Eventually someone will be caught who will explain the events surrounding this sad crime, usually after getting off the hook for some other crime. Until then idle speculation or unfounded implications should be avoided by all. Put yourself in Dana's shoes; he would gladly forgo all the money to simply again be with his family.

Dana along with the attorney for the Ewell estate have set up a reward fund; however any response must go through the Sheriff's Department ... We challenge the Bee to set up a proper Secret Witness program to ensure all leads are then pursued.

Our family loves and supports Dana as one of

*our own. Before this crime and since he had been
a very welcomed guest in our home. The harm that
has been done to him within Fresno, and at Santa
Clara University will pass but none of it has been
beneficial to solving this crime. The challenge is to
solve every aspect of the crime to then identify the
perpetrator not to simply take aim at Dana in light
of one's own limitations or inabilities.*

John Zent
Morgan Hill

Souza felt his blood pressure soar. He tossed the newspaper across the room, pages scattering, fluttering to the
floor.

"... 'in light of one's own limitations or inabilities'!"

Bad enough he'd heard that Zent had joined Dana in
deriding the detectives as "Bert and Ernie," but this letter!
From a fellow law-enforcement officer, someone whom
Dana's uncles believed might be helping Dana derail the
investigation!

Souza took a call around Christmastime from the owner
of the Avenue of Flowers shop on Kings Canyon road.
Harry, the shop owner, said he'd delivered an FTD sympathy offering to the Ewell's East Park Circle residence a
few months after the murders.

Harry told Souza he'd called the home and a young
man answered who described himself as a friend of Dana
Ewell's. Harry asked the fellow if Dana would prefer a
plant or flowers. The young man said a plant would be
fine.

On June 6, Harry delivered the plant, with a card that
read "Dear Tiffany, we're always with you," signed by
friends of Tiffany's in Japan. The man who'd taken the
call signed the form, thanked Harry, and retreated inside
the Ewell home with the plant. Souza asked Harry if he
could recall a name.

Sure, Harry said. That's why I'm phoning. I saw his name in the *Bee* a few weeks ago. Joel Radovcich.

Also in December, Dale Caudle was contacted by the television show *Unsolved Mysteries*. Caudle told Souza that researchers at *Unsolved* wanted to air the Ewell story in the hope that leads would be produced. The FSO offered to help, but the final decision on whether a segment would air was in someone else's hands. An *Unsolved* researcher wrote, "Until I have contacted the Ewell's son, Dana, and received his cooperation to do a story on him and his family (which may not be possible), I will not even be able to propose the idea to the Executive Producers. We cannot do such a story as this without his permission . . ."

But Dana apparently did not give his consent, and the story never made it to the air.

1993

". . . bring your parents and your sister. We'll have a party at your house . . ."

ONE

THEY ARRIVED, LIKE A STEALTHY INVADING army, in the San Fernando Valley area on the first of February 1993. Fifteen vehicles and fifteen detectives. Most were personnel from Narcotics Enforcement—shaggy-haired undercover cops dressed in baggy shirts and worn jeans, driving tired pickup trucks and plain-wrap cars.

Half were deployed outside the Canoga Park office of the Department of Motor Vehicles, half waited near the home of Judy Radovcich.

When Joel's black Honda CRX was spotted pulling into the DMV parking lot, Souza immediately called the team outside the Radovcichs'. They roared over to join their compadres at DMV.

It was a setup.

Souza had flagged Joel's car registration at Motor Vehicles and written a letter to the DMV station asking for assistance in bringing Joel in to the station. With Joel's registration due for renewal that month, a DMV officer phoned Judy Radovcich, handing her a tale that someone had duplicated Joel's registration—could Joel come in on Monday and straighten it all out?

But Judy called back later and said she would bring the Honda in herself.

This left Souza with a decision. He'd gone to his immediate superiors with the idea of a Los Angeles surveil on Radovcich. Now, after making a presentation to the captain and receiving approval from Sheriff Magarian himself, could Souza risk hauling fifteen detectives down to LA only to spy on Radovcich's mother?

In the end, on the premise that Joel would eventually end up behind the wheel of his own car, the team assembled for a briefing. Everyone got a photo of the primary subject, and the detectives spent hours poring over maps of the San Fernando Valley.

Souza made sure the team realized it was preferable to lose Radovcich during surveillance rather than risk discovery, which would compromise the entire Ewell investigation. The FSO convoy hit the freeways on a Sunday. They selected a valley motel as their headquarters and staging area.

At daybreak Monday, the early-morning sunlight pink against the hazy Los Angeles sky, they had been up and staking out Judy's house and the DMV, happy to see Joel himself appear.

After a short wait, Joel exited the station and headed for his car. A point car jockeyed into position, picking up the CRX as it cleared the parking lot. The rest fell in behind in pairs.

Souza brought up the rear, where he could coordinate the operation with a minimum chance of being spotted by Radovcich. This was the first he'd seen of Joel in months; he had to know where the kid lived.

He cursed himself again for not following up immediately after Joel was seen at Dana's, but at the time it had just seemed crazy that Joel would move into the Ewell home if he'd been involved in the crime.

From the DMV, Joel cruised convenience stores and fast-food restaurants in what appeared to be aimless meanderings. He stopped at his mother's house, then began to make rounds of area phone booths.

Souza knew Joel's mother had a telephone—why did Joel need to use pay phones?

Radovcich stopped at booths in Canoga Park, El Segundo, Seal Beach. He covered a lot of ground, and he covered it at breathtaking speeds.

As Joel talked on one pay phone, Souza got on the cell phone to Detective Sergeant Jeff Hollis.

"We have to know what this kid is talking about."

"What should we do, get a shotgun mike?"

"I don't think so," Souza said. "I'm afraid it might get tossed out on evidentiary grounds."

"Well," Hollis said, "what then?"

Souza was trying to think.

Hollis said, "How about we just listen to the guy?"

"What do you mean, listen to him?"

"Just that. Next pay phone he stops at, I park around the block and walk up and use the phone next to him."

"I can't believe the kid would be stupid enough to say something incriminating with someone right next to him."

It was well into the evening before one of the detectives got the opportunity to test Radovcich's reaction to eaves-dropping detectives.

Detective Rick Pursell stepped up to the greasy pay phone next to Radovcich. The drug cop fed thirty-five cents into the slot and dialed randomly, thumbing the hook. From a distance, through Souza's binoculars, Joel seemed animated, in a good mood. Souza laughed, watching Pursell standing there talking to himself. He wondered if Radovcich was suspicious about the guy next to him, but Radovcich gave no indication of concern.

After ten minutes, Joel hung up and strolled into the 7-Eleven. Pursell continued to jabber away into a dead line, then he cleared out.

When Souza got him up on the radio, Pursell said, "Hang on a sec, let me write this down."

Souza waited, looking over the neighborhood and wondering why anyone would want to live in Los Angeles.

"John?"

"Yo."

"Okay, the kid was talking about the weather—"

"Come on, the weather?"

"Hang on. The weather over the Grapevine on the way here from Fresno. Sounded like he was saying the road was clear and whatnot. He said, 'Come on down, you ought to be here.' Then he says, 'I don't know, a helicopter.' You know, like he's telling someone to take a chopper down."

"I get it."

"So it went on like that for a while."

"Nothing else?"

"Oh yeah, there was."

Souza saw Radovcich emerging from the 7-Eleven. "Spit it out. He's getting back in the Honda."

"Starting up now. Oh . . . no shit, he said, 'bring your parents and your sister. We'll have a party at your house.' "

Joel was followed to an aging apartment building in Huntington Beach, thirty minutes south of Long Beach, before the surveillance was terminated. Afterward, in their hotel's underground parking lot, Pursell and Souza and the other surveillance-team detectives held an informal debriefing session.

"I can't say for certain he was talking to Dana, but it was a hell of a coincidence if he wasn't," Pursell was saying.

"Jesus," Souza said. "Your parents and sister? A party at your house? If these clowns really were talking about Dana Ewell's family, they are a couple of stone-cold characters."

"He sure as hell looks sneaky, running around to all those phone booths. If I didn't know better, I'd say Radovcich was one of the dealers we go after."

Souza nodded. "Also interesting? He drove countersurveillance, but only for the twenty minutes or so before he made the call that Pursell listened in on."

"Hey," Pursell said, "at least it looks like we made the place he's living."

"Tomorrow, let's set up outside the Huntington Beach apartment complex."

By Wednesday evening, Joel Radovcich's habits were becoming clear: He would depart his Huntington Beach apartment at 11:00 or 12:00 A.M., spend much of the day driving without apparent destination, eat at Taco Bell, visit the Long Beach Aviation Center (though exactly what he was doing at the airport remained a mystery), and stop regularly at pay phones.

Souza wondered what to make of this kid. A graduate of a prestigious business school, son of a Ph.D. engineer, yet from all appearances unemployed, aimless, living a meaningless life. Who the hell would want to spend their days like that?

The surveillance continued the next day. Souza hit the gas and blew through a yellow street light, bringing up the rear of the team that shadowed Joel's every move.

It was an exhausting effort; not only did Radovcich run "fresh red" lights and exceed the speed limit, but the team was on foreign turf. They knew Fresno's streets cold, but greater Los Angeles was another story. Team members learned to drive at eighty miles an hour while struggling to read a road map.

On February 3, 1993, after four days of tailing Radovcich, Souza terminated the effort. On the drive home, as he traveled north over the Sepulveda Pass between Los Angeles and the Valley, a cloudburst blew in, dumping blinding sheets of rain and forcing him to pull over until it subsided, although the crazy LA drivers seemed unconcerned by zero visibility as they rocketed past Souza's parked car.

Listening to the whine of tires on the wet pavement, Souza lamented that he had found no hard evidence linking Radovcich to the Ewell murders. But the suspicious activity of the brooding young man in the black Honda had confirmed, at least in Souza's mind, that Joel was involved. Unfortunately, the detective had no idea what his next move would be.

He started by taking a chance. By returning to the south-land and contacting the manager of Joel's apartment building. Helen was aging and tough, but Souza found her a pleasure to spend time with.

"Helen, I hope I can trust you with this information. It's gotta be kept secret, or this whole investigation could go down the toilet."

She shook a cigarette free from a pack and lit up with a chrome Zippo lighter. "Detective," she said, smoke curling around her face, "it won't leave this room."

"I can't thank you enough. So, how do we find out what Joel's status is here?"

"Easy. He's renting a room from a trucker. The guy's name is Rick. Joel moved in the end of January. I'll tell Rick his roommate will have to fill out a rental form if he wants to stay here."

Yawning, still beat from the drive home from Los Angeles the night before, Souza whipped the county car into the taco stand parking lot at lunchtime.

He ordered combo plate #3, beef taco, pork burrito, rice, and beans, and carried his fragrant food over to a picnic table. A carload of gangsta kids cruised by in a lowered Chevelle, stereo thumping out rap music at about two hundred decibels. Chewing his burrito, Souza winced at the racket and glanced over at the car. The punks weren't anyone he knew; one of the boys stared back idly.

"I knew I'd find you here," said a voice behind him. It was Burk. "Man, I got news, I got news."

Souza forked up some frijoles. He wanted lunch, not news. "Yeah?"

"Hang on, that swill looks good."

Burk was back in five minutes with his own plate. He plopped down opposite his partner. He asked, "How'd the LA surveillance go?"

Souza gave Burk a quick rundown, and said, "I thought you had big news."

"Damn tasty," Burk said.

"It doesn't look so good inside your mouth."

"So I ran down a friend of your boy Radovcich."

"I was beginning to think he didn't have any friends. Except Dana."

"Not many," said Burk. "Joel ain't exactly Mr. Popularity. So I called this guy 'cause someone—who was it?—anyway I called a guy named Tom Duong up in San Jose."

"Another oddball?"

The gang cruiser was back, "music" louder than ever.

Burk turned for a look. "Assholes. Anyway, no—this kid seems to be a straight arrow, ROTC candidate. Wants to work military intelligence. Radovcich stayed at Doung's parents' house in summer of '91. While Joel was staying there, he asked Duong if it would be all right if Joel had some books sent to the address."

Burk had Souza's full attention now. "And?"

"Damn good grub. And, Duong says sure, what does he give a shit? Joel said he had some magazines on the way, and to please not open the package when it arrives."

"But Duong did."

"Right. Tom says he mistakenly opened it. Who knows?"

Burk filled his mouth again.

"Ernie," Souza said, "if you don't stop eating that fucking food and tell me what was in the package, I am going to shoot you."

Big swallow. "Might be worth it. It was handbooks, man. Fringe handbooks. On making homemade weapons, explosive devices. And, here we go: on building silencers."

TWO

SOUZA WAS ASTONISHED.

Burk said, "Duong claims he was pissed, Joel sending this crap to his parents' house. He apparently bitched Joel up and down, and Joel apologized."

"Who was the company that sent the material?"

"Not sure yet. Presidio Press or something."

"Silencers, huh?"

"Duong said one book cover featured a big photo of a weapon with a homemade silencer."

"We gotta find those books."

"One more thing. Before Joel moved out, he asked Duong if he had any weapons for sale, or if he knew someone who did."

Burk's information from Duong was a major break. Souza was all but certain that they had their shooter. He believed it wouldn't be easy to implicate Joel; he knew success wouldn't come quickly, but the detective felt his confidence, so battered during the trudging investigation, surging once more.

They'd need to keep track of Joel, and Souza would soon learn he'd be doing just that. The relative success of earlier surveils on Dana, and then Joel, gave Souza's bosses at FSO the confidence to open up the county wallet and fund additional surveillances of Radovcich.

* * *

On March 18, Souza opened an interoffice memo from Gary Hoff of the District Attorney's Office. Hoff wrote:

> *The District Attorney's Office received the enclosed note and the attached letter. The anonymous sender obviously finds the part highlighted (done by the sender) suspicious. Mr. Hunt asked me to pass this along to you for your consideration.*

Gary Hoff was Fresno County Senior Deputy District Attorney. A Post-it note was stuck to the attached letter.

> *I hope you are investigating him! Isn't this an interesting statement considering the situation?*

The letter itself bore the imprint of Western Piper Sales, Inc. It appeared to be part of a mass-mailing marketing campaign, and was addressed to "Dear Aircraft Owner." The first line, which had been highlighted in yellow by the anonymous sender, read:

My name is Dana J. Ewell and I own Western Piper Sales in Fresno.

Souza raised an eyebrow. The letter was packed with hyperbolic prose singing the praises of Western Piper's "highest level of service and professionalism available today."

The mailer closed with an invitation to aircraft owners to call Jack Whitman in service or Bob Pursell in sales, and was signed, "Dana J. Ewell."

Souza had heard that Dana was hanging around Western Piper, using his father's office, driving his father's car. It occurred to him that Dana's assumption of his father's life was now complete.

And the Ewell brothers again contacted Souza, requesting that he and Burk meet with Kathlyn Rhea, a psychic who had been used in other police investigations. Souza, understanding that the family was willing to try just about anything that might solve the case, agreed. During the meeting, Ms. Rhea didn't provide anything that Souza felt would be of assistance in the investigation, but she did insist the gun used in the murders had been buried somewhere.

As the focus of the case narrowed to Dana and Joel, fellow detectives told Souza to be wary. If Dana was the type to hire a hit man, maybe he wouldn't hesitate to take out a cop, too.

Souza wasn't particularly concerned. Killing cops wasn't the best way for a suspect to deflect attention from himself. Still, stranger things had happened, and more than once he'd nearly died while on duty.

Back when he had been a constable, Souza responded to a street disturbance where local police, fearing a potential riot, had radioed for assistance. Souza rolled up in his cruiser, parked nearby to assess the situation, and someone stepped out of the shadows and screwed a .357 Magnum revolver into his ear.

He suddenly believed all the stories he'd heard about one's life flashing before one's eyes. What will the newspapers say? What will happen to Sharon and the boys?

Of course, he didn't die, but it took twenty very slow minutes, and a great deal of chatter on Souza's part, to convince the gunman to back off.

"You kill a cop, pal," Souza said perhaps a dozen times, "and you will be hunted down like a dog."

As suddenly as the man had appeared, he vanished, and Souza wondered if picking cotton hadn't been a pleasant job after all.

Souza hoped media pressure might lead Joel to panic and make a mistake, and the detective decided to turn up the heat by contacting reporters. The California Album section of the March 22 *Los Angeles Times* headlined:

SLAYING OF FAMILY REMAINS A MYSTERY
Fresno police have mostly discounted possible ties of wealthy businessman to drug dealing or disgruntled

Filipino investors. They now focus on the lone surviving son.

That leaves burglary-gone-bad or a theory involving Dana Ewell, the sole heir to an $8-million estate.

Detectives traveled to Southern California and
Utah and spent a week at Santa Clara University trying to glean information about Ewell and a college
buddy, Joel P. Radovcich, a San Fernando Valley na-
tive who dropped out of sight after being questioned.
Investigators said they are trying to find Radovcich
to question him again.

Of course, the detectives had found Joel, but the tone
of the article—that Radovcich was avoiding investigators—was essentially true.

Souza made a copy of the piece (which featured a large
photo of himself at work on the case) and set about planning the next rolling surveillance of Joel Radovcich.

Nearly every week, at least one of the Ewell brothers took
the time to call Souza and offer support—unlike Dana,
who never once called to inquire if the police were tracking down his family's killers. The calls were always cor-
dial, and Souza was glad for the opportunity to keep
relatives advised on the investigation's progress.

Richard phoned one morning to let Souza know the
Ewell family intended to double the $50,000 reward
they'd offered for information that would convict the
killer or killers; Souza assured Richard the increased reward would not impede the investigation. Later, however,
Souza learned that Dana had refused to contribute toward
the hundred-thousand-dollar reward.

With the investigation's long hours, Souza was picking
up considerable overtime. But his absences from the ranch
were costing more than the overtime pay brought in. His
sons were busy with their own lives, working as correc-
tion officers in preparation to moving over to the FSO,

and Souza brought the onion harvest in late, which meant a missed market and a correspondingly weak price for the crop. Afterward, he and Sharon barbecued a couple of steaks and sat out on the deck. Souza didn't have much to say.

Sharon prodded him to share the latest about the Ewell case.

"I feel like I'm never here, and you're the one that's paying for all this," he told her.

"Stop worrying. Besides, when you are here you're cranky."

"Great. Firing on all cylinders aren't I?"

"I have my sisters and my family. I'm hanging in. Guess I'm just not as whiny as the new generation of girls."

"Rollin', rollin', rollin', " Souza was singing as he drove, "keep them dogies rollin'. Raw-hiiiiide!"

The undercover detectives ahead of him were hitting it hard as they struggled to keep Radovcich's black Honda CRX in sight. One thing that amazed the entire team, all of whom had ridden patrol before moving to detective work: Joel had not once been ticketed by local traffic enforcement, despite his annihilation of posted speed limits.

Souza got on the horn to Sergeant Ron Adolph.

"He's headed back to the airport, huh?"

"It looks like it. I'm afraid we lost Hollis a while back. One of the locals stopped him for speeding, but then cut him loose."

"You think he's taking flight lessons?"

"It had crossed my mind."

"Okay, Sarge. I think I'll try to find out soon."

Souza would always feel indebted to Adolph. It was Adolph who had been most instrumental in getting Souza into the Homicide Unit.

When Souza first put in for the position, his superiors favored bringing in someone younger. But Adolph reminded the brass how Souza had made a name for himself.

While still in uniform, Souza pioneered a uniquely successful procedure for solving residential burglaries: he'd memorize the often mismatched tire tracks left at a scene, then study the tires of cars encountered on neighborhood patrol. When he located tires matching those tracks found at burglaries, he'd monitor the cars, often taking to the skies in patrol planes, and in so doing managed to catch scores of burglars.

When the brass still hesitated to move Souza into Homicide, Adolph related a tale that had become legend at the FSO.

As a young deputy, Souza responded to the report of a theft of five gallons of gasoline at a farm pump. The temperature was over one hundred degrees in the shade, Adolph told his superiors, and most lawmen would have scribbled a report and gotten the hell out of there. But not John Souza.

Souza spotted shoe prints near the farmer's gas pump, followed the tracks nearly a mile to a house trailer, and found a full gasoline can. He rounded up a teenager who lived at the trailer, made the frightened kid haul the gasoline back to the farmer, and then Souza went on his way.

Johnny was the kind of cop everybody would want as their cop, Adolph said. And he'll be as dedicated and relentless as any homicide detective you could find.

Souza finally realized his dream: he got the nod as a homicide investigator.

Joel spent an hour at the airport and then tore off again in the CRX. What, the investigators continued to wonder, was Joel doing at the airport every day?

Surveillance vehicles were tailing him in pairs, and they had constant problems with Joel's propensity for running fresh reds and leaving chase vehicles at traffic lights. Souza never saw any indication that Radovcich knew he was being surveilled; the kid just drove that way.

At one point Radovcich raced up Pacific Coast Highway and ran the yellow, as usual. Vehicles in pursuit fell into what was now routine—they'd fan out in pairs and slip into the outermost lanes—one in the left turn lane, one in the right. Both drivers would check for cross-traffic and then jump the red light in an attempt to catch Joel.

This time, Souza saw an older gentleman in a twenty-year-old Cadillac stopped at the light. On each side of him, pairs of surveillance cars screeched to a stop, then blasted through the red-lighted intersection.

The man in the Cad, his head swiveling as if he were at a tennis match, watched the first pair go, then the second. Souza could see that the old guy was getting steamed. By the third pair, the driver's hands were high on the wheel, his elbows out, a look of angry determination on his face.

"Oh, shit, Pops," Souza whispered, "don't get your panties in a bunch."

As the next pair, which included the huge, long-haired, biker-outfitted Ross Kelly in a clapped-out old pickup, pulled up beside the Cadillac, the light turned green. Souza guessed what was coming.

The old guy punched it, the huge V-8 roared, and Kelly found himself in a race. The drug cop was glaring at the driver in the Cad, his jaw going, and Souza knew Kelly was shouting at the codger to yield before his lane terminated.

But the Cadillac, obviously superior in horsepower, held off the pickup. Kelly found himself being squeezed into the divider. He hit the brakes and skidded across two lanes, nearly taking out the Cadillac and some poor bastard in a Pinto. Souza knew he shouldn't be laughing, but with the tears in his eyes almost drove off the road himself.

Back in Fresno after the latest surveillance, Souza perused a report from one detective who'd followed Joel into the UCLA library. Joel had asked the librarian where he could find copies of the *Los Angeles Times*; this after his name had appeared in the *Times* as a possible suspect in the Ewell case.

Detective Avila then tailed Joel from UCLA to the beach at Malibu. Avila's follow-up report:

FSO 92-15285
Det J Avila
On Saturday, March 27, 1993, at approximately 1431 hours, I was involved in a moving surveillance involving the subject, who was driving a black Honda CRX in the area of Pacific Coast Highway and Coastline Drive, Topanga Canyon.

At approximately 1434 hours, I observed subject Radovcich walking across the Pacific Coast Highway toward the ocean. As I watched through the binoculars, I saw him walk to the edge of a cliff located near the intersection cited above. Radovcich walked toward a vehicle that was parked there. His head was bowed, and he seemed to be very upset. He kept looking down toward the ground and then would look over the cliff as if contemplating jumping. He squatted down and appeared to be looking out over the ocean.

He was not talking to anyone in the area, he just seemed to be very self-confined, and at one point I felt he may [sic] jump over the cliffs onto the rocks below. He appeared very, very upset and it was my personal feeling that he may be contemplating suicide.

At 1445 hours, I observed Radovcich walk back across PCH into a residential area and out of my view.

During the course of my observation of

Radovcich, at the time he was near the cliff, I felt he was in a very lonely state and it would not have taken much for him to jump off the cliff and into the rocks.

Another observer echoed Avila's observations. Souza felt that the *Times* article had sent Radovcich into a fit of despair, and the detective hoped this would lead Radovcich to make a strategic error.

In late March Souza received a note from estate attorney Russel Georgeson. Georgeson handled a Mitchell family trust account that had been set up for Glee Ewell, and since her death, had used Dan Ewell, not Dana, as trustee.

The copy of a letter to Georgeson made clear Dana's dissatisfaction with the attorney's choice as trustee of his mother's account:

Dear Mr. Georgeson,

I would appreciate it if you could tell me in what century you and Dan Ewell plan to wrap up the James J. Mitchell Trust. Being only 22 years of age, I would like to do some early estate planning and want to know how much money will be squandered away in attorney's fees...

Right now, you are wasting my time, my money, my attorney's time, your time, Dan Ewell's time, etc., etc., etc. Please give me your intentions! As you know, a trustee is accountable to a degree of fiscal responsibility. Technically, Dan Ewell is opening himself up to personal damages by continuing in this manner. Does you [sic] client realize that, Mr. Georgeson? Do I have to file a complaint against you to get some action? Please do something, in this century.

Dana J. Ewell

*   *   *

Another rolling surveillance operation.

Ten-forty A.M., March 31, Joel was moving out of the Huntington Beach apartment. Helen, the apartment-building manager, had kindly contacted Souza and informed him of the date of Radovcich's impending move.

Souza (who now, as he did typically during the surveillances, waited in his car at a distance where he wouldn't be spotted by Radovcich) listened as Bob Moore gave him a report via radio.

"He's stacking a futon and clothes in the Honda," said Moore, a quiet, extremely capable investigator.

"Well, shit," said Souza, "let's be sure not to lose him when he takes off."

At eleven-twenty, Moore reported, "Okay, looks like he's done here. He's in his vehicle and away. Let's get ready. Wait a minute, he pulled up. Getting out near a Dumpster. Okay, yeah—he tossed a trash bag into the Dumpster."

Excellent, Souza thought.

Moore again: "We're rolling."

Souza said over the radio, "I'll catch up. Got a pickup to make."

"What?"

"On second thought, Moore, you stay put. Can you identify that trash bag?"

"Wouldn't want to have to pick it out of a lineup. But yeah, I can still see the bag in the garbage."

Souza whipped his car in next to Moore's in the alley.

"My Christ, what's that stench?" Moore said.

"Probably disposable diapers," Souza said. "Where is it?"

"Man, what are they feeding babies nowadays, anyhow? There it is, right there."

"This it? Let's get out of here."

Souza tossed the bag into his trunk, and he and Moore joined the surveillance team again. They caught up at

John's Hamburger Stand. From John's, Joel visited the Long Beach Aviation Center, this with an enormous streetside parking lot. Then they followed him north on the 405 freeway to an office complex on Sunset Boulevard. Souza saw signage that indicated Joel was visiting a lawyer's office.

At around three o'clock, Joel led them to his mother's house, where he unloaded his things.

"Moving back in with Mommy," Souza announced into the radio.

They waited for hours. Souza wondered who would win the Series this year, and remembered he'd made no provision to have his crops watered while he was away.

At 9:30 P.M. the itinerant Radovcich was back on the road in the Honda, returning to the 7-Eleven at the northwest corner of Saticoy and Fallbrook. The strip mall on the fringe of West Hills, surrounded by modest apartment buildings, was near Joel's favorite Taco Bell. Joel hustled to the far-left phone on the outer wall of the convenience store. His back to the nearby alley, he lifted the receiver.

"Man, he must carry a zillion dollars in quarters," Souza said to Moore, as they watched Joel feed coins into the phone.

Moore said, "I'm telling you he keeps looking down at his belt and grabbing something, then dialing. He's using a pager."

"I think he got a new pager," said Souza.

"That explains it."

Joel hung around the 7-Eleven for an hour, gassed up the Honda, and buzzed back to his mother's house. Souza terminated the surveillance and drove back to the motel parking lot to sort through Joel's trash.

Souza had both gloved hands in the bag when a well-dressed woman walked by. He was unsure if her look was one of fright or disgust or both, but he gave her a big loopy grin. She hurried along.

Souza wasn't surprised to find numerous paper bags from Radovcich's favorite restaurant.

"Taco Belch," Moore said.

"Kid's stomach must be made out of stainless steel."

Moore pulled out a handful of notes. "Female handwriting," he said, reading. "Notes to Joel . . . looks like Joel's roommate has a girlfriend and she wants to play a little bouncy-bouncy with Radovcich!"

"Joel doesn't seem very aggressive in chasing the babes."

They found two plastic water bottles, an empty box of granola bars, a local newspaper. Certainly nothing dramatic, until Moore found a copy of the *Recycler*, a regional free classified advertising paper.

"What's he shopping for?" Moore said.

Souza rooted through the detritus at the bottom of the trash bag.

"Holy shit, John. Check out the artwork."

Souza, reading over Moore's shoulder, saw just below the Roommates Wanted section a display ad about five inches square. The ad touted the effectiveness of the *Recycler* (Advertising that Pays!) and featured a retro-style graphic of a family—Dad, Mom, son, and daughter—together reading a newspaper. Near the border, scribbled in ink, were the words, Unfurnished Util, sec dep $400, fone, how my living, occupation.

Someone, presumably Radovcich, had also doctored the display ad. Dad was given a long tongue, with which he licked his daughter's face, slurp, slurp, as he says, "nice beef, Honey." The young blond daughter says, "Dad, you suck." The dark-haired son says, "Mom FARTED."

But it was the depiction of Mom that startled Souza.

She'd been given eyeglasses by the doodler (and Souza immediately thought of Glee Ewell, lying dead in her office with her glasses on) and a hideous smile had been drawn on her face.

The back of her head now featured a mushroom cloud–like explosion and the word POW!

Souza sat on the cold concrete, suddenly aware of the bitter taste in his mouth. Moore got up and examined his fingernails. Neither said anything for a while.

THREE

THE QUESTION REMAINED: WHY WAS JOEL SPEND-
ing so much time at the airport? Souza paid a call at the
Aero Plex Aviation Center in Long Beach, a coastal city
less than an hour's drive from Los Angeles. He told the
manager that he was a police officer and wanted to speak
with Joel Radovcich's flight instructor.

"That must be Everything Flyable," the guy said, dialing his phone. "His instructor's name is Fabrice Allouche."

"Allouche?" Souza said.

A trim dark man with the appearance of a European
race-car driver walked up to Souza and stuck out his hand.
"I'm Fabrice Allouche."

Souza pulled the leather tab ID out of his pocket so
Allouche could get a look.

"What can I do for you, Detective?"

"There somewhere we can talk?"

"Sure. Come on."

Back in a conference room that overlooked helipads
and choppers, they each found a seat.

"This is about Joel? Radovcich?"

"Mr. Allouche—"

"Fabrice."

"Fabrice, then. I need to speak with you about an ongoing investigation. I'd like your assurance that what we
say will remain confidential."

"Whatever you say, Detective. I can keep my mouth shut."

Once again, Souza took the risk of informing an outsider who might warn Joel, rather than assisting investigators.

"I get the feeling you can. Sir, Joel may have information about a multiple homicide that occurred in Fresno last year."

"Jesus."

"Yeah. And we need to keep tabs on him without his discovering it. Do you get me?"

"Sure I do."

"Super. And anything you can tell us about Joel could be a big help."

"Okay," Allouche said. "Where should I start?"

"How long has he been coming here?"

"Let me see. I believe he got his private chopper license up in Fresno, around September of last year. But around the beginning of this year he left uh . . . Mazzie up there and started with me when I was at CSR Aviation."

So it was flight lessons, helicopter no less. And Souza reckoned it was no coincidence that Joel had switched from a Fresno flight school to Long Beach flight schools at the end of 1993—right after the *Bee* article named him.

"Okay," Souza told Allouche. "Then what?"

"Well, then I came here to Everything Flyable in May, and Joel stuck with me."

"He's pretty loyal. And now he's going for what . . . ?"

"His commercial license."

"Really? Make a lot of money when he gets it?"

"Won't be The Donald or anything. Maybe forty-five, fifty a year."

"How much are the lessons?"

"Five hundred an hour."

Souza nearly choked. "How much would you say he's spent so far?"

"Oh, this is April . . . maybe seven, eight thousand."

"Okay," Souza said, thinking that was a lot of cash to

throw around for a guy without a job. "How does he pay?"

"How?"

"I mean check, cash—"

"Oh," Allouche said. "Pays cash."

Souza was taking notes. "And is he close to getting his commercial license?"

"He's got a way to go. Probably cost another five thousand."

Souza said, "How do you get in touch with Joel? Does he have a phone number?"

"Not to my knowledge. Just a pager."

"Oh? Could I get that number?"

"Sure. Hang on."

Fabrice flipped through his day planner and read a phone number aloud.

"Great, that's a big help," Souza said. "And that number is in working order?"

"Sure, last I tried. Yesterday."

"Fabrice, we appreciate your help. I don't believe Joel's dangerous to his friends, but please remember my admonishment about keeping this to yourself."

"Well, Joel's pleasant enough, but if he's involved in murder, he'll get no sympathy from me."

When Souza called Mazzie Flying Service, where Joel had taken flying lessons until following Fabrice Allouche over to Everything Flyable, Mazzie representatives said Joel had paid with money orders and cash. Another young man named Dana Ewell had come in initially with Joel, negotiating a cut-rate deal for both customers by offering to prepay for lessons.

Mazzie faxed over copies of two cashier's checks. When Souza saw the dollar amounts—$5,660—the numbers struck a chord. He examined financial records and found the amount matched exactly a withdrawal from Dana's grandmother's trust.

*   *   *

In early April, through his attorney, Dana Ewell would issue the following press release:

> On April 19, 1992, four wonderful lives ended in tragedy. My father, my mother, and my sister were brutally murdered. My world was shattered and my life was changed forever. The reality of a loss like this can hardly be imagined even after this length of time.
>
> I am grateful for the loving help and support from the rest of my family and my friends. They have helped me get through this most difficult year.
>
> I must say that this tragedy has been deepened by those in the media who have spread gossip and innuendo which was unsupported by fact or distorted reality. These reporters who have been inaccurate or sensationalist in their stories are doing a disservice to the public, my family and me.
>
> I understand the Sheriff's Office is following all possible avenues of investigation. They have said they are eliminating no one until the killer or killers are found and I understand this to be the usual method in such an investigation. I have spoken with them and posted a large reward and I hope this will assist the Sheriff's detectives.

April Fool's Day, and Joel was back on the phone at the 7-Eleven on Saticoy and Fallbrook, less than a mile from his mother's home. Hollis let Joel talk a few minutes before he took up position at the adjoining phone and dialed the number for FSO, narcotics.

Joel was saying ". . . so I'm staying at my mom's until I find a place. No, I don't want to stay here long in case they drive by and see me."

Hollis asked for Mr. Brown and started babbling about how he had to have the kids at soccer practice pretty soon.

Joel said, "Let me ask you something. Are you getting any heat yet? They want a chain saw on the table or something. They want glitz and glamour."

He went on about flying and computers, then Souza had

trouble making out words until he clearly heard, "Make twenty-five big ones for not doing anything? Why not?

"Got this lawyer down here so it doesn't look like the buddy-buddy system . . . I'm out fourteen hundred already, three hours yesterday and one today . . . no, I didn't tell them anything. Can't you find anyone cheaper?"

Finally, Radovcich signed off with, "See what you can find out and get back to me."

Radovcich returned home until three that afternoon. When he took off in the direction of the 7-Eleven, Souza got on the radio to Lee.

"Hustle over to the Famous Phone before our boy gets there."

Lee was in position, faking a call when Joel arrived. But the 7-Eleven was suddenly bustling as three cars pulled up, one with the radio blasting. By the time the area had quieted down Joel sounded excited.

"It's a news blitz! Things are going to blow up, I'm telling you." He pumped more quarters into the phone.

"This guy looked like a Fresno newsguy . . . you never know. I don't want no fucking stock options! I want a quarter million and I want it now . . . What? I want to go around the world. We know how much your thing was, right? Then tell this guy to step on it!" Joel slammed down the phone and stomped back to the Honda.

Souza cracked his knuckles, turned off his radio, and smiled.

FOUR

JOEL'S STATEMENT ABOUT NEEDING "TWENTY-five big ones" provided Souza with the ammunition he needed to request a search warrant, which would require the phone company to hook up a Dialed Number Recorder (DNR) to the booth at Saticoy and Fallbrook.

The DNR would document every outgoing number dialed from the pay phone, and would be pivotal in helping detectives prove who Joel was speaking to during his overheard conversations.

The telephone company told Souza they would hook up a DNR immediately, but before they could release the records, they required a signed search warrant.

A frustrated Souza, writing his first DNR warrant, holed up in a local motel, eating vending-machine sandwiches and faxing material back and forth between the motel and Caudle at FSO. When he'd finally drafted a complete affidavit, Souza faxed the document to Chris Curtice, who secured a judge's signature and faxed a signed copy to Pac Bell.

April 2, Joel on the Famous Phone:

"I have the feeling this thing is going to blow up, Dana . . . what about that? I need money."

DNR records showed Joel had made a two-second call to Dana's dorm, followed a short while later with a call to a pay phone in a Wendy's in Santa Clara.

April 5 on the Famous Phone:

"Is Mr. Woolf there? I'm a referral from Mr. Berman. I need to see him . . . Just tell him it's Joel, he'll know who it is . . . It's in regard to a homicide . . . Radovcich, R-A-D-O-V-C-I-C-H. Who is this? Well, be careful you don't tell anyone."

Listening to Joel talk on the phone was fruitful, using the DNR to track numbers he'd dialed was a bonus, but investigators pondered how they might document calls made to him, via his pager.

The detectives needed to know who was paging Joel, and when. Soon after the DNR installation, Souza and Hollis discussed the narcotics team's use of cloned pagers—virtual duplicates of pagers used by known dealers, placed in the hands of detectives through court order.

But Souza learned that a warrant for securing a cloned pager had never been issued in a homicide case. Still, sitting alone in his spa at night, Souza realized he had to clone Joel's pager. And common sense, it seemed, would dictate that a warrant should be approved; why would the use of a clone be limited to drug cases, and not be legal for a triple murder?

Perhaps, he thought, the need for the use of a clone had simply never arisen in a homicide case! But could the communications company that provided service to Joel duplicate his pager? Souza, on unfamiliar ground, had no idea.

With help from the narcotics team, Souza labored over the next week to draw up a warrant requesting permission to receive a clone, based upon the fact that Joel was observed using a pager and then making return calls from pay phones. Since surveillance of Dana in Santa Clara suggested that he was the one who generally paged Joel, this constant communication pointed to a conspiracy between the two.

A judge agreed. On April 12, Fresno County Superior

Court Judge DeWayne Keyes affixed his signature to the search warrant.

Curtice and Burk served the warrant on Communication HQ in Beverly Hills. The staff was intrigued. And helpful.

They said, "We can do this," and the FSO detectives walked out with a working pager, programmed with a cap code (the computer-generated code inside a pager that defines its number) identical to Joel's. Souza and HQ ran a series of tests using simple sequences of digits, such as 1111 or 1234, but the pager simply did not work. He visited HQ on April 21. The company assured him they had the bugs worked out, and reprogrammed the device. A few hours later, Souza took a call on his cell phone.

"Detective," the HQ manager said, "we've just had a visit from Joel Radovcich."

The first thing that crossed Souza's mind was that he was glad he hadn't shown up two hours later than he had at the HQ offices and run right into Radovcich.

"Radovcich told us he's been getting strange pages over the last few weeks."

"So what'd you say?"

"We told him that maybe his number was being usurped by drug dealers."

"Good answer, good answer."

"He was a bit paranoid, this guy. Frankly, so were we, what with him possibly involved in killings. I expected him to pull out a chain saw or something."

Souza laughed. "No, I don't think he's your thrill-killer type."

"But we almost fainted when he asked if we'd been served with a search warrant on his pager."

"What?"

"Yeah. Don't worry, we know the warrant says we can't tell anyone. Hell, we wouldn't anyhow."

"And he fell for the drug-dealer line?"

"Sort of, but when he saw his name on the computer

screen, he squirmed and asked us to relist his account under the name, 'Mike Smith.' "

"Smith. Creative."

"Hey, I wasn't about to tick this guy off. We changed his name on the computer and gave him a new number."

"Shit, and I just got this one done right."

"Remember that cap code we talked about? That's how you get your calls. And we didn't change Joel's cap code, so you'll still get whatever pages he gets."

"Great!" Souza said. "You folks really came through."

No sign of Joel recently, and Souza was getting worried. The already considerable pressure on the department mounted, as did incidents of frayed tempers. At one point, Sergeant Adolph spotted a woman dumping trash into the Radovcichs' garbage. On a hunch she might be a courier in a payoff to Joel, Adolph ran the car's plate and told Souza he was going to check out the owner's address. Souza, concerned that any such action might compromise operation security, disagreed, and the disagreement escalated into a heated argument between the two friends. It would be months before the two managed to patch things up in a meaningful way.

The surveillance detail continued to observe the comings and goings of members of the Radovcich family, but Joel did not appear. Souza had no choice but to postpone the southland surveillance.

Then on April 12 Souza got a call from Detectives Moore and Lyons, who were phoning from their car in Fresno.

"We're in the Von's parking lot," Moore said, his voice racing.

"Congratulations."

"I'll say. Adolph's in there watching your boy Radovcich."

"He's here?"

"Lyons and I were sitting at a light at Fresno and M

Streets, and Lyons says, 'Jesus Christ, is that Joel Radovcich?' "

"Where was he?"

Moore was laughing. "Sitting in the Honda, right next to us."

Souza was giddy, too. Sometimes the bad guy just got unlucky, and it was always fun.

"I looked over and almost pissed my pants," Moore said. "It was Joel all right, but he did something to his hair, dyed it shoe-polish black. As if no one'll recognize him now."

"Oops, he's moving," Moore announced. "This boy doesn't let any moss grow on him."

Souza stayed on the line with Moore.

"Okay—man, it appears he's headed over to Sunnyside . . . here we go, here we go! Damn, John. He must have a garage door opener or something, 'cause we can't see his car in the Ewell's driveway."

Then, at 12:25: "He's vacating the Ewells'."

12:56: "We're blowing town."

2:25: "John, arriving Santa Clara city area. Okay he's pulling into, what else, a 7-Eleven. Going to the phone."

3:14: "We're driving through the dorm area at Santa Clara University."

3:24: "Another 7-Eleven! Looks like he's just waiting . . . oops, he grabbed a phone. Must've been waiting on an incoming call."

3:50: "We got something, John. Gold Mercedes rolling up into the 7-Eleven lot! Lordy-Lord, it's Dana Ewell himself! They're having a little rap session by the cars."

4:00: "Okay, we're hanging back and Manny Ybarra's got them . . . Shit, he lost them! He lost them!"

4:12: "Okay, Ybarra's got the Mercedes again, in the lot outside something called Aris Helicopters."

4:30: "We got them coming out of a one-hour photo. They're looking at pictures and laughing. Damn, I'd like to get a look at those shots! Now they're going into El

Pollo Loco. Guess Joel couldn't find a stinking Taco Hell."

6:22: "Back at the 7-Eleven. They're having some kind of powwow in the Mercedes. Been in there for nearly an hour. Joel's out, getting into the Honda. They're taking off."

Surveillance was eventually ended, but it had been quite a day for the FSO. These stealthy ways and cheap Spy-vs-Spy theatrics were the stuff of conspiracy, and would be instrumental in bolstering the case against Dana and Joel.

Another surveillance, in late April, found Joel moving to an apartment in Costa Mesa, south of LA. He was soon frequenting a 7-Eleven pay phone a mile from his apartment, this at the corner of Bristol and Baker Streets. Souza amended the DNR search warrant, moving the DNR to the Costa Mesa pay phone. It was no mean feat keeping up with Joel, but the investigators weren't resting either.

On May 12 Chris Curtice had an idea that he hoped would rattle Dana's cage. Curtice related ensuing events to Souza by cell phone from the Santa Clara University campus:

"Osborn and I get to campus about 9 A.M. and we check in with campus security. Then as we're walking across the parking lot, we spot Dana coming the other way. He was supposed to be in a class at that time, but he wasn't. Osborn says to me out of the corner of his mouth, 'Does he recognize you?' and I say, 'Probably.'

"So we just keep on going like nothing's up, but Dana takes a long look at us. We stop near the library for a quick peek back, and Dana's doing the old private-eye routine, standing by a light pole pretending to read a paper, but checking us out.

"So on we go on our merry way again, but we spot Dana at a fast walk toward us, you know, with that weird Dana walk—chin out, head jerked forward, fists going back and forth.

"We duck into the campus bookstore and he practically runs in after us. Osborn hangs around a rack of postcards. I'm at the southeast corner of the place, pretending to look through textbooks.

"Then, bingo, Dana's standing right next to me, as if he's looking to buy a textbook. I mean, nobody's fooling nobody! I cruise over next to Osborn. Dana follows, and he sort of bumps Osborn. I look at a rack of cards, Dana's next to me, brushes my arm. Finally, at one rack, he gets on the opposite side of me and just stares at me, like I'm supposed to be terrified or something. I wanted to drag his skinny ass outside and pound the shit out of him, but, you know, regulations. He finally cleared out and we heard over the radio that Dana was leaving the campus.

"Osborn and I were laughing our asses off afterward, saying, 'What's that all about?' Dana the Intimidator."

Later, Burk now with him, Curtice put his scheme into action. It was eight that evening when they asked Campus Public Safety to escort them into the exclusive Casa Italiano building. They passed under the arched entryway of the tile-roofed, Mediterranean-style dorm, through a white doorway, and found room number 340.

One of the campus security officers knocked on the door.

"Who is it?" said someone inside.

"Officer Molina, with Public Safety."

The locals stepped back as the door opened and Dana Ewell faced the detectives.

"Hi, Dana," Burk said.

"What are you doing here?"

"Dana, we have information on who might have killed your family."

"This hardly seems the appropriate place or time."

The Public Safety officers exchanged glances.

Dana said to them, "Why did you bring these men here?"

"Dana," Curtice said, "I think this is an appropriate place for you to learn who our suspect is."

"Well I don't."

Curtice glanced into the dorm room. Monica Zent sat quietly on the bed.

"Aren't you interested in learning who killed your family?"

"Of course," Dana said. "Of course I am. But I need to make some phone calls."

Burk almost laughed. "Phone calls? Who do you need to call?"

"My attorney. Okay?"

"Go ahead," said Curtice, "but I don't think it's necessary. I just don't understand why you're being uncooperative. I figured you'd want to know who killed your parents and sister."

Dana turned to Officer Molina. "What's the procedure for bringing these guys into the building?"

Molina shrugged. "They asked for assistance."

"So, Detective," Dana said to Curtice, "did you enjoy your visit to the campus this morning?"

"Very much, thank you."

"Well, I filed a report against you with campus security. Now, if you have a local number, I can give you a call."

"Dana, you know how to reach us. I think you have the number."

"I'll do that. How would you like it if someone came banging on your door at eleven at night like this?"

Curtice took a look at his watch. "Uh, Dana. It's only eight, first off, and generally family members are happy to receive this kind of information at any time."

Dana pleaded with the campus officers, "I have my rights here, and I don't wish to speak with these men right now."

Turning away, Curtice said, "Okay, Dana. You know how to get hold of us."

But as Dana started to close the door, Curtice stepped forward. "By the way, just so you know. The information we have leads us to believe that Joel Radovcich killed your family."

*   *   *

Souza, on stakeout near the Radovcich home in West Hills, listened on the cell phone as Curtice described Dana's reaction to hearing Joel's name. (Souza was hoping a page would come in for Joel. If Dana were upset enough, he might page his cohort, and the link between the two would be tightened.)

Curtice, now solo, said, "It looked like someone punched Dana in the gut. I mean he was fish-belly white. And for once he was speechless."

"Knocked the wind out of him, huh? You're in the parking lot now?"

"Yeah, so . . . uh-oh, here he comes. Got Monica with him, in a little red dress. Hey, she's got damn nice legs, you know that? They're heading for the Benz. Let's see what he's up to."

Souza kept the line open. He wished he was in Santa Clara, too, instead of hanging out in LA where nothing was happening.

"He stopped at the Public Safety office and he's looking through the windows," Curtice said.

"Seeing if you yahoos are in there."

"He went inside."

Souza waited.

"Okay, coming out . . . we're rolling."

Curtice tailed Dana and Monica to the 880 freeway, southbound.

"He's in the number one lane, moving pretty good," Curtice told Souza. "Shit! He just darted across three lanes and caught the exit. Shit! I can't make it across without killing a few motorists."

"Lost him?"

"I have to admit, Dana used solid countersurveillance driving techniques. Goddamn it!"

"Maybe Moore can pick him up," Souza said. "Let me know."

*   *   *

Souza grabbed the buzzing pager and pushed the light button: 408 area code, 998 prefix. Santa Clara.

He dialed Curtice. "Okay, got something, buddy. Someone from Santa Clara just paged Joel."

"Gee, I wonder who that could be? You know the location?"

Souza shuffled pages that listed Santa Clara public phone numbers and locations (a list that Curtice and Detective Scott Jones had compiled previously by scouting every phone booth in the campus area).

"John, we have a location?"

But the number wasn't on Souza's list.

"Nothing, damn it. You better start doing a visual. Scope out all the booths you can."

"For what it's worth. I'll radio Moore, too." Curtice hung up.

Souza was double-checking the lists when Curtice phoned back. "All right, all right! We got an address."

"Found him?"

"Not yet, we're scrambling. Moore called someone he knows at Pac Bell and they made the address on the pay phone. Damn it, I'm trying to read the map . . . okay, found it."

Souza hung on for the five minutes it took Burk and Curtice to reach the target area.

"Got him," Curtice said. "He's pulling out of a parking lot. Looks like an office complex of some kind. The whole area is dark as the wrong side of the moon. Moore's picking him up. We'll go verify the number on the phone."

FIVE

PERHAPS DANA HAD PAGED JOEL TO CONFRONT him, to ask him if it were true that he was involved in the murders, but Souza doubted it. No, the reason seemed much more sinister. A check of phone records showed that Dana had telephoned his attorney after the detectives visited his room—yet, he'd run out to a darkened pay phone to contact Joel. Souza could see the nooses tightening around the necks of Dana and Joel. But they'd have to stick around long enough to get snagged.

Joel's May 18 Costa Mesa conversation with someone named Jennifer started out lighthearted and casual, talk of her car and her parents. As Detective Toby Rein listened in, a wire in his pocket, Joel told a rambling joke that made no sense to the detectives.

Things got more interesting halfway into the conversation, when Joel's mood changed abruptly.

"What? Say it, say it . . . oh, did he? With them? Oh my God, Jen! Jen did you talk with your parents about this? Oh, Jen, lie-detector tests are very false. If this says you're wrong, oh boy . . . Jen you are not taking this test."

He listened intently for a minute.

"You're trusting them? Jen, you're getting in way too deep. They cannot demand you take a lie-detector test . . . Jen, they can't . . . I know you're not part of this, but you should have told me. When . . . when did they ask? Jen,

Dana Ewell and family: *(left to right)* Dale, Tiffany, Glee, and Dana

The Ewell Family

Overhead shot of the Ewell home

Crime scene photo of the Ewell master bedroom. Note the portraits of Dana and Tiffany on the wall.

A picture of the possible murder weapon, plus a layout of the Ewell home that indicates where the bodies were found.

KJED TV—Newsphoto—Fresno

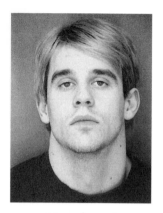

Mug shot of
Joel Radovcich

Monica Zent
Political Science

Monica Zent's yearbook
photo with the eyes shot out

The Famous Phone

Detective Chris Curtice (*left*) and
Detective John Souza

Jon R. Haugan

Allen Boudreau

Michael Giberson

Recovering the barrel of the murder weapon

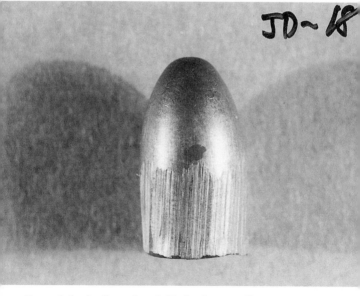

One of the bullets that killed Glee Ewell

Crime scene murder bullet comparison

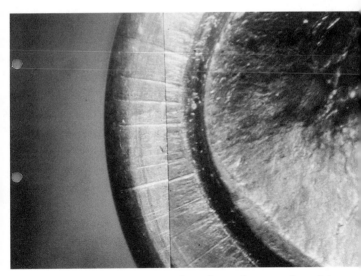

Comparison of ammunition from box of ammo found in the Ewell home with a recovered murder bullet

Detective Souza and Detective Curtice escort a hand-cuffed and stiff-lipped Dana Ewell

KJED TV—Newsphoto—Fresno

listen to me. I'll call you right back, okay?"

Radovcich hung up, trotted to his car, retrieved a piece of paper. He made another call and asked to speak to Terrence Woolf.

"Yeah, this is Joel. It's sort of an emergency. The Fresno sheriffs have been harassing one of my friends to take a lie-detector test.

"What? They think she knows something, and she's going to take a test . . . so, if she doesn't nothing will happen to her? Well, she said they told her she has to . . . all right . . . she can call you? All right, thanks a lot. You're welcome."

More change and another call. "All right, Jen, this is what I want you to do. What time tomorrow will they do it? Two. Okay, what you do is talk to my attorney . . . they're very unreliable . . . obstruction of justice is a bunch of bullshit.

"Jen, this is some serious shit." He gave Jen his attorney's number.

"Jen, this isn't funny. Look at what they're doing to me. People get put away for lifetimes and find out later, oops, they made a mistake . . . Jen, it isn't funny! They will destroy your life. I advise you to call my guy and seek his advice.

"Okay, I gotta go. Get this straight, okay? All right, I love you, I love you. All right, gotta go."

Jennifer's name came up again in a May 19 surveillance of a pay phone at Harbor and Nineteenth Streets, with Detective Haroldson eavesdropping on Joel as Souza listened from his car:

"Been up all night, haven't slept."

Haroldson later told Souza that Joel appeared exhausted.

"I called my guy at twelve. He's serious . . . Okay Dana, okay . . . She says, okay she'll think about it.

"I called her parents and told them what kind of deep shit she's into, I called her, then I called my Woolf guy that he was going to call her back . . . I know, dude, I figure they got a tap or something . . . I got one quarter left."

An hour later:

"Okay, Mr. Woolf . . . I can assure you she knows nothing, but what if they find me? Can they arrest me?"

Again, detectives had gotten a reaction to applied pressure. "Jennifer" in this instance (it turned out that Joel knew three different women named Jennifer) was Jennifer Nunikkoven, a close and apparently platonic friend.

A few nights before, Curtice and Burk had approached her and asked her about Joel. Had Joel mentioned anything about guns or the Ewell crime?

Jennifer said Joel had said nothing of the kind.

No problem, Curtice told her, then you wouldn't mind taking a lie-detector test?

Nope, she said. When?

We'll set it up for later in the week, Curtice said. We'll give you a call.

The polygraph test would never take place—Joel's warnings had put her off. But with Joel's reaction, the effort hadn't been completely for naught.

Curtice interviewed Jennifer again a few days later, with her father sitting in. She swore Joel had said nothing about the Ewells, but she did admit he'd bragged that he'd be a millionaire by age twenty-five.

On May 28, a surveillance team followed Joel to an Ontario TGI Friday's restaurant. Joel spent some time at the bar, and a few minutes in the kitchen, out of sight of investigators.

A few days later, Joel was back at the Famous Phone. Souza watched through binoculars as Detective Toby Rein, wearing a wire, strolled up and lifted the handset on the left phone.

Joel turned toward Rein.

"Hey. I'm using that phone."

"Excuse me?" Rein said, holding the receiver.

"I said, I'm using that phone."

"Aren't you using that one?"

"I'm using both of them. Use the phone across the street."

Souza knew Rein would have loved to punch Joel's lights out, and the blond-haired Rein had three or four inches on Joel.

Souza thought, Just get out of there, Toby.

But Rein wasn't folding yet.

"You go use that phone," he told Joel. "I'm using this one."

"I'm waiting for a call," Joel said. "There's another phone right over there."

Souza muttered, "This is all I need."

Rein hesitated, but then he slammed down the receiver and stomped off.

At least, Souza thought, Toby didn't shoot the kid.

The surveillance team returned to Fresno, but Souza stayed behind, taking a fifth-floor room in the Costa Mesa Red Lion Inn, located directly across the street from Joel's current favorite 7-Eleven phone at Bristol and Baker.

He set up a tripod-mounted spotting scope just inside the sliding glass door leading to the balcony. The DNR search warrant on the pay phone specifically stated that police should witness pertinent calls, and Souza wanted his evidence to stand up in court.

If he couldn't have a surveillance team, he would watch the kid himself and record the times Joel used the booth.

Typically, the workload would have been shared with Burk, but the demands of Burk's personal life were taking a toll to the extent that Burk was available only one day a week.

During discussions between the partners on "common day"—the day they worked together—it was clear that Burk could not put in the time this case required. Burk wondered aloud if he should ask Dale Caudle to excuse him; he was feeling increasingly guilty that Souza had to take up the slack for an absent partner.

An empathetic Souza knew what it was like to work endless hours; at times it seemed your kids would grow up without you.

The surveillance itself was mind-numbing, and its restrictive nature made it a claustrophobic chore. He worked in fear that, like the baseball fan who misses a home run when he dashes to the bathroom, Joel would show up and make a case-breaking phone call as soon as Souza stepped away.

On Souza's last day at the Red Lion, he munched a pear and watched Joel pull into the 7-Eleven and make a few calls. Souza noted the time. A lush-bodied young woman in tiny cutoff jeans swiveled by Joel. Joel didn't seem to notice, but Souza let the scope follow her for a few seconds.

Some of the other detectives had noted Joel's indifference to women and surmised that the kid was gay. But Souza didn't think so. He had the feeling that Joel was one of those emotionally broken individuals who was mostly asexual, who seemed to have no real interest in physical contact with others of either gender.

Joel hung up the phone and wandered inside to play a round of pinball on his favorite machine, one emblazoned with *Terminator 2* graphics. He seemed to be having a rough game. He threw his hands in the air, paced a circle, played another round, bobbed his head as if cursing the machine.

When the game ended, Joel bounced the bottom of his fist on the glass. Looking about, he slipped behind the machine and yanked the electrical cord out of the wall.

He grinned and strode away, stopping a few feet from the pinball machine. Then he turned and raised his hand as if aiming a handgun, "shot" the pinball machine with his forefinger, and blew imaginary smoke from the barrel.

*   *   *

New rolling surveillance, June 3: Long-haired Detective Avila, wired with a remote monitoring device that sent a signal to Souza's car, stood next to Joel Radovcich at a pay phone at Sherman Way and Shoup.

"Then why don't they pick us up?" Joel said. He put more coins into the phone. "I gotta talk to my guy and see, ah, see if they can actually charge me, in that um"— he grasped for words here—"three-shirt deal."

Three-shirt deal! Souza was stunned.

"Okay," Joel continued, "but I wish I could find a place . . . no, I was just calling to say we got to be extra, extra careful. You never know what they might hold.

"Ha-ha. Yeah, okay if there's anything you need . . . that's the deal, we just got to hang tough . . . all right. Later."

At the same time in San Jose, Detective Dadian observed Dana using a pay phone in the Jet Center, a corporate jet operations area at the San Jose Airport. Souza and the surveillance team felt this episode would be extremely damning if presented at trial. And, as far as he was concerned, Joel's "three-shirt deal" comment blew away any last shred of doubt that Radovcich was the killer.

On June 8, Detective Haroldson was surprised when Joel dialed without having first fed quarters into the pay phone.

Radovcich studied a piece of paper. The first part of the conversation was unintelligible, drowned out by the whining gearbox of a delivery truck on the street. When Radovcich turned toward the detective, Haroldson heard, "Yeah, four hundred thirty-one dollars and eighty-nine cents."

Haroldson hoped the recorder was picking this up.

"How much for the cover charge?" Joel said. "Three hundred sixty-nine dollars? That's the difference?"

The team knew the DNR would record the number Joel had dialed. Probably an 800 number, it would be easy to spot.

Joel said, "We just had three hundred sixty-nine dollars . . . okay, grand total, four hundred thirty-one dollars, eighty nine cents. How long will it take to ship? Okay, thank you very much."

Joel shuffled inside the 7-Eleven, where he purchased two money orders before driving away. The investigators couldn't wait to find out what new toy Joel was buying.

After requesting and receiving a DNR printout the next morning, Souza dialed an 800 number and reached a Georgia company called Bookmasters. He identified himself and asked the manager what products the company sold that would total $431.89.

"That including tax and shipping?" she said.

"I believe so."

"Hm. That would have to be the electronic lockpick."

What're they up to now? "Okay. Ma'am, this would be used how?"

"Um, by a locksmith? This device will unlock most types of locks in seven seconds."

This Joel ain't no locksmith. "Look, this person ordered a lockpick on June 8, about two your time. Could you pull the order and give me a name?"

"I don't know that we're supposed to do that, frankly."

"I don't know that you're supposed to be sending out lockpicks to just anyone."

"Hey, it's legal."

"Listen, I'm involved in a triple-homicide investigation here. How about a little help?"

The woman at Bookmasters sighed. "Okay, we'll do what we can."

"This guy apparently is paying with a money order. Would you have a record of the call?"

"Look, if he's sending us a money order, we have nothing yet."

"Great," Souza said.

"But when we get his order, we can call you then. How's that?"

Souza thanked her and hung up. Why a lockpick? Did Dana have another job for Joel? Perhaps involving Dana's grandmother and her fat trust fund? Or was this Joel's doing, Joel's alone? Was he burglarizing homes, or worse, starting a murder-for-hire business?

One thing was certain: Souza's hopes that Joel might crack under pressure had turned out to be wishful thinking. Far from folding, Joel appeared to be quite capable of taking care of business. Exactly what that business was remained to be seen.

SIX

J‌UST IN CASE D‌ANA AND J‌OEL HAD PLANS TO TEST
out the lockpick by eliminating Dana's grandmother,
Souza phoned the Turlock nursing home.

He explained to the director that Dana and his friend
Joel Radovcich were now suspects in the death of Mrs.
Mitchell's daughter and family. He described Joel, insisting that the staff be diligent in watching for anything, or
anyone, suspicious with regard to Glee Mitchell.

After nearly a year on the case, Burk was finally out. He
just couldn't keep up, what with his family obligations,
and he didn't want Souza doing the work of two. With
the brass's approval, he'd still be around to assist, but
would no longer be a primary investigator. Chris Curtice,
who'd videotaped and assisted at the scene in 1992 and
confronted Dana at the SCU campus, would be Souza's
new partner, which was fine with Souza.

Curtice had been born in Tulsa and spent his early years
in St. Louis. At the age of eight his life was shattered
when he lost his father in Vietnam (Curtice remembers
cursing the night sky and God Himself for taking his father). His mother eventually remarried, moving with her
son and new husband to the Monterey Peninsula in California. For a time, Curtice wanted to be an actor, but
soon after he began studies at Fresno State, he decided
that he would pursue a career in law enforcement. Starting

with the Sheriff's Reserves before graduating with a degree in criminal science, Curtice rode patrol from 1982 until 1989, when he accepted a position with the Homicide Unit. He also began a sideline career as a country music singer.

Souza and Curtice had been friends since the mid-eighties, attending Cardinal baseball games together when the team was in California. Curtice was as polished as Souza was casual, as aggressive in his job as Souza was conservative, and he didn't know one end of a plow from the other, but the two had an easy camaraderie from the start.

On June 11, 1993, in response to an inquiry from estate attorney Michael Dowling on the status of the investigation, Captain Ken Houge of the FSO wrote to Dowling:

> *After lengthy investigations and with deliberations with the Fresno County District Attorney's Office, it is the position of our department that Dana Ewell is to be considered a prime suspect in the investigation.*

Dana's status as a prime suspect was now official, and Dana would know it.

Souza and Curtice wondered: How would Dana react? Just blow it off, since he was so much smarter than a couple of dumb cops? Stay away from Joel? Run?

Dana Ewell graduated summa cum laude from Santa Clara University on June 12 (after taking a temporary leave of absence following the death of his family). The next day, he and Monica boarded a commercial jetliner and flew to Cancún, Mexico. Souza believed Dana would return, but who knew for sure?

Eleven o'clock the next evening, as Souza relaxed at home with Sharon, the cloned pager went off. Souza checked the page: 222. Multiple pages came moments later: 111, followed by 000.

Then, a number Souza recognized as one Dana had been using in Santa Clara: 984-9059.

Souza got on his home phone and called the Costa Mesa PD. He asked a Sergeant Pherrin if a patrolman could check the pay-phone location at Bristol and Baker, and report back if they saw a caller who matched Joel's description.

The Santa Clara number, or variations on that number, came in on Souza's clone four or five more times before Sergeant Pherrin called Souza.

Pherrin himself had rolled to Bristol and Baker in time to see a young white male fitting Joel's description hop in a black Honda CRX, license #2MGN911, and drive away from the 7-Eleven.

Souza thanked Pherrin and hung up. The pages were certainly unlike others received in the past—and Dana was in Mexico. Was it some system designed to test if the police had a cloned pager?

The next morning, Souza requested the DNR records from the Costa Mesa phone. The record showed the pages had come from the Bristol and Baker phone. Joel had been paging himself. Souza slumped back in his chair.

Why the hell was Joel paging himself?

If there was some logic behind this, it escaped Souza. He hoped this was a sign that Joel, desperate for Dana to call, had finally begun to sag under the weight of the investigation. The risk was he might bolt, as he should have already; the upside was that he could do something dramatically stupid, something that might give investigators a substantial break.

Four days later, Dana and Monica returned from Cancún. The game would continue, but most of the pages to Joel would not; after Dana's graduation, Santa Clara–area pages to Joel ceased completely.

*   *   *

Shortly thereafter, Bookmasters called Souza.

The manager said, "My operator remembers this guy. Apparently, he called a few times. Got a catalog sent out and then he mailed in his order. We sent one lockpick to a Jack Ponce in San Bernardino."

Jack Ponce? Souza asked her to fax the address. He wouldn't immediately pay this Ponce a visit, not while it could risk revealing the surveillance, but he certainly looked forward to meeting Ponce in the near future. Anyone receiving items for Joel was someone Souza wanted to meet.

Burk burst into Souza's office. "Okay, bud. Tom Duong just called. It seems Joel, that is, Tom Duong, received a catalog from the company that sent Joel the silencer books."

"Presidio Press? We contacted them, and they don't publish those kinds of books."

"But Paladin Press does."

The name rang a bell, and Souza wondered why he hadn't remembered Paladin himself. Had they been sued for selling books that taught hit-man tactics? Maybe not, but that type of book was their specialty.

"The catalog has books on silencers, bombs, how to dispose of a corpse, how to spy on people. All kinds of nasty shit."

Souza took down the toll-free number for Paladin. Considering that the company published what some considered handbooks for criminals and terrorists, Souza didn't know what to expect, but he found the people at Paladin eager to help. Despite this, it soon became clear his search wouldn't be easy. The financial manager at Paladin, also named Joel, said the computers were purged of order records every year.

Souza winced. "Are you saying you have no records of orders older than a year?"

"We have them in hard copy. The original order forms, whether they're coupons out of magazine ads or handwritten pages or crayon on paper bags, are collected and stored in a manila envelope at the end of each day."

"Oh. How many average in each envelope?"

"Well, we get about three hundred orders a day, so . . ."

"So, if I want to see this particular order, I'd have to sort through a ton of order forms."

"Um . . . right."

"Can I get permission to come in and do that?"

"Sure," the Paladin rep said. "If you have the patience, feel free."

"Oh," Souza said wistfully, "I have patience."

On June 24, Souza hopped a jet to Denver and picked up a rental and drove into the quaint mountain town of Boulder. Paladin's Joel shook the detective's hand and led him to a dusty, windowless room.

"Where do I start?" Souza said.

"Give me a month and year."

Tom Duong felt that the books had come in mid-1991. "Let's start with June of '91," Souza told Joel.

And he was soon looking at thirty bulging manila envelopes. About nine thousand order forms. Souza slipped on his reading glasses.

He put in a mind-numbing half day of work before Paladin closed down. The next day, eyes burning, he struggled through twenty more envelopes of orders. By quitting time, he'd finished another batch.

And come up empty.

In his hotel that night, he sipped a beer and watched television without knowing what program he was staring at. A call to Sharon made him feel better. The next morning, he awoke still dressed in the clothes he'd worn the day before. He showered and got on the road to the Paladin offices.

"Ready for more?" Joel said when Souza arrived.

"I'm a real party animal, huh?" Souza said.

"What month this time?" Joel asked.

"I figure May. Just got a feeling that'll be paydirt."

"Better you than me," Joel said, and he produced another month of orders.

It took hours. And hours.

But May it was.

"Yes!" Souza shouted. The titles and prices had been typed:

```
    Please send me the following titles
```

Name:	Price:
Homemade C-4	$12.00
How to Get Anything on Anybody	$30.00
Improvised Explosives	$10.00
Radio Detecting Techniques	$10.00
Smart Bombs	$12.00
The Anarchist Arsenal	$12.00
The Hayduke Silencer Book	$10.00
Home Workshop Silencers	$12.00
Deathtrap	$15.00
New ID in America	$15.00

Attached was a four-inch-by-two-inch coupon from a May 1991 issue of the *American Survival Guide,* with the handwritten name and address of Tom Duong.

Souza's elation deflated as he scanned the titles a second time. It looked as though Joel Radovcich had been preparing for war.

The company produced another order form. This, for a later shipment of books sent to the same address, but ordered in the name of Tony Duong: over four hundred dollars' worth of instruction on lockpicking, surveillance, eavesdropping techniques, and even Whispering Death, whatever that was. Souza purchased a copy of each book; he would turn them over to Allen Boudreau. Then he glanced at the order form again. In handwriting identical to that on the first order, the customer had added: I wish to have the letter opener for my purchase of $65.00 or over.

Upon his return to California, Souza began to exercise more caution in his day-to-day routine.

According to friends, Dana continued to deride the detectives (since Curtice was in, "Bert and Ernie" were now "Mutt 'n' Jeff"). Joel was ordering lockpicks, reading books about gas bombs, car bombs, revenge. Souza warned Sharon to be wary, and he frequently searched the underside of his car for explosives before driving into work.

"Maybe the case was spooking me," he admitted to her, "but I'll be damned if these assholes are going to get me or mine."

Following Souza's trip to Boulder, Boudreau studied the particulars of silencer construction. In December 1993, he applied for an ATF permit that would allow him to build a silencer, a process so rare the local ATF office was unsure if they possessed the necessary form (they did).

When ATF approval came through, the forensic scientist did an exhaustive study of the types of silencers outlined in the Paladin books. One required steel wool as a sound baffle, and some recommended more exotic materials. (Baffle materials reduced the decibel level of the shot, as well as altered the sound. A second component of a gunshot report, the shock wave produced by the projectile breaking the sound barrier as it exits the barrel, could be eliminated by using subsonic ammunition.)

One design featured tennis balls, cut in half with the centers removed. The rubber hemispheres were stacked inside one another, stuffed into a section of plastic PVC pipe, and packed tightly with steel wool. The pipe would then be capped on both ends, the caps bored out to accommodate the barrel, and the whole unit slid over the ported barrel of a firearm and wrapped with duct tape for strength.

Boudreau went to work. He would write in his report:

On June 24, 1993 I received two Paladin Press books from Detective John Souza:
   The Hayduke Silencer Handbook of Quick and Dirty Homemade Silencers
and
   Home Workshop Silencers
   Working from the information in these books, experiments were planned to challenge the theory that a silencer was incorporated into the murder weapon.

INTRATEC, TEC-9 EXPERIMENTS:
   I obtained a 9mm Luger caliber, Intratec Model Tec-9 pistol, serial number 40142. This pistol came with a screw-on flash suppressor. The suppressor was modified to serve as a test fixture. Three experiments were performed on the Tec-9 to determine the cause of the stria on the murder bullets.
   Screen wire discs with a perforation were packed into the suppressor and test-fired. The markings were not like the stria on the murder bullets.
   Automobile freeze plugs were fit into the suppressor. Damage to recovered bullets was not like the stria on the murder bullets.
   Nine, 3/16" holes were drilled into the barrel from the outside. As expected, drilling left burrs around the drill hole inside the barrel. Recovered bullets from test-firing are remarkably like the murder bullets.

In fact, the significance of "burrs" left after a drill bit had passed through metal came to Boudreau not during firearms experimentation, but while working on his son's Ford Bronco truck.

A master mechanic, Boudreau was modifying the Bronco for extended off-road use when he ran a finger across the ragged underside of a hole he'd just drilled in a suspension component.

The sharp edges around the hole sparked an idea: he remembered details of the Paladin silencer-construction books. A common technique in these "how-to" manuals called for the crude "porting" or drilling of holes in gun barrels before sliding the silencer over the barrel. Through porting, the explosive effect of gases exiting the barrel is reduced significantly. The high-decibel shock wave is vented more evenly and quietly through the holes along the barrel.

Boudreau immediately inserted a Tec-9 barrel into a machinist's vise and began porting it with a drill press. First thing Monday morning, he was in the lab test-firing the ported Tec-9. The jackets on the first few bullets were nearly shredded by the fresh burrs inside the barrel; thereafter, however, the results were heartening.

Souza yawned. He'd never loved meetings, sitting inside under tube lights, listening to blah, blah, blah. His mind wandering, he remembered an interview with a Ms. Freebody that he and Curtice had recently conducted. Freebody was the former owner of Joel's Honda, and a stunner. She answered her door in a flimsy nightgown, but Souza caught only fleeting glimpses while Curtice conducted the brief interview from her doorway.

As they left her place, Curtice said, "Wow, did you get a load of her?"

"Not for long," said the frustrated, and much shorter, Souza, "with you blocking the goddamned doorway the whole time."

The briefing dragged on. Allen Boudreau passed by in the hallway, giving Souza a lingering, oddball grin.

What's he so happy about?

After what seemed an eternity, the meeting adjourned and Souza wandered back to his office. He sat, shuffled papers, then his eye caught a shiny copper object on his desktop. Souza picked up an expended bullet. "What the . . . ?"

It was a copper-jacketed nine-millimeter, the bearing surfaces etched with stria. A Ewell murder bullet. Christ, did I pull this out of evidence?

He slumped back in his chair. He'd been overworked for months, often dulled with fatigue, but certainly he'd recall taking a murder bullet out of evidence. And he sure as hell wouldn't have left it sitting there on his desk!

The phone rang. "You find it yet?" It was Boudreau.

"Jesus Christ, Allen! You can't just leave evidence lying around on my desk."

"Ah, that isn't evidence. I made it."

It took a second for the significance of Boudreau's statement to sink in. "I'll be right down," Souza said. He grabbed the bullet and trotted down to the crime lab. Boudreau sat behind his desk, glasses perched low on his nose, shit-eating grin on his face.

"Look pretty good, huh?" he said as Souza rushed in.

"Hell, to my eye they look just right. How about under the scope?"

"They're almost identical to the murder bullets, pal. Not identical, but almost."

"Son of a bitch!" Souza shouted. "Come on, show me how you did it!"

"Burrs," Boudreau said.

"Huh?"

"From the porting of the barrel, right?"

Boudreau handed Souza a gun barrel with over a dozen holes drilled into.

"Last night I stuck it in a vise and drilled those holes.

I was in here at seven today, test-firing it. Look inside the bore. Burrs. From when the drill bit chews through the barrel."

Souza held the barrel to his eye and looked at the jagged points of steel that had been produced by a drill bit piercing the barrel.

He whooped so loud Boudreau jumped. The two pumped hands. It would be best, of course, if they had the barrel from the actual murder weapon. But, considering what he had to work with, the Mad Scientist had succeeded spectacularly.

The massive, moving surveillance of Radovcich could not go on forever; the cost to the Sheriff's Department would soon precipitate the end of the mission. As it turned out, the actions of Radovcich himself brought the operation to an unexpected conclusion in mid-1993.

The detectives waited in a park about one-quarter mile west of Judy Radovcich's house. The point man, Chris Osborn, sat inside his red Toyota pickup on the cul-de-sac that marked the park's boundary on Bobbyboyer Street.

Souza waited in his car in a lot at the far end of the park, watching a few kids toss a baseball back and forth. Dingy clouds were strung along the horizon and a lone jetliner climbed above them.

His cell phone rang. It was Osborn.

"Hey, Joel just came barreling out of the house. He stopped in the middle of the street, kind of frantic, looking up and down the road. Then he ran back . . . oops, here comes the Honda."

"Toward you?"

"Yeah, and he's got me cornered in this damned cul-de-sac. Hang on, I'm dropping the phone a minute."

Souza cursed softly. How had Joel made the point guy? Did a neighbor tip him off?

"John?" Osborn said. "He drove up and just stared at me for a minute. I'm taking off."

Souza radioed Toby Rein and watched as he crossed the park on foot, heading toward Bobbyboyer. Then the Radovcich family van, Judy at the wheel, screeched to a stop at the cul-de-sac. Joel jumped out and hustled toward the park gate. Toby scrambled up a tree.

Souza hoisted his binoculars. Joel had something in his hand and for a moment Souza feared there would be gunplay. But Joel carried only a camera. Toby jumped from the branches, shouting something as he headed for the merry-go-round, and Souza knew Toby was calling for an imaginary child. Joel sauntered right by without giving the undercover detective a glance (though of course the two had nearly come to blows months before over the use of a pay phone).

Joel trotted back to the van and he and his mother drove off. Now where are they going?

A new point man had been unable to take up position, what with Joel and his mother driving up to the gate. But out of the corner of his eye, Souza saw the van coming.

"Ah, balls," Souza said, sliding down in his seat.

Joel hung out the window with his camera. Surveillance cars started up and began clearing out one by one. The van stopped a few feet from Detective Tom Inchaurregui. Incharregui stuck his arm out the window and raised his middle finger.

Souza laughed and wished he could ask Joel for a print. A few minutes later, the van was gone. Souza called Detective Sergeant Hollis, and they decided to regroup a few miles away at a health-club parking lot.

When everyone was there, Souza leaned against a car and folded his arms over his chest. "Damn it! What was that all about?"

Toby Rein said, "It was like he got a phone call or something, telling him we were there."

"So now what?" said Souza. "Do we just go back to Bobbyboyer like nothing happened?"

"Look who's coming," Toby said, gazing up the street. The black Honda rolled to a stop ten yards from the detectives. Inside, Joel seemed to be jotting down plate numbers. Then he fumbled with his camera as if trying to do two things at once but not succeeding.

"The hell with this crap," Hollis said. Heavily muscled and deadly, the SWAT team leader stomped off in Joel's direction.

"Hey! Asshole! What the fuck are you looking at?"

Hesitant, Joel stared at the walrus-mustached narcotics detective.

"Yeah you, dickhead!" Hollis shouted. "Looking for someone?"

Joel dropped the Honda into gear and sped away. Everyone roared with laughter, but Souza knew the party was over.

Souza, back at the office and cleaning up loose ends shelved earlier to avoid warning Joel about the surveillance, received copies of Joel's financial records. Anything Joel had purchased before the date of the murders was of primary interest, and Souza noted that Joel had shopped at a pool-supply company and also filled a set of acetylene tanks. Had these purchases been necessary for the construction of a silencer?

And once again unabated tension from the case frayed nerves. When Souza all but ordered Curtice to write up a series of overdue reports on the case, Curtice slammed the files down on Souza's desk, shouting, "I'm not your goddamned secretary! Do your own reports!"

Where was Joel? Souza now began to worry that Joel had finally smartened up and left the state for good. Souza and Curtice made follow-up calls, to Nick Johns at the body shop ("I'm still sure I didn't see Joel on Easter"), to Peter Radovcich ("Yeah, Joel told me he got an attorney"), and to Joel's previous flight school ("The lunatic took out a million-dollar JetRanger helicopter and taxied around the runway without authorization. That kid didn't give a shit about anything").

Souza interviewed Joel's former roommate from the Costa Mesa apartment. The roommate said that Radovcich had first contacted him in response to a "Roommate Wanted" ad (like the one Souza had found festooned with a drawing of a woman's head exploding.) Joel always paid in cash, Rick said, and never used the phone, but it did seem odd that Joel had no interest in incoming calls.

"It can't be for me," Joel had said. "No one knows I'm here."

Joel had been no trouble and was always polite, if a bit closemouthed. The weirdest thing about him, according to the roommate, was that Joel slept on a futon. In his closet.

That summer, Dale's brothers showed up at Souza's office with their father, Austin. Souza had seen Austin at the funeral service, but hadn't met him.

Souza liked Austin Ewell immediately. A lanky, leathery old bird with gnarled fingers on hands the size of fry pans and a palpable strength despite his eighty-odd years, Austin brought to mind the salt-of-the-earth dairymen Souza had known as a child.

The old farmer wanted to know—what did Souza think, was Dana behind the killings?

Souza admitted he was suspicious of Austin's grandson. Dana certainly hadn't been eliminated as a suspect.

Austin thanked Souza, and the old man and his sons left. A day later, Austin hired the Russ Georgeson law firm—the same firm that handled the James J. Mitchell Trust—to deny Dana access to any inheritance money.

Souza was livid. He reread the obtuse letter, sent to the DA's office by Mitchell estate attorney Georgeson, shortly after Austin had contacted the attorney. Georgeson was pressing for detailed information about the ongoing investigation.

He required it, he wrote, to determine whether sufficient evidence had been uncovered to justify a civil action against Dana. Georgeson questioned "if there is a continued aggressive, diligent investigation being undertaken" by detectives, and further questioned the likelihood that an arrest could be made after so much time.

"It is my honest heartfelt belief the Fresno County Sheriff's Department has engaged to some extent upon a course of deceit in dealing with the various attorneys as to the quality and quantity of evidence acquired . . ."

"The inevitable conclusion being substantial assets will be delivered to Dana Ewell . . ."

After a few relatively uneventful months (Joel was still unaccounted for) Souza and Curtice boarded a jetliner on September 29. Despite its being struck by lightning in midair, the jet landed safely in Cleveland, Ohio.

The detectives drove a rental car to Dale Ewell's boyhood home. His kids gone for decades, his wife long dead, Austin Ewell lived alone in the sturdy old farm home.

Austin told Souza and Curtice he'd gotten calls and letters from Dana, but only after he'd contested Dana's receiving his inheritance. Dana was furious, the grandfather said, which only increased his suspicions that Dana was involved in the murders.

He produced a letter from Dana:

Dear Grandpa,

Hello . . . I hope your part of the country gets some rain soon. Enclosed is a copy of the objection I told you about on the phone the other day . . . I don't understand what Ben and Dan have talked you into doing but you should know what your attorney is doing. My father would be absolutely disgusted at the course of events that Dan and Ben have caused, Grandpa . . .

> *Very truly yours,*
> *Dana J. Ewell*

*   *   *

It had been a tradition for the Ewell brothers to bring their families to Ohio for a few weeks each summer. Even as a kid, Austin said, Dana seemed to believe he was above working around the farm, though Dale would rise at dawn and labor in the fields as he'd done when he'd had nothing. But Dana was always a strange one, conniving, lazy.

So when Dana called and said he planned to visit, Austin told his grandson it would be better if he didn't, not until these matters were settled. Austin claimed that Dana continued to call, and, the Ewell patriarch added, some of the calls had a threatening undercurrent.

Dale's sister Betty was another story.

She told Souza and Curtice that Dana was innocent until proven guilty, and she was upset with her father and brothers for their presumptions of guilt.

Souza asked if perhaps her brothers didn't have reason to be suspicious of Dana.

"Sure," she said, "they're greedy for the money."

From the fields of Ohio, the detectives traveled to Atlanta and a hotel lobby where Joel Radovcich's father Nick waited. Souza could see Joel's features in Nick's face, thick eyebrows and hair, although Nick was taller and leaner and certainly grayer, and as neat as Joel was slovenly.

Whether their differences were educational (Dr. Radovcich had a doctorate in aeronautical engineering, Souza had been forced to drop out of college to go to work) or simply a product of opposing personalities, Souza found they simply could not communicate on a substantial level. Curtice was no more successful.

Souza, in language as diplomatic as he could manage, told the elder Radovcich that Joel had information on the Ewell case that could put Joel's life in mortal danger. He hoped Dr. Radovcich's intervention might move Joel to assist investigators.

Dr. Radovcich asked what the detectives had found that led them to believe Joel was involved, but Souza demurred—he simply stated there was sufficient information to persuade investigators that Joel was at least materially involved.

Radovcich waited until he'd heard everything the detectives had to say, then he would only offer that he and his son were estranged, and he was the last one in the world who could help.

With time to kill until their morning flight, the detectives caught a Braves-Rockies game at Fulton County Stadium, and later partied in the hotel nightclub until the wee hours, Curtice dancing nonstop while Souza (a beer-only drinker whom Curtice had discomfited into drinking tequila shooters) fell asleep standing up at the bar. Curtice later paid for his application of peer pressure: what little rest he had that night was fractured by Souza's foghorn-decibel snoring.

Home again. Souza and Curtice had had enough. They felt they knew who was behind the murders. They wanted to arrest Dana and Joel and browbeat Joel into rolling over on his partner. Souza decided to go to the DA and ask that arrest warrants be issued for the pair.

Souza wrote out a probable cause affidavit, and he and Curtice presented it to District Attorney Ed Hunt and chief criminal prosecutor James Oppliger.

It's time, Souza said. We want to pick up Dana and Joel and convince a jury to send them to prison.

Hunt and Oppliger listened politely, then gave it a thumbs-down.

We think you're right about these clowns, they said. But we can't convict with what you've shown us. And if we screw this up, Dana and Joel will walk, and we won't be able to try them again. Sorry.

That evening, Souza sipped a beer in his hot tub. Frustrated, angry over the DA's refusal to bring in Dana and Joel, Souza knew he had to give these attorneys something on a silver platter. Something indisputable and powerful. And Souza thought he knew where he might find it.

SEVEN

ERNEST JACK PONCE WAS SLIGHT, HIS DARK HAIR slicked back like a leading man in a Depression-era film, his eyebrows cocked high as Souza and Burk introduced themselves. Ponce seemed surprised that homicide investigators had shown up on the doorstep of his mother's home.

"May we come in, Mr. Ponce?" Souza said.

It was October 8, 1993. The home was located in a prosperous neighborhood of San Bernardino, south of Lake Arrowhead and a few hours east of Los Angeles. Ponce motioned Souza and Curtice inside. They took seats around a wooden coffee table. The young man relaxed and folded his arms.

"I don't know Joel that well," Ponce offered.

"You're friends with him, aren't you?"

"I didn't say that, did I? I'm best friends with his brother, Peter. That's how I know Joel, through Peter."

The kid was cocksure and smirking, and Souza was rapidly losing patience, but he was going to give Ponce a chance to lie about the lockpick.

"Ever bought or received any goods for Joel Radovcich?"

"No."

"Never?"

"No, never."

"You knew him through his brother? So the three of you must have spent time together."

"Occasionally," Ponce said, pretty damn sure of himself.

Souza played a hunch. "Jack, did you ever go shooting with Peter and Joel?"

"You mean at a range?"

At least a bit off-balance now.

"Wherever."

"Yeah, we went shooting a few times."

"Okay. You own a lot of guns?"

"A few."

"What do you have?"

"Let me see." Ponce crossed his ankles. "A rifle. Just a .22. A 12-gauge shotgun. I have two handguns—.380 and a .44 Magnum."

Souza pounced. "Jack, why are you holding out on us? You say Joel never had anything sent to you. What about the electronic lockpick?"

Ponce's composure collapsed. His mouth fell open, and his body stiffened. Souza read the kid's face: How the hell did they know that?

Ponce stammered, "Huh?"

Souza didn't say a word, just gave Ponce his cop look.

"Lockpick?" Ponce said, recovering. "You must mean a locking device, right? That's what it is."

"What's a locking device?" Souza said.

"Shit, I don't know." His laugh was hollow. "Ask Joel."

"Why did he say he needed it sent to your home, instead of to his place in his own name?"

"I guess he didn't want the cops to know."

Souza laughed. "Jack, why wouldn't he want the cops to know? You're saying the device is to be used for illegal purposes?"

"No. I . . . he moves around a lot, and I suppose it was easiest to send it here."

"Uh-huh."

Ponce hopped up. "Look, I have to go to work."

"Fine," Souza said. "Where do you work, Jack?"

Ponce, looking back and forth across the room, seemed to be weighing his answer.

"Jack?"

"At the Ontario TGI Friday's. I'm a bartender."

Souza remembered that Joel had visited the very same TGIF months before.

At the front door, Souza said, "Okay, Jack. We'll be talking to you again."

The October 11 page had come from the 619 area code. From his home, Souza made the number as the San Diego Hilton, then he called the Hilton and asked the hotel's assistant security chief to check the phone booths for a man matching Dana's description. The physical matched right down to the aluminum briefcase Dana favored.

The next day an identical page came in, and Hilton security followed the caller outside to a Mercedes 190 with Dana's plates.

Souza and Curtice decided these sightings added up to a sound reason to visit San Diego at the end of October—perhaps they could learn what Dana was up to now. Besides, a few days at the bayfront Hilton sounded tolerable after all those nights sleeping in cars.

The hotel was lovely, but Dana never showed. Still, the detectives found a certain logic in Dana's use of the Hilton public phones: the booths were of a vanishing design, completely enclosed and secure, offering the caller total privacy and anonymity.

Further, the detectives remembered that Monica Zent was now attending law school in town. They rolled to her house on October 21. Dana's car wasn't in sight, but they spotted Monica backing out of her driveway and followed her to a post-office complex. She parked and entered, and Curtice pulled into a parking spot directly adjacent to hers.

When Monica returned minutes later, Souza and Curtice approached her, gold badges displayed.

"Hello, Monica," Souza said. "You remember me?"

She nodded.

Souza noted a marked improvement in her appearance: expensive clothes, meticulously applied makeup, and she'd gone bottle blond. Now she seemed much more the "flashy blond" type that Dana reportedly favored.

He said, "Do you have a few minutes to talk?"

"No," she said, keys out, approaching her car.

"We'd just like a few comments."

"I have nothing to say. My father's with the FBI. He told me not to talk to you."

Curtice showed his palms. "Hey, we can't make you talk. Monica."

They watched her drive off, and Souza said, "What I wouldn't give to find out what she knows."

Next, Souza and Curtice paid a visit to Dana's grandmother at the Turlock rest home. Glee Mitchell was in her late eighties and her attention faded at times, but she was generally coherent. As Souza spoke with her, Curtice paced the room, alert, noticing correspondence from Dana and Monica.

Souza asked about the two checks for $5,660—did she okay this kind of expenditure for flight lessons?

Mitchell said she would have for Dana, but certainly not for Dana's friend. Souza told her he was sorry that her family had been killed.

"Oh!" Mrs. Mitchell said. "I thought they got sick and died."

Souza thanked her for her time and told her to call if she needed anything. A few days passed, and Dana learned of the detectives' visit. He fired off a letter threatening the rest home with legal action if any persons "pretending to be police officers" were again allowed to see Mrs. Mitchell.

The rest-home director telephoned Souza and said the police would no longer be welcome. Souza had been up most of the night, unable to force the case out of his mind, and he'd already warned these people about Dana and Joel.

"Listen," Souza told the director, "I'm working a triple homicide, and to do that I may need to talk to Mrs. Mitchell. If you get in my way, I'll throw you in jail."

The director loosened up and agreed to keep Souza informed of any moves by Dana.

In late October of 1993, a call came into the FSO from a Radovcich neighbor whom Souza had befriended during the surveillance. It seemed the Radovcichs were loading up a trash Dumpster outside their home.

Souza called the refuse service, who informed him the Radovcichs had said they were cleaning out their garage. The heaping Dumpster was still in the service's Dearing Street yard; because of a driver's illness, it was never emptied. Souza told them he would send Ernie Burk over to baby-sit the trash until it could be searched.

The service called Souza back a short time later.

"We had a call from someone asking about the Dumpster."

"Besides us?"

"Yeah, a young guy, wanted to know if cops were searching the Dumpsters."

"You're kidding. What'd you tell him?"

"I told him yeah. What was I supposed to say?"

Souza sighed into the mouthpiece.

"Listen," said the manager, "I didn't know what to do. I don't want to get sued if it turns out you guys don't have the authority or something."

"I'll tell you what. We'll get a search warrant. Okay?"

"Yeah, great," the guy said, and hung up.

When Souza wrote the warrant on a pile of trash, he also asked for authorization to search Judy Radovcich's house. On October 28, Souza, Boudreau, Criminologist Jack Duty, and Detectives Burk, Curtice and Harrera went through the trash container—and turned up nothing useful.

The next day, Souza called LAPD Homicide and let them know about the impending house search.

"You might send a patrol car over," Souza suggested to the LAPD captain.

"Hell, yes, we'll get someone over there."

Souza was in Judy's front yard when ten LAPD cruisers screeched to a stop on the street. A chopper swept overhead, whump, whump, whump, bending palm-tree fronds and kicking up dust, and it must have appeared to neighbors that the Symbionese Liberation Army had resurfaced in West Hills.

"I said, a patrol car," Souza whispered to no one.

Burk, Curtice, and the LAPD officers had their hands on their weapons when Souza did the knock and notice. The door opened, and Judy appeared.

"Judy, we have a warrant to search the premises," Souza said, handing her a copy of the paperwork signed by Judge Chip Putnam.

Her face as white as flour, she stared at the pages and then at the helicopter and the small army before her.

"Judy, please have Joel come out into the living room."

"He's not here."

"Now, Judy, are you sure? If he's here, tell us, or things could get dangerous for everyone. Do you understand?"

"He . . . he's not here."

Moving inside, Souza said, "Okay. Take a seat, please. We'll get this over with as soon as we can."

Jack Duty photographed the interior to protect the FSO from charges that they'd trashed the residence. The Radovcich children stepped out into the backyard as Judy huddled on the sofa. Souza sat across from her, as he'd done on their first meeting here.

"Judy, I'm sorry you're being put through this, I really am. But we're investigating a multiple murder. This isn't a game. As long as Joel won't talk to us, as long as he keeps coming here, he keeps you in the middle of our investigation."

"Joel isn't here. I don't know where he is. I've told you that and I've told you that."

"I'm pretty sure you're holding out on us, Judy."

She didn't argue the point.

"And if Joel has the kind of information we think he has, he could be in danger."

"You keep trying to scare me, don't you?"

"He should talk to us, ma'am. It would be best for everybody, best for Joel, if he'd talk to us."

Burk emerged from one of the bedrooms. "Been working Joel's room. Found this letter."

Souza looked it over. It was a receipt from the law offices of Terrence Woolf, whom the detectives had overheard Joel calling from the Famous Phone. The receipt had been drawn up in April—an acknowledgment of three thousand dollars received as a retainer. Burk whispered that he was hesitant to seize the document, lest they whip up controversy about attorney-client privileges. Souza suggested that Duty photograph the letter.

Curtice had found a locked briefcase, which he broke open. Inside, he found an article about a defense lawyer famous for springing killers, and a batch of material about the model Claudia Schiffer. He showed the items to Souza.

"Maybe I better interview her," Curtice said, grinning.

"Who?"

"This Claudia Schiffer. Could be important."

"Yeah," said Souza, shaking his head. "You get right on it."

"Where would Joel get three grand to pay for a lawyer?" he asked Judy Radovcich.

"I'm sure I don't know."

"Have you or your husband been giving Joel money?"

"I don't know how he's surviving. I don't think he has a job."

"Are you aware he's been taking helicopter flying lessons?"

"No. It . . . it doesn't really surprise me. His brother is a military pilot."

"But, Judy, these lessons are expensive as all get-out."

"If you're asking how he pays for his training, I can't speak to that."

When the search was complete, and Duty had taken another set of photos, the "after" shots, the team filed out.

"Judy, I'm sorry about this, I really am," Souza said, stepping outside. "I think you better talk some sense into Joel."

Without another word, she closed the door. The garage was open, and Souza wandered in, nosing around, studying the machine-shop equipment inside. Joel's younger brother Daniel came up and shook his head.

"You won't find anything in here."

Souza believed the kid, and the investigators departed.

Souza, Curtice, Boudreau, and Duty had rooms at the Woodland Hills Marriot during that time. After the search at Judy Radovcich's, they gathered in a quiet lounge near the hotel bar, sipping bottled beer and brainstorming the case.

Even within the Sheriff's Office, only a small group of detectives—Lieutenant White, Sergeant Caudle, and Detectives Souza, Burk, and Curtice—were privy to all aspects of the case, and they had been ordered by the sheriff not to discuss the case with anyone.

Souza decided to bring Boudreau and Duty up to speed; he needed all the help he could get. They sat quietly as he took them through the investigation to date.

Duty said, "It looks like you can show these two are in cahoots."

"The surveillance on Joel accomplished much of that—Dana pages Joel, Joel calls from a phone booth, to a phone booth. And financially, we're finding Dana's name on Joel's expenses and flight lessons. Shit, Joel was even living at the Ewell home for a while."

"Well, that was stupid," Boudreau said. "Why don't

they just steer clear of each other for a year or so?"

Souza shook his head. "Let's just hope they don't, or we're dead in the water."

"But," said Duty, "you've gotten nothing solid out of listening in on Joel's phone calls?"

"Not an out-and-out admission of guilt. Everything but."

"So who's the third guy?" Boudreau said.

"Jack Ponce. I've had a feeling about Ponce. Joel sent that electronic lockpick to Ponce's house, right? So, maybe that's just a part of the pattern. Maybe Joel's been using Ponce to pick up other things."

"Like a gun," Duty said.

"Like a gun. I'm gonna keep squeezing this Ponce kid. One of these bozos has to crack sooner or later."

Boudreau said, "It's already later."

They went to dinner, came back, and continued. Boudreau was talking about his firearms experiments. "The porting. I don't know why I didn't think about it earlier."

"Now what?" Souza said.

"Now I need you gentlemen to find the murder weapon."

"If only," Souza said. He drank his beer and wondered what Jack Ponce was thinking about at that very moment.

Before returning to Fresno, Souza drove to Ponce's home, where he spotted a white Ford van in the driveway. He motored by, parked for ten minutes, then made another slow pass and noted the plate number.

A Ewell neighbor had reportedly seen a white or blue van around the time of the murders. So how long had Jack had one?

Souza followed up the raid on the Radovcich residence with a bit of deception. The move was strategic, but it wasn't all business. A recent medical checkup had shown Souza's blood pressure rising to dangerous levels.

"Let off some steam once in a while," the doctor had said.

And Souza knew who he was steamed at: the whole gang of spoiled, amoral little bastards who seemed as concerned about murder as they might have been about a bug hitting a windshield.

He dialed the number of Peter Radovcich and his wife Danielle. The answering machine picked up; he knew it would, since he'd waited until their scheduled work hours before calling.

"Yes, this is Detective Souza of the Fresno County Sheriff's Department. Anybody home? Peter?"

He paused. "Peter, are you in? I really need to talk to you."

"Okay, Peter. You remember me. I wish you'd pick up, or at least give me a call right back. We have some new information, and I think your brother Joel may be in jeopardy.

"The point is, we've gotten word from an informant up in the Santa Clara area. This guy claims that Dana has put a contract out on Joel. A hit. If this is true, Joel could be in serious danger.

"Okay, Peter. You have my number. I don't want any harm to come to Joel, and I'm sure you feel the same, so if you see him, try to get him to come in and talk to me, okay? See you, Peter."

Making up a tale about a possible hit on Joel wasn't exactly kosher, but it wasn't as though he were beating suspects with a rubber hose, either. Detectives considered it standard practice to "mislead" suspects if that could result in a break in a case. But would any of this make Joel crack?

On December 8, with Joel remaining scarce, Souza and Chris Curtice waylaid Jack Ponce as he left his mother's house.

Ponce saw the detectives and stopped in his tracks. "Hey, what is this?"

"And a good day to you too, Jack," Curtice said.

Ponce's eye twitched. "Goddamn it, you can't just

come around here whenever you want! This is harassment."

"File a complaint, Jack," said Souza.

"I just might do that," he said, fists knotted at his sides. "You cops are running roughshod over everybody, even Joel's mother. Searching Judy's house really pissed off Joel."

"He's mad, huh?" Souza said, smiling. But he didn't find it all that amusing. Joel was unpredictable, and if he'd killed three innocent people, dangerously so.

"You know, Jack, we found some of the things you told us last time to be a bit questionable. And you left some things out."

"I don't think so."

"Why didn't you tell us you sublet your apartment to Joel Radovcich a few years ago?"

"You . . . you didn't ask."

"But you did rent him your room in Santa Monica?"

"No."

"You're saying no?"

"I don't even know if he ever stayed there or not. I can't really remember at this point." Ponce's speech had suddenly become quite rapid.

Souza said, "Would you be willing to take a polygraph test in regard to the Ewell murders?"

"A lie detector?" He snorted, hands on his hips. "Sure, I'd take a lie detector. When?"

"Right now."

Flustered, Ponce glanced at his watch. "Now?"

"We've got it all set up."

"I can't run up to Fresno now."

"No, it's set up right here in town. Just take a couple of hours."

"This isn't the time."

"When is the right time?"

"January. Sometime in January would be better."

"Well, we can't force you, Jack. Don't know why you need to put it off, though."

Turning his back to the detectives, Ponce hurried to his car.

"Have you seen Peter or Joel recently?" Curtice called out.

"Not since October."

"We'll see you in January, then."

Souza watched Ponce drive away. "Jack," he said quietly, "you're up to your ass in this."

The next day in Fresno, hoping to shore up a paper trail on the ammunition used in the crime, Souza contacted Harry Massuco, whose father had once owned the hardware store where Dale Ewell purchased the now missing Browning Hi-Power nine-millimeter in 1971.

Harry was a former peace officer. Souza went through the case and asked Harry if the elder Massuco had retained his sales records from the hardware store.

Yes, Harry said, he believed his father boxed up his sales receipts, though it would take some time to sort it all out. Harry said he'd get to work, nevertheless, and call when and if he had something.

The long shot paid off. To Souza's astonishment, Harry called back two days later. He'd found the original sales slip for the Browning. More important to the Ewell murder investigation, Harry also had located the paperwork for the Winchester nine-millimeter ammunition.

Now, the history of the bullets used to kill Dale, Glee, and Tiffany could be traced with certainty right back to 1971.

1994

". . . a Menendez-type deal . . ."

ONE

Nineteen ninety-four began as oddly as 1993 had come to a close.

Souza and a small surveillance team—only four detectives—rolled to Judy Radovcich's West Hills home. A tiny red KIA blew out of her driveway, and detectives recognized Joel behind the wheel.

"Hey," Souza said over the cell phone. "Where's the Honda?"

Joel drove at his usual raceway speeds, parking at the Long Beach airport. When he was gone, Chris Curtice pulled closer to the KIA—or rather, two of them, both red, side-by-side.

Souza didn't think there were two KIAs in the whole state.

When he ran the plate numbers he found one was a stolen car, the other a rental. And if Joel was driving the stolen KIA, the FSO would have to report it and their whole case might go down the drain.

"He's back in view," another detective radioed a half hour later. Souza pulled back and waited.

"He's getting in the rental!" someone said over the radio.

Breathing a sigh of relief that his prime suspect wouldn't be off the streets courtesy of the taxpayers, at least not on a two-bit vehicle-theft charge, Souza dialed the Long Beach PD and reported the location of the stolen KIA.

Shortly thereafter, all but convinced that Ponce had furnished the weapon used to slaughter the Ewells, Souza phoned Ponce to schedule a polygraph examination. But Ponce wasn't going for it.

He said people close to him had advised him not to take the test. Souza asked if Ponce had seen the Radovcich brothers lately.

"No. Not at all."

"Well, Jack. You know I'm disappointed with your decision, but that's your right."

"Yeah," Ponce said. "Good-bye."

Souza picked up his trash can and bounced it off a wall.

On January 11, flight instructor Fabrice Allouche telephoned Souza. Joel had graduated from flight school and received his commercial license.

Souza thanked Fabrice for the information. At least someone cared enough to offer information without it being pounded out of them.

"Funny thing though," Fabrice said. "We always take a graduation photograph. You know, for our records, and to hang on the wall. Another happy graduate."

"Didn't get the picture, did you?" Souza said.

"Hey, how'd you know? He took off, said he didn't like pictures."

"Oh, I guess I've gotten to know old Joel over the past few years."

Boudreau's firearms experiments continued.

He secured and tested an Uzi nine-millimeter carbine, with results similar to earlier tests. However, when he modified a Browning Hi-Power (like the one stolen from the Ewells') with an extended barrel and ported chrome molybdenum tube, he found he was unable to reproduce the coarse stria on test bullets. In fact, the added weight of the improvised barrel extensions interfered with the Browning's autoloading action; ten out of ten times, the Browning failed to eject the empty cartridge case and load another round from the magazine.

That night on the ranch, Souza unbolted the generator from his tractor. It would take an hour or two to rebuild it, and the work would be a welcome change from the Ewell case.

Then, pop, pop, pop, pop, the sound of gunshots near the front of the house. Automatic weapon fire.

Sharon came out the back door.

He shouted, "Get back inside! And stay down."

A car blew by on the blacktop.

Souza dashed to the unmarked cop car, roared off after the shooters, his visor flip-light flashing. The only weapon on hand was the backup five-shot .38 he carried in an ankle rig.

He caught up with the car a mile down the road, hit his siren, and the car pulled over on the shoulder. His tiny weapon drawn, he ordered three young men out of the car.

But he found no guns. He was fairly certain they had tossed it during the chase. He took their names (to check for ties to Dana and Joel) and cut them loose.

"Hey, man," the driver called out before driving off. "You thought we had a machine gun and you was gonna shoot it out with that bitty gun?"

Souza shrugged.

The kid put the car in gear. "Man, you are crazy!"

Souza leaned against his car and sighed.

In early 1994 Boudreau turned his attention to the heels of the murder bullets, where the bullets fit into the shell casings. Here, too, Boudreau found odd markings—an asymmetric distribution of deep and faint lines that

formed a radial pattern on the base of the bullet jackets.
Boudreau would write:

```
Jacketed bullets, like the murder bul-
lets, may have toolmarks present on their
bases from manufacture. These toolmarks
are impressed by imperfect, damaged or
worn tooling during the manufacture of the
bullets. When such marks are present, re-
producible and have sufficient identifying
characteristics, they can be compared and
may establish a relationship between two
or more bullets.
```

This method of "establishing a relationship between
two or more bullets" was not merely applicable to the
murder bullets. He reported:

```
It was now important to determine if the
murder bullets, were, in fact . . . from
the ammunition found on the bedroom floor
and in the night table at the Ewell resi-
dence. The manufacturing code number,
3EB91, stamped on the box established that
the ammunition was packaged at the Win-
chester Ammunition plant in February of
1971. The ammunition was 21 years old at
the time of the Ewell homicides.
     The existence of sporting ammunition of
that age would not be common and could be
rare. Determining if this 21-year-old am-
munition was rare would require communi-
cation with the Winchester Group of the
Olin Corporation.
```

Using a kinetic bullet puller, Boudreau disassembled all
nineteen of the bullets found in the Ewell bedroom, sealed
the powder charges in plastic, and examined the heels of

the bullets under the comparison microscope. He concluded in his report:

> The radial pattern toolmarks present
> . . . were found to match, establishing a
> relationship between two of the murder
> bullets, the bullet found on the bedroom
> floor, and five of the bullets from the Winchester ammunition box.

In other words, he now had more compelling proof that the murder bullets had come from the box found in the bedroom. Consulting with representatives of Winchester to learn the exact nature of these toolmarks, and then assaying the trace metal content of the lead cores, would be required to further establish his belief.

Boudreau packed up the murder bullets and the bullets found in the Winchester box at East Park Circle, and shipped the package to the FBI Laboratory in Washington, DC. FBI lab tests would determine the exact metal content of the bullets through neutron-activation analysis; that is, the test would quantitatively measure minute amounts of trace metal impurities in the lead, a virtual signature of the batch of lead from which the bullets had come. As Boudreau reported:

> These elemental compositions vary from
> one melt of lead alloy to the next . . .
> by determining the elemental composition
> present in specimens of lead bullet cores,
> comparisons can be performed. This can be
> helpful in establishing the existence, or
> absence, of the relationship of the lead
> between two or more bullets.

The test results came back from the FBI laboratory in late March. From these results, Boudreau concluded:

> There are only two elemental compositions represented in the eight evidence bullets with the radial toolmarks. These results are consistent with, and support, the previous observations and findings.

TWO

"I KNOW WHY YOU'RE HERE," SAID DR. ERNEST Ponce when Souza and Curtice appeared at his home on February 15.

"Why are we here?" Souza asked the dentist.

"Jack's been worried sick. I thought he had AIDS."

Curtice frowned. "AIDS?"

"I told my son I would stand by him, that he could count on our support no matter what."

"Does he have AIDS?" Souza said.

"No. He's been under a great deal of stress since you've spoken with him. He's been very depressed."

"Did you ask your son why he's been depressed?"

"Of course. As I just indicated, it was the police questioning. I asked him what the police wanted with him, if he had done anything. But, Detective, Jack has assured me he isn't involved with Peter Radovcich in any way criminal."

"What about Peter, Doctor?"

"According to Jack, Peter has gotten involved in what he called a Mendendez-type deal. I asked if that meant that someone had killed their parents, like those sons had in Beverly Hills."

"And what did Jack say?" Curtice asked.

"He said yes."

The detectives left. On the drive home, both voiced wonder that so many people had heard information that could be vital to solving a triple homicide, but no one had bothered to pick up a phone. And they made plans to have another talk with Jack Ponce. Souza sensed something was about to break wide open.

"Mr. Ponce, is it true this is our third interview?"

"Yes."

It was February 18, 1994, at Jack's mother's home.

"Okay," Souza said, "you've indicated you were close friends with Peter Radovcich, and you're aware his brother Joel is possibly involved in a homicide?"

"Yeah."

This time, Ponce had told the detectives, he wanted his own tape of the interview. He produced a recorder and turned it on.

"All set, Jack? Last time, we talked about the lockpick you had received under your name that was actually bought by Joel. Is that correct?"

"Yes. I believe it was a locksmith device."

Chris Curtice snorted. "Jack, it was a lockpick, all right? Did you ever talk to Joel about it?"

"No, I haven't. Mentioned something to Peter, and he felt bad my family's affected by it, like his. You know, people coming around and all."

"Like us?"

"Yeah," Ponce said.

"So what did Peter say about the actual homicide itself?"

"Uh, he's always maintained, that . . . that there's other possibilities, that he doesn't believe Joel's involved. He said, you know, Joel's always been kind of an odd person. But Peter thinks there's all kinds of other things that could have happened."

Curtice said, "Yet you guys have a question mark."

"There's so many questions being asked about Joel. I mean, Joel's not an open person, so . . ."

"Yeah," Curtice said. "Do you think Peter would talk to us?"

"Uh, I don't know. He was angry about you guys at his mom's house."

"Is he blaming us?"

"No, there's just problems, I guess."

"Okay." Curtice was silent a moment. "Jack, have you purchased anything else for Joel or Peter?"

He grew quiet. "Uh, I'm trying to think—"

"Any books?"

"No, no. No mail order other than the lockpick, and I'm trying to think really hard."

"So how did that transpire?"

"He showed up at TGI Friday's and kind of surprised me. Said what's up, how you doing, and asked if he could send some locksmith thing to me, because Peter's wife was kind of weird about everything."

"Okay," Curtice said. "You indicated in your first statement that he didn't want the cops to know."

"Uh, maybe, but I think it was more a thing with Peter and his wife. Maybe I'd assumed that, what I said. I mean, you guys looking into him, and he was moving around."

"So he was avoiding us?"

"Uh, yeah, I think so. He didn't want people asking him questions."

Curtice asked, "About the murders?"

"About the homicide, yeah."

"Well, do you know why he wouldn't want us to ask those questions?"

"He answered them the first time, then . . . I don't know why, if he wasn't involved or anything."

Souza said, "Joel was spending time at Peter's house, right?"

"Yeah, his dad shows up at home, gives him hell. His dad had a really dominant personality at one time. Wouldn't let anybody go outside. I guess when they got older, they got to be their own people."

"Okay," said Curtice. "You indicated earlier that Joel went shooting with you."

Ponce glared at them. "No, just Pete and me."

"Jack, your father indicated to us that he was concerned about your weight loss since we talked to you."

"I had the flu, that was all."

"And he said you mentioned Peter and a Menendez-type deal," Souza said.

"No, sir, I never said that! If anything, I said that Peter's brother might be involved in a Menendez-style deal. I never said Peter's involved."

Curtice asked, "Where is Joel staying?"

"I think at his mom's."

"Anything else you want to tell us?"

"Uh, just that I don't know anything about Joel being involved. I don't think Pete knows anything, uh, either. Anything can happen, but I don't think so. I've never met the Ewell guy, I've never been up in that area. If someone had told me Joel, you know, Joel did this, I wouldn't have got it sent to me. I try to open up, but I'm stoic sometimes, but I'm sorry if it seemed I was hiding from you. I'm not, and, uh, if you . . . if you have questions go ahead and ask me."

Souza thought, What's with the sudden sincerity? "Okay. Have you ever been to Fresno?"

"No."

"Okay."

"You ask me the same question. I guess you're supposed to do that. I've never met the Ewell guy, never seen him and Joel together."

Souza said, "Have you ever lent Joel a gun?"

"No, never."

"Have you ever owned a nine-millimeter weapon?"

Ponce went rigid, struggling to answer. "Yes."

The detectives also struggled to maintain their composure—they knew this was very big.

"Do you own one presently?" Souza said.

"No, I do not."

"What type was it?"

"It was an AT9 rifle."

"Rifle?"

"Yes." Nodding a few times.

"I'm not familiar with that," Curtice said. "AT9? Nine-millimeter?"

"Yes. By Featherlite."

"Did you ever loan it to Joel?"

"I did not."

"To Peter?"

"No."

"Did you sell it to somebody?"

"I did not sell it."

"Who has it?"

"I don't know. It was in the trunk of my car in LA, and someone broke in and it was taken."

"You filed a report on it?" Curtice asked.

"Yes, to West LAPD. I got it, um, probably April of '92. Around my birthday."

"Was it a gift?"

"No, from the, from National, around the corner."

"Did you get it fully equipped?" Curtice said.

"Yes."

"I don't know what it looks like. Like an AR-15? Does it look like a machine gun?"

"It's the kind you can shove in the barrel, like an A-10. It had the little shroud."

"Oh, the flash suppressor?" Souza said.

"Oh," Ponce said, "wait—no."

"Did Joel ever see it?"

"No, no."

"Jack," Curtice said, "any other times when Joel has just appeared at Friday's while you were working?"

"No. At Pete's, maybe," Ponce said, contradicting the observations of investigators.

"Anything then that struck you as unusual, anything he was into . . ."

"He wanted to be an economics major. Wanted to be wealthy. I guess he hasn't had a job."

"Ever say how he's going to get wealthy?"

"Uh-uh, no," Ponce said. He shrugged. "You'd think he'd get a job."

"He into metalworking or anything?" Curtice asked. "Got oxygen, acetylene tanks?"

"Yeah. He's a good mechanic."

Souza said, "Any way Joel would know the gun was in your trunk?"

"No one knew. They couldn't have known. The thing I was gonna do, there were possums in my mom's attic, and I was going to sneak up and grab Pete and take him, but I didn't get to. He wasn't meant to be a possum killer."

Curtice stared. "What?"

"He wasn't meant to be a possum killer."

"Possum killer."

"Yeah."

"Oh, really?"

Souza said, "Uh . . . uh, okay. Jack, do they call you at work?"

"Just Pete. Never Joel."

"Does Joel have a pager?"

"Uh, Joel had one."

"What if we told you we know Pete and his wife are hiding Joel?"

"That would surprise me. Danielle and Joel don't get along that much. Anyway, they got divorced in December."

Souza asked about the white van he'd spotted in Ponce's driveway. Where was it now?

Ponce claimed he had bought the van hoping to make five hundred dollars on resale, fixed the transmission, and sold it.

"Okay. Anything else, Jack?"

"Only it would surprise me that they'd do that."

"Okay. The time is 1223. We're terminating this interview."

THREE

ELATED BY THIS NEW INFORMATION, SOUZA AND
Curtice called Allen Boudreau from the car. When Boud-
reau heard the story of the Featherlite AT9, he told Souza,
"Buy one!"

"We're on our way to National Gun Sales right now.
We need permission from the office, but if the store has
an AT9, we'll get them to hold one for us."

"Great. Call me as soon as you can."

Souza and Curtice badged the manager at National Gun
Sales and asked whether the store had a Featherlite AT9
in stock.

They did. The manager pulled a used model off a shelf.
Souza immediately phoned Boudreau.

"Get a flashlight," Boudreau told Souza.

Souza borrowed one from the store manager.

"Now light up the barrel," Boudreau said. "It should be
six, right."

Souza held the flashlight and Curtice squinted down the
AT9 barrel. Grinning, Curtice nodded to Souza.

Souza told Boudreau, "It's six, right twist."

"Bring it on in," Boudreau said.

Souza and Curtice asked the store manager to hold the
weapon for pickup by the FSO.

"One other thing," Souza added.

He explained that investigators needed a copy of a purchase slip for an AT9 the store had sold to one Ernest "Jack" Ponce in April, 1992.

After a short wait, the manager produced an original sales slip with Ponce's signature.

Souza's elation was short-lived. Upon contacting Feather Industries, manufacturer of the AT9, Souza stumbled upon yet another problem: Feather subcontracted out the manufacture of the AT9 barrels; the barrel of the weapon purchased (a used gun made in 1990) had been made by a different manufacturer than the company that had produced Ponce's barrel.

Allen Boudreau verified that the land widths of test bullets fired from the purchased weapon differed from the land impressions on the murder bullets. Now he needed a barrel of the same manufacture as the one on the Ponce weapon.

Two steps forward, one step back. It seemed to Souza that every break in the case simply dumped another complication in his lap.

When Souza interviewed Ponce's former girlfriend, Leticia Gonzalez, on February 2, she claimed no knowledge of Ponce's involvement in the Ewell crime.

And, if Jack's car had been burglarized at her apartment, he'd said nothing to her. He never even mentioned buying an assault rifle, something Leticia found odd. Souza, of course, found Jack's secretive manner somewhat less surprising.

The detective paid another visit to Peter Radovcich. They showed him a brochure photo of the AT9. Never saw it in my life, Peter said.

A few days later, Souza and Curtice brought the surveillance tapes of Joel to a professional sound studio. They hoped technicians could clean up the background noise and perhaps notch up the volume on Joel's words a bit, so transcript typists could take down a more complete account of the phone calls than they'd managed so far.

(They'd considered the use of sophisticated, remote eaves-dropping equipment, but ruled against it for fear its use would violate privacy laws and any recordings would be ruled inadmissible.)

After days of manipulating the sound track, the studio people said there was just too much "crud" on the tapes. Enhancement was out of the question.

Trying to relax in his backyard spa that night, Souza knew the "wrong" barrel on the AT9 they'd bought—it being of a different manufacture than the Ponce barrel—presented a major problem.

He sat back in the steaming tub, a can of Miller Lite in his fist, and watched the dark rural sky. He spotted the unique reflection of a satellite hurtling through space, and remembered the night of the first Apollo moon landing. That landing had amazed him, a quarter century earlier. It still amazed him. He felt that spoke to his better nature, that he hadn't lost his childlike wonder at the world around him.

And then his mind went right back to the Ewells, to Tiffany, who sure as hell would never get a chance to see the stars again, and he remembered those gun barrels . . . "Damn, that's it!" he said, jumping up, dripping wet.

The next morning, Lieutenant Ron Wiley (who had taken over from White as chief of detectives) looked at Souza as if he'd just suggested hiring Dana Ewell as a deputy sheriff.

Wiley, a handsome African-American so powerful he'd once tossed a belligerent suspect over a car, tilted his head back and laughed. "John, you're out of your mind."

"What's that got to do with it?"

"I'm telling you, you will never find the barrel that was manufactured right before Ponce's."

"Or right after."

"Whatever. Ain't going to happen, John."

"Look, I'll find them."

"Them?" Wiley said.

"I need two, according to Boudreau. One to port and one to keep in original condition."

"If you say so."

"So I need authorization to purchase two new replacement barrels from Feather's supplier."

"You just said you need the old barrels—"

"I need new ones to swap for the old ones."

Wiley leaned back in his seat. "Oh. Pretty good idea."

"Hey, thanks."

Wiley cleared his throat. "Two barrels might be pricey. Find out what they cost."

Souza did. They were available for thirty-five dollars each. Wiley had no problem authorizing that little. Now all Souza needed to do was get a list of every Feather Industries AT9 assault rifle sold before the crime, track down every owner, call every damn one of them.

He wondered if he wasn't crazy, as Wiley had suggested.

Lucky for once: Souza found that Feather had shipped to the West Coast only fifteen guns of the series he sought, and all of those to Interstate Arms, parent of National Gun Sales. Ponce's weapon (#407) was the highest number shipped. Souza obtained from Interstate the names of purchasers of weapons # 395–406.

A woman in the San Fernando Valley provided the barrel from AT9 #395. She seemed glad to help, and thrilled to get a spanking-new barrel for her assault weapon.

Souza tracked down the owner of #406 through the Department of Motor Vehicles. The Tujunga man quickly agreed to swap his barrel for a fresh one, and confirmed that the old barrel was of original manufacture.

Number 406 was significant: in the manufacture of gun barrels, "rifling buttons" are pulled through the bore to create the land-and-groove characteristics. But with each barrel machined, the rifling button wears slightly, altering the ballistic "signature" of each successive barrel.

Therefore, the signature of barrel # 406 would more closely resemble that of barrel # 407 then would, say, # 524 (assuming the barrels were fitted to the weapon in the same order as manufactured).

Souza delivered the barrels to Boudreau. With # 406 in hand, the criminalist said he could really get to work.

FOUR

CURTICE TURNED ON THE TAPE RECORDER.

"Okay," Souza said. "The date is February 28, 1994. This will be an interview with Jack Ponce as regards case number 92-15285. Present will be Detective Curtice, myself, Detective Souza, and Mr. Ponce. We're presently at Mr. Ponce's residence in San Bernardino. Jack, I believe this is like the fourth time we've talked to you, correct?"

"Yeah, it is."

"Yeah, okay. Basically, we want to go over a few things from the first time we talked. You said you knew Joel Radovcich through his brother Pete. Correct?"

"Yes."

"We covered the issue of the electronic lockpick—"

"I, uh, believe it was a locksmithing device."

"Right, yeah," Curtice said, obviously struggling to hold his temper. "You also indicated you knew Joel was a possible suspect in the homicide. It didn't enter your mind, anything foul going on in reference to this lockpick, right?"

"That's correct."

"Okay, then we got into something about Peter and Joel at an indoor shooting range."

"See, you keep saying that, but he's never been anywhere like that with us."

"Okay, your dad brought up an issue that Peter was involved in a 'Menendez-type thing' with Joel."

"I don't know why he brought that up, but he goes, 'what's upsetting you?' and I told him it's a Menendez-type parent-killing thing. I would have said Pete's brother Joel was a suspect, so maybe he just remembered Pete."

"Okay, and last time you said you were a onetime owner of a nine-millimeter, uh . . ."

"AT9."

"And, ah, it's curious to know why you didn't bring up the gun the first time."

"I did."

"Jack, you didn't say anything about the AT9."

"Yeah. I did."

"Listen," Souza said. "We would have definitely caught that."

"No, I listed all my guns, and I said a nine-millimeter rifle."

Curtice huffed turning away, rolling his eyes. "I want to talk to you about the AT9. I think the receipt said you bought it in April of '92?"

"A little before that. Bought it for my birthday."

"What was the reason you bought it?"

"I could pack it up and go hiking, you know, you can fold that one up."

"I don't know," Curtice said. "The last time you told us you wanted to kill possums in your—"

"Yeah. That's a good reason. We still have possums in the attic."

"All right. You got it with the shroud?"

"You take the barrel on and off. I guess there's a shroud."

"Did anyone ever go with you to look at it?"

"No."

"No one?"

"Uh-uh."

"How many times did you shoot it?"

Ponce made a face of intense concentration. "Like twice. Up in a canyon a few miles from here."

"And you say you had it between April and October.

Did you show it to anybody? Peter or your girlfriend?"

"No. And she doesn't like guns."

"But it was stolen from your car at her house?"

"Yeah, they jimmied my door and used the trunk release."

"And LAPD didn't come out?"

"They just took a counter report."

"Was there any other loss?"

"Um, it was just like, I think my razor was there and the rest was just my clothes—"

"They took your clothes?"

"No, no. My clothes were there."

"Did you ever lend it to anyone?"

"No."

"Did Joel ever shoot it?" Souza said.

"No."

"Jack," Souza said, "obviously we have some concerns."

"Yeah."

"And you told your dad you lost weight 'cause you had the flu."

"Uh," Ponce said, straightening up, "a lot of people at my work had it, too."

"Jack, you ever given your fingerprints for anything?"

"No. Like a driver's license?"

"Well, we have to eliminate some prints found at the residence. You know, we don't think you were there, but it would eliminate you."

Ponce was suddenly very wide-eyed. "Okay, that's not, that's not a problem, but just that uh, um, okay. Keep going on your apparent line of questioning."

"Okay. We had to tell you about this lockpick and Joel. Yet you knew about his being a suspect in a triple homicide. We know from others that you've been stressed out. You agreed to take a poly, then declined to go through with it. Then you bought the AT9 down the street from Peter's house. Did you use your own money?"

"Yeah."

He's lying again, Souza thought.

Curtice said, "Do you know about ballistics?"

"Uh, no."

"The problem we have is, ironically, this AT9, ballistic-wise, is identical to the murder bullets we have from the victim's bodies. It's got a right twist and six lands and grooves. You picked it up April 8 of '92, eleven days before the homicide. Everything is so damned coinciden-tal here."

"That is."

"Isn't it? We can't help but believe you bought this AT9 for Joel, and maybe in October Joel told you to re-port it stolen. Okay? Then all the other facts we just gave you about the interviews and such."

"It's all—"

"And the fact about possums," Souza added. "With an AT9, you'd be knocking holes in the roof—"

"It wasn't my gun. I don't know what he did or any-thing, but it wasn't my gun. I had my gun. I mean, if he used an AT9 or if he did something like that, it wasn't my gun."

"I think you, as a logical person, would share the same suspicions as us," Souza said, staring Ponce down.

Ponce seemed to shrink a little under Souza's gaze. "I understand, it's a little upsetting to hear that."

"And our feeling is you didn't have anything to do with the homicide. We think you bought this gun for Joel and maybe Joel told you he was going hunting or something. And we don't really care that you bought it for him; we need you to tell us and eliminate yourself as a suspect, and be a hero and solve this thing."

"I didn't buy that gun for Joel." He folded his arms.

"The only way to show that is to take a polygraph. If you fail it, it can't be used in court, but—"

"Can I take it if I have asthma?"

Hoo, boy. "Sure," said Souza.

"You sure?"

"We've run out of options," Curtice said. "You can

choose not to take it but then in our minds, you are a suspect. That's the way we're going to pursue it."

Souza said, "But then again, if you did buy it, now is the time to come out with it. Because if we find out down the road, I guarantee we will get you for conspiracy to commit homicide. That's not a threat, I'm just putting it out there. This is your last opportunity to say, 'I fucked up, I bought the gun, and this is what happened.' You know, if you did this, you're probably going to get some money—"

"What are you talking about?"

"If Joel asked you to buy this gun, he would probably pay you some money."

Ponce made a dismissive motion with his hand. "I'm not that interested in money."

"Oh."

"They can keep it, fuck the money."

Souza wondered who "they" were. He said, "Everyone's interested in money. 'Cause it pays the bills."

"No, it doesn't pay them that way."

Souza thought the high moral ground wasn't Ponce's territory.

"If you didn't, then just show us," Curtice said.

"Right now, I'm just . . . no, flat no. For the reasons I gave you. Uh—but that's not a definite no."

"Okay, I ran the scenario down for you. You understand where we're at, trying to solve a homicide, whether we get your help or not. The time is 1653. We'll go ahead and go off tape."

FIVE

ALLEN BOUDREAU'S NEWS MADE SOUZA FEEL that victory was finally in sight.

The forensic scientist had conducted a series of exhaustive studies with the "new" barrel, number 406, the one that had come off the line right before Ponce's. The bullets were all but indistinguishable from the murder bullets. Here, Souza and Boudreau agreed, was evidence the DA could use.

The case against Dana Ewell and Joel Radovcich—and probably Jack Ponce—was moving into its final stages.

On February 28, the detectives followed up with another visit to Jack's father at his home. Had he, they asked Dr. Ponce, given Jack the money to buy a rifle for his birthday in 1992?

"No," Dr. Ponce said.

Had Jack told him about the weapon?

"No."

Did he know about any nine-millimeter guns his son owned?

Again it was "no."

They showed Dr. Ponce a picture of the Feather Industries AT9 assault rifle and said Jack claimed he'd bought the gun to shoot possums in his mother's attic.

"That's just bullshit," Ponce said, laughing.

Souza advised Dr. Ponce that the ballistics from an AT9

matched the bullets from the Ewell murder scene. Dr. Ponce stopped laughing.

Curtice said, "We're going to ask him again to take the polygraph. I hope you'll advise Jack to take it and prove he wasn't involved in the actual murders."

Pale, Ponce said, "Well, obviously I'm quite concerned. I'll . . . I'll talk to him. If he didn't have anything to do with the killings, I'll try to persuade him to go ahead and take the polygraph."

Three days later, Dr. Ponce phoned Souza.

"I talked to Jack."

"And?"

"And, he said he had to consult someone before he'd take the test."

Shit.

"I asked who he was talking to, but he wouldn't say. I told him he'd have to face the consequences even if he wasn't involved, because you guys think he was in it somehow."

"But he still said no?"

"He didn't say no, exactly. But . . . he wants to think about it. That's what he says."

"Sir, I hope he comes around. I'm convinced he can help break this case, but if I have to, I'll arrest him, and he'll be looking at three counts of murder, with special circumstances. You understand, sir?"

After a moment of silence, Ponce said, "I'm afraid I do. You can imagine how upset I am—"

"Yes, sir."

"But I can't make him take it."

"I know the feeling, Dr. Ponce. Thanks for your call."

In mid-March, 1994, estate attorney Georgeson sent Souza a copy of another letter he'd received from Dana. It began:

Soon after the tragic loss of my family, [attorney] Bill Keeler, against my recommendations, created the circumstances such that Dan Ewell became trustee of the James J. Mitchell trust.

After claiming that Dan was abusing his discretion as trustee, Dana continued:

The trust document indicates the money from the James J. Mitchell trust should have been distributed to me already, as you stated the last time we met. Yet, in his attempts to financially benefit from my parents' tragic deaths, Dan Ewell has used this trust money to fight the distribution of estate assets into the trust for my benefit. Aside from my moral disgust at his actions, I am concerned that his actions constitute a breach of his responsibilities as trustee by exceeding the realm of reasonable discretion exercised in good faith.

Dana continued to rail against the conduct of Dan and his other uncles in regard to his parents' estate, and what he considered conflicts of interest. In closing, Dana wrote:

I would like to see what suggestions you and Bill Keeler have on this situation regarding the James J. Mitchell trust, as well as the Pajaro Dunes beach house in question, with which Dan and Ben will be extremely difficult in dealing with, I am sure. In any event, I beg of you not to ever repay the $140,000 loan back to the James Mitchell Trust anytime in the near future as I am sure I would never see it again. Dan Ewell would certainly use this money as a continual "free ride" to pay his attorneys to fight me and the estates of Dale and Glee Ewell for the next ten years!

Dana J. Ewell

Souza filed the letter, hoping the uncles would continue to battle Dana for control of the estate until Dana and Joel could be brought to trial.

A March 16 phone call to Souza generated a great deal of excitement at the Sheriff's Department.

Souza had "flagged" the passports of both Dana and Joel—that is, placed a memo on the Customs computers that he be notified should these men leave the country. He learned, however, that Customs could only notify him when the subjects were returning.

Customs agent Liz Bannigan told him that Dana Ewell and Joel Radovcich were waiting to take off from Los Barrollos, Mexico. Souza was glad they'd decided not to stay in Mexico forever. But now what? What were the "boys" up to? Just a little joyride in Dana's new hundred-fifty-thousand-dollar airplane?

Souza asked Bannigan, "Can they track them in?"

"I'm certain they can. Let me put you through to air traffic control."

A controller came on the line. "You want us to keep this aircraft on screen?"

"If you can."

"I can track them while they're in our range, then I'll hand them off."

Which the controllers did, each city bringing Dana's aircraft, wing number N9129Z, up on their radar until the next zone picked it up. All the while, Souza hung on the line as control towers updated him on the plane's position and heading.

When it was clear Dana was headed for Fresno, Curtice reached narcotics detective Osborn, a veteran of the LA surveillance on Joel and Dana. Osborn raced out to Fresno Air Terminal.

SIX

Souza quickly got word that Dana's plane was on final approach. He thanked the controllers and reached Osborn on the cell phone.

"They're on the ground," Osborn said. "I'm getting some great pictures of Dana and Joel together on the tarmac. Dana is talking to some guy from the fuel truck. Ah, shit! Looks like the fuel geek is ratting us out. He's pointing at me. Here comes Dana. Want me to shoot him? Hello, John?"

"I'm thinking."

"Oh well, party's over. I'm history."

Osborn spun the undercover van around and made for the exit, Dana in hot pursuit, but came to a locked gate and had to pull a fast K-turn. Dana——chin leading the way, arms swinging high——cut through the aviation complex, apparently hoping to head off his observer, but the van screeched out on the highway as Dana rushed through the doors.

Osborn told Souza he was coming back in.

"What would you have done if Dana caught up with you?" Souza asked Osborn.

"I was gonna hop out and knock him on his ass."

Souza hung up the phone, and he and Curtice laughed like schoolboys.

* * *

Souza, Curtice, and other FSO members stepped up their efforts to find something tangible on Ponce.

Souza felt Ponce wouldn't roll over until he was arrested, but the detectives needed solid probable cause to make that arrest. Much of May 1994 was spent learning more about Ernest Jack Ponce, a recent UCLA graduate, who'd known the Radovcich brothers for years.

Ponce's relatives told the detectives that Jack had been with family on Easter Sunday. And Souza learned that Ponce used a pager—interestingly, first rented just days before the crime. Souza wrote a search warrant and cloned the pager. Then he wrote another so Ponce's financial records could be audited.

Souza also pulled the registration history of Ponce's van: Ponce had bought the van from Sketchly-Mason Plumbing (Peter Radovcich's employer) on April 10, 1992—again, just days before the murders. Ponce in turn sold it to a San Bernardino janitorial service in October of 1993.

A Sketchly-Mason manager told Souza Ponce had paid $2,000 for the van and later installed an alarm system in it. (This puzzled detectives—why would Ponce buy an alarm for a van he claimed he had bought to fix up and sell for a quick five-hundred-dollar profit?)

Souza followed up by contacting the van's new owner. He learned Ponce had sold the van for $1,500 (a five-hundred-dollar loss). Souza asked the owner if any ammunition had been found in the van. One .22 caliber cartridge, the owner said, but he'd tossed it in the trash months before.

Souza had no way of determining with certainty if it was Ponce's van that had been spotted near the Ewell residence on Easter weekend 1992. Witness accounts were sketchy and contradictory. It was just another piece of the puzzle that didn't fit.

Determined not to lose track on Ponce, Souza called TGI Friday's one slow, gray afternoon and asked if Jack Ponce still worked there.

"No," came the response.

"Okay. Who am I speaking with?"

"Habib."

Souza smiled. "Yeah, okay. Thanks, Habib."

He hung up and laughed. He knew Ponce's voice, and he got quite a kick of the little weasel claiming his name was "Habib."

On May 9, in order to seek a different perspective on the ongoing investigation, Souza, Curtice, and Sergeant Dale Caudle joined an FBI/Department of Justice criminal profiling team in a conference room at the Holiday Inn Centre Plaza in Fresno.

The FBI/DOJ team listened to a detailed, relatively unbiased account of the murders, scene, evidence, and the current state of the investigation.

The Fresno County detective wanted to know: Did the three-member profile team agree with the tack of the FSO's investigation? Did the team see something significant that might indicate other suspects had been overlooked? Finally, did the FSO's focus on Dana, Joel, and Jack Ponce seem logical and appropriate?

By midafternoon the FBI/DOJ team members had rendered their collective opinion: Souza, Curtice, and the FSO seemed right on target.

But all displayed shock when told that Monica Zent represented a weak link in the investigation; none were aware that John Zent had insinuated himself into the homicide case, and FSO members were encouraged to contact Zent's superiors at the San Francisco Bureau office.

Following that meeting, investigators and Sheriff Magarian wrote Zent's Regional Supervisor and listed actions that they believed Zent had taken "to interfere/obstruct our investigation," including: using FBI identification to access the scene, writing a critical letter to the *Bee*, instructing his daughter not to cooperate in the investigation, and "Strong indications that he is advising Dana Ewell on how to handle investigators."

*   *   *

In mid-1994 a fellow detective handed Souza a copy of
a True Crime/Pocketbooks paperback, *REWARD: You
may collect $500 to $500,000 helping police solve these
True Crimes,* by Paulette Cooper and Paul Noble.

Souza found "The Fresno Murders" on page 187 of
REWARD, which included information about the crime,
the suspicions of Philippine or CIA involvement, and rumors that Dana was involved. The chapter closed with:

> In Fresno the rumors have quieted from a roar to a whis-
> per. Sheriff's spokeswoman Margaret Mims says, "We're
> looking at everything and everybody. We can't rule any-
> thing or anybody out."
> REWARD: $50,000
> FROM: Ewell family relatives
> FOR: Information leading to the arrest and conviction of
> the killer or killers of the Ewell family.
> CONTACT: Detectives Ernie Burk or John Souza

The publicity couldn't hurt, but Souza knew that after
all these months the likelihood of an informant stepping
forward was slim indeed.

Just a few days after he saw the *REWARD* paperback,
Souza received a dozen calls from friends and colleagues,
all insisting he check the Miscellaneous section of the *Bee*
classified ads. He borrowed a paper from Curtice and
found an ad that read:

> FUR COATS Gorgeous Normart's. Beige opossum $400,
> ranch mink, $450, Mahogany, $1000, white fur, $500.
> 432-4500 ask for Dana Ewell

Souza asked Curtice, "But why the fuck would Dana
put his name in there? Nobody puts their name in the
classifieds!"

Curtice considered this. "One reason I can think of.
Some people might look at his dead mom's furs as col-

lector's items. He probably realized he'll get more money by using his name."

Souza felt sick.

Later that month, Chris Curtice's private life became another casualty of the far-reaching ripples of the Ewell case. He came home one night to find that his live-in girlfriend of four years had moved out, taking her son, whom Curtice had come to love as his own. He found a "Dear John" note. She wrote that she could no longer tolerate his extended absences. It would be months before Souza saw the pain fade from Curtice's face.

Souza was perusing Boudreau's firearms notes one morning when he took a call from Royal Caulkins, a *Fresno Bee* reporter who had been covering much of the Ewell story.

"Did you hear about Austin Ewell?"

"What about him?"

"He was killed."

"What?"

"Yeah. Back on the Ohio farm. He was killed in an explosion."

The Ohio coroner, Elizabeth Balraj, ruled on the death of Austin Bert Ewell, father of the late Dale Ewell:

```
CAUSE OF DEATH: Bronchopneumonia
Due to: Explosive injury to head and upper
extremities with thermal burns ACCIDENTAL.
```

But Souza knew that Austin had battled to prevent Dana from receiving any inheritance money. Souza also remembered Joel's electronic lockpick and books on remote explosions, including gasoline bombs. The detective strongly suspected Dana planned to get his maternal grandmother out of the way so he might control her oil revenues. And now Austin was dead in an explosion.

Ohio authorities explained that on June 28 (and now I'm just hearing about this? Souza thought) Austin entered the basement of his Wellington, Ohio, farmhouse. Local fire-department volunteers believed Austin was refilling a generator gas tank (the generator drove a sump pump that helped prevent flooding) when fumes were ignited by a water-heater pilot light.

As was his murdered son, Austin was found by a neighbor. The elderly farmer lingered for two months before succumbing to pneumonia. Souza told himself it probably had been an accident. But timing and circumstance . . . And what about opportunity?

He couldn't be sure where Joel and Dana had been on the evening of June 28; they'd flown to Mexico at least once, might they not fly to Ohio if there were millions in it for them?

Souza learned that no police report had been filed. The incident had been looked into by a volunteer fire department. The small-town firefighters in Wellington, even if experienced as arson investigators, certainly had had no cause to suspect homicide, and the blast was not investigated as such.

But Souza questioned Austin's death. Where did all the gas fumes come from, anyway, unless Austin had left the can open for hours? And how many times had Austin used that generator and sump pump without a problem?

The skeletonizer was dead.

This year, the county agent had formulated a pesticide mix that was knocking the costly pest dead all over Fresno County. Souza's crop was hefty, the sugar levels excellent. He and the boys dried the grapes, boxed and packed the raisins, and Souza felt flush with cash for the first time in years.

He decided to skip the onion planting for the season—hadn't had much luck with it anyway—and he and the kids and a few friends drove up to his old forty-foot houseboat. They partied in the middle of a thousand miles of waterway that comprised the rich Sacramento delta, where Souza could lose himself in the glory of acres of peat moss blazing orange under the setting sun.

In mid-November, Souza and Boudreau boarded a jetliner at Fresno Air Terminal, bound for Pennsylvania. They'd already located two Green Mountain barrels, manufactured before the one Ponce had bought. Now, in order to bolster their firearms case statistically, they would buy two barrels made after Ponce's.

Souza had contacted every dealer who had received a shipment of the weapons, listing the names and addresses of buyers and dates of sales, generating over forty handwritten pages tracking the distribution of AT9s.

While most of the AT9s were in private hands, some remained unsold, many had been reported stolen, some had gone to the ATF when dealers folded, and one shipment was untraceable, as the sales records had been destroyed by fire during the Los Angeles riots. Numbers 408 and above had gone to private buyers in Pennsylvania.

While on the East Coast, the pair would tackle two other evidentiary tasks: they'd visit Green Mountain Barrel in New Hampshire and learn more about the characteristics of the AT9 barrel, and they would stop at Winchester's massive Olin ammunition plant and discuss the properties of the nine-millimeter cartridges that had been used to murder three-fourths of the Ewell family.

The trip began inauspiciously. At a stopover in Salt Lake City, the flight was delayed by mechanical problems. Then the wings required deicing before takeoff. When Souza and Boudreau finally landed in Cincinnati, they'd missed their connecting flight to Baltimore. An alternate flight into Baltimore, via La Guardia, found the pair aboard the same plane that had broken down in Salt Lake—broken down again. After an hour's wait, they flew into La Guardia—too late for that connection.

They caught a commuter to DC, only to find that their baggage was missing.

Souza was known to keep a cool head in aggravating circumstances, but he was furious, and let the agents know it. The airline provided a voucher for taxi fare to Baltimore. They arrived only after a harrowing journey through the roughest sections of DC, in a taxi that sputtered and jerked as if it might run out of gas at any moment.

The next morning, November 14, after a few hours of sleep, they drove a rental car to Hanover and Three Rivers, and picked up barrels 412 and 419, respectively.

Then it was back to Baltimore for a flight to Portland, Maine, and a road trip to Center Conway, New Hampshire, home of Green Mountain Barrel Company.

For the next two days, Souza and Boudreau met with Branch Meanley, president of Green Mountain. As big as Dale Ewell had been, confident, educated, and articulate, Meanley provided manufacturing records and technical information about the rifling characteristics of his company's barrels. The FSO representatives were given a tour of the plant and witnessed the rifling process.

Meanley then produced the rifling button, with the actual pull-rod assembly that had been used in the manufacture of Ponce's AT9 barrel.

"Keep it," he said.

The bombshell of the day fell when Meanley casually mentioned that these barrels had a one-in-twelve rate of twist, that is, the rifling inside the bore made a complete rotation every twelve inches.

Boudreau sat up. "I've never seen that in this caliber."

"To my knowledge this rate of twist has not been used in other nine-millimeter barrels."

"I checked with Browning before we left," Boudreau told Souza. "It's a turn in ten on those models, not twelve. I think this barrel is unique."

"I agree," said Meanley. "You'll need to do some research, no doubt, but that rifling could be of significant investigative value."

Once back on the road, Boudreau said, "I'll compare the rate of twist on the murder bullets with test bullets fired from the Browning, then the AT9. Then I'll start contacting other nine-millimeter barrel manufacturers to see if anyone else makes a one-in-twelve twist."

Souza and Boudreau traveled on to East Elton, Illinois, and the Winchester/Olin ammunition manufacturing plant.

They signed confidentiality agreements that would protect Olin's proprietary rights, and witnessed the manufacture of ammo from lead block to boxed product. A meeting with company engineers followed. The engineers explained that impressed radial lines on the bases of some of the murder bullets were formed during production.

The shift foreman showed Boudreau engineering drawings of a tool called a coning punch—a device used to crimp the bullet jacket around the lead core. He explained that the marks were formed as the coning punch began to wear; the punch used on the murder bullets had been badly worn, and would have been replaced soon thereafter.

The foreman estimated that a maximum of seventy-five hundred rounds (out of millions over the years) with these unique marks had been produced in 1971. Here, too, the company provided Boudreau with a tool sample.

Souza and Boudreau enjoyed their flight home. There were no flight delays, and the value of the information gathered during the journey had raised their spirits.

Boudreau later wrote of his need to visit the Winchester plant:

> I did not know the specific origin of the radial pattern toolmarks; how many bullets with these had been made or how many toolmarks remained in April of 1992. Without some knowledge of these things I could not

evaluate the significance of the match. It was apparent I should go to the Winchester Ammunition plant to research these issues.

Boudreau reported after the trip to Winchester:

Winchester Group engineers and the production foremen had examined the (murder bullet) photographs and identified the source of the toolmarks in question.

Mr. Eberhart (a graduate engineer) showed us engineering drawings of a tool used in the making of 9mm full-metal jacket bullets. This tool is called a CONING PUNCH and serves a function of the closing of the bullet jacket around the lead bullet core.

Det. Souza and I were told that the marks . . . would have been made by a badly worn coning punch.

Mr. Eberhart and general foreman Greeling concluded that the maximum number of bullets with these marks would be about 7500.

The FBI lead analysis, his own matching of toolmarks, and information gathered at the Winchester plant led Boudreau to sum up:

Logic and reason lead us to the conclusion that twenty-one years later, the time of the murders, very few rounds of this ammunition would remain in existence.

These remaining rounds could be anywhere in the US, Canada, or other countries.

Consequently, the chance of a burglar or

other intruder bringing ammunition with
radial pattern toolmarks to the Ewell residence is so slight as to be beyond reason.

And in Boudreau's follow-up report about the Green
Mountain trip, he wrote:

Mr. Meanley pointed out that the 9mmP
Feather barrels were rifled with a turn in
12-inch rate of twist. Mr. Meanley said to
his knowledge this rate of twist in 9mmP
caliber was not used in other 9mmP caliber
barrels.
   The bullets fired from the (AT9) barrels
demonstrates a rate of twist the same as
the (murder) bullets.

Even with these compelling findings, Boudreau continued to test-fire and measure the rates of twist of hundreds
of bullets. He also studied the rates of twist of the AT9
barrels in his possession, using an ingenious design of his
own to build a measuring device from a barrel brush,
cleaning rod, and an eight-inch protractor.

Boudreau and Souza attended a number of SHOT
(Shooting, Hunting, and Outdoor Trade) shows. They met
with dozens of weapons manufacturers and importers to
determine the rifling characteristics of myriad nine-
millimeter barrels. At one show, the pair ran into Branch
Meanley. Meanley assured Boudreau that the criminalist's
extraordinary rate-of-twist experiments on the AT9 barrel
had been accurate—in fact, Meanley said the barrel had
a nominal one-in-twelve rate of twist, and tiny variances
in twist from barrel to barrel would be expected.

Even Boudreau's Herculean efforts could never be
enough to prove that somewhere there didn't exist a nine-
millimeter firearm with rifling characteristics identical to
those found on the Ewell murder bullets. Still, his relentless search turned up only one firearm—an Interarms Star

pistol—with a one-in-twelve, right-hand twist, and that weapon was manufactured with an enclosed barrel that "was not suitable for the barrel modifications, crude porting, giving rise to the coarse stria."

Another nine-millimeter weapon came to light in late 1994.

The District Attorney's Office had written additional search warrants on Dana's financial records. One substantial purchase stood out—a 1993 VISA card transaction from the Target Range in Van Nuys, just a few miles from Joel's neighborhood.

Target Range employees told DA investigator Pete Chavez that the buyer had purchased a Heckler & Koch model SP89 nine-millimeter pistol, a black, low-recoil weapon of paramilitary design.

But one clerk said the HK wasn't bought by a guy, it was a tall blond gal. "She must have been in here six different times."

The Target Range pulled their records, and Chavez produced a photograph.

"This her?" Chavez asked.

"Yeah, I think so. Here's the ATF form. The credit card must be a joint account with the Ewell guy, 'cause her name was on it. Here it is: Monica Zent."

Boudreau was confident his research had been sound, but as some of his work had involved areas new to him, he wanted a second opinion from a fellow criminalist and firearms expert. The main issue was to determine the truth about the physical evidence. There was a risk, of course, that he would be proven wrong in his conclusions. But he was prepared to take it, and if he were wrong, it was better to learn it now than in court.

Investigators and Boudreau's superiors at the Sheriff's Department had serious reservations about Boudreau's plan. Blatantly negative test results would make their case difficult even before arrests were made. But in the end, they agreed to seek a second opinion on the firearms work, and Boudreau contacted famed independent forensics expert Lucian Haag, who had re-created the shooting scenes in the notorious Ruby Ridge FBI case.

On August 4, Haag accepted the case. Boudreau asked Haag to:

1. Examine the physical evidence
2. Examine and critically review Boudreau's analysis of the evidence
3. Examine and critically review the research, experiments, and conclusions
4. Make recommendations concerning the work completed and suggest other experiments or examinations to be performed.
5. Prepare written reports of findings

On October 6, Souza, Boudreau, and Lieutenant Ron Wiley drove the evidence to Carefree, Arizona, the home of Luke Haag's Forensic Science Services. For the entire day, the quiet, unassuming Haag discussed the case with the detectives and Boudreau, and evidence was turned over to him and a receipt taken by the FSO representatives. Boudreau later provided Haag with a complete list of questions, the answers to which would provide the backup he needed to bolster his case—if his work had been accurate.

On December 7, 1994, Haag reported his findings to the FSO.

In short, he concluded:

1. A single firearm had fired all six evidence bullets.
2. The stria on the bullets were produced by porting the barrel of the murder weapon subsequent to manufacture.
3. The murder bullets were 9-millimeter, full-metal jacket, probably Winchester.

4. The Browning probably could not produce bullets identical to the murder bullets.
5. The marks at the base of all bullets found at the scene constituted a match, probably due to "damage or defects in the tool that rolls the heel of the bullet jacket into its final shape," from a "very limited population of bullets formed on the same tool."

Haag recommended studying evidence bullets under the electron microscope, as "minute chips of barrel metal might be imbedded in the bullet jackets." He also could not eliminate the AT9 as the weapon that had fired the bullets used in the murder.

In essence, Haag had effectively verified nearly all of Allen Boudreau's conclusions.

1995

". . . a fifty-fifty split . . ."

ONE

FROM CHILDHOOD, SOUZA HAD KNOWN THE crushing weariness of farm work, and later, the sting of sweat in his eyes as he slung rolls of roofing paper in triple-digit Fresno heat while earning extra money for his family.

But as the new year came, he felt an exhaustion more complete than any he'd experienced from the drudgery of menial labor. He lay back across his bed, staring at the ceiling, and at that moment realized it was at an end—the investigation had run its course. He'd done all he could think of, all Curtice and the brass could conjure up, gathered whatever evidence there was to gather, watched Boudreau work his magic.

Now the bosses would decide whether the almost three-year investigation had been fruitful. In turn, the District Attorney's Office would pass judgment on the likelihood that the evidence would produce convictions in a court-room.

Souza, Curtice, and Caudle, so that they could labor undisturbed, took a motel room across the street from the office and constructed a time line of the investigation.

Curtice, the talented one, worked with rolls of butcher paper, felt-tipped markers, and tape. Souza shuffled case papers and spewed out dates and facts from his remarkable memory. Caudle oversaw, probed, pushed, polished.

After two days of work, the trio produced a detailed time line that covered nearly three years and 140 feet of paper, to be added to as the case wound down.

As they viewed their handiwork, Souza found even he was surprised at the extent of circuitous, bizarre events that had been case number 92-15285.

When Souza wrote up a fourteen-page arrest declaration Undersheriff John Swenning rejected it outright. He wanted far more detail. Swenning ordered his staff to work with Souza (admittedly not a born writer) to produce a precise, professional draft for submission to the district attorney.

The days dragged on as draft after draft was rejected, and all the while the Undersheriff needed constant assurances about Ponce.

"What if Jack Ponce doesn't roll and give up Radovcich?"

Souza told Swenning he felt certain that Ponce would come through once the kid learned he'd be facing homicide charges.

"How certain?" Swenning wanted to know.

Souza picked a number. "Hell, eighty percent."

But Swenning continued to push for more information, more assurances on Ponce. Souza finally reached his boiling point; when Caudle asked for what seemed the ten-millionth draft, he exploded.

"Fuck this! I'm in my third year on this goddamned case. My farm is a disaster, my family thinks I'm the world's biggest asshole, and my bosses want to grind me into hamburger over a couple of goddamned sentences on the warrants. I quit! You guys finish it. I'm going home and see if my wife even recognizes me!"

But Souza did not quit. Caudle, ever diplomatic and understanding, let his detective blow off steam, and then it was back to work as if nothing had happened.

* * *

The end result of hundreds of hours of labor: a Declaration in Support of Warrant of Arrest that ran to forty-seven pages (an extraordinary length, even for a homicide case; most were five or six pages), including a fifteen-page preface that outlined the crime and the evidence against Dana and Joel.

Caudle and Wiley used the massive time line they'd produced to make a formal presentation to District Attorney Ed Hunt (known as a cop's DA) and Deputy DA Jim Oppliger.

When the detectives finished their presentation, Oppliger and Hunt remained silent.

Then Hunt grinned. "Go get 'em," he said.

One urgent situation developed before the arrests. Souza learned that Dana had moved his grandmother out of the Turlock nursing home and into a rest home in Studio City—less than ten minutes from the home of Joel Radovcich.

He ran down the number of the Studio City rest home and contacted the manager. How was Mrs. Mitchell? he asked.

Fine, the manager said, but her grandson had only brought two changes of clothing when he dropped her off. And, she'd just had hip surgery and wasn't supposed to be moved, but he ran her all the way down here in the backseat of his car.

Jesus, Souza thought. "Where is she? What part of the home?"

Got a nice room, the supervisor said. Dana said his grandmother liked fresh air, and her room has a door that opens right to the outside. The 7-Eleven is just next door.

The lockpick.

Souza immediately faxed a photo of Joel down to the rest home, demanding that the supervisor post extra security around Mrs. Mitchell, and asking him to call the police at once if Joel were found on the premises.

First Austin, now Glee?

TWO

OPERATION THREE STOOGES EVOLVED INTO A complex multiple-arrest scenario.

Three arrest warrant teams were dispatched on Thursday, March 2, 1995: Mindy Ybarra headed the team that would pick up Dana at 5663 East Park Circle Drive. Ernie Burk, Sergeant Hollis, and backup drove to West Hills to arrest Joel Radovcich. Chris Curtice's team was charged with arresting Jack Ponce.

But first the arrest warrants, completed after business hours, needed a judge's signature. Souza and Caudle tracked down Superior Court Judge Lawrence O'Neil at his residence, where he and his wife were hosting a dinner party. The judge asked the detectives to wait while he slipped into his bedroom and studied the arrest declaration.

As Souza and Caudle were cooling their heels, Sergeant Hollis paged them. Souza phoned Hollis, who said that he and his heavily armed surveillance team had tailed Joel Radovcich and his brother Peter to—where else?—the Taco Bell restaurant across from the 7-Eleven Famous Phone, at Fallbrook and Saticoy near West Hills.

"How many civilians inside?"

"Just the staff and one long-hair at a table, beside the Radovcich assholes."

"Are you going take him at the Taco Smell?"

"We've gotta take him here," said Hollis, a SWAT

commander. "The way this bastard drives we may never catch him again."

"You can't move," Souza said. "We don't have the warrant yet."

"Shit! What's the holdup?"

"Hang tight, Sarge. The judge is going over the papers as we speak. Should be any second."

"I'm hanging, I'm hanging. Looks like Joel's about to tear into another green burrito. Belch."

The minutes dragged by. The judge's wife left her guests and came looking for her husband.

"Has he given you an answer yet?" she asked.

"No, ma'am."

Mrs. O'Neil held up a forefinger. "Let me check."

She went into the bedroom, closing the door behind her. Souza and Caudle paced and compulsively checked their watches. They kept a cell-phone line open to Sergeant Hollis.

Then the door opened a crack. The judge stuck his hand out, giving the detectives a big thumbs-up sign.

Souza shouted to Hollis, "Go! Go!"

"My pleasure, Johnny boy."

Hollis and two team members, assault rifles in hand, burst through the doors of the Taco Bell. As frightened employees scattered, Hollis shouted to Joel and Peter, "Police officers! Get your hands where we can see 'em! Now!"

The Radovcichs were ordered into a felony arrest position—facedown, fingers laced behind their heads. The poor long-hair had to rush into the men's room—he'd wet his pants.

Once Joel was cuffed and dragged to his feet, Ernie Burk strolled into the restaurant. Hollis nodded toward Burk, and asked Joel, "You recognize this gentleman?"

Joel, silent, simply hung his head.

As Souza would later see, Joel had bright orange hair when arrested; Souza was contacted by a Beverly Hills hairstylist who said Joel had requested that she bleach his hair blond. She asked Joel if he had previously dyed his hair black. He lied, claiming he hadn't, and when she applied the blond hair coloring, the reaction turned his hair a shocking orange hue, infuriating Joel.

While Peter Radovcich wasn't under arrest at that point, Hollis detained him so he'd not have a chance to warn Ponce.

At the same time in Fresno, Souza, Caudle, Lieutenant Wiley and Deputy District Attorney Jim Oppliger rushed to the Fresno Air Terminal. They boarded a private jet bound for Ontario, California. (Use of the aircraft had been donated by the CEO of Harris Ranch, a local cattle and meatpacking operation.)

The jet touched down at nine-thirty that evening. Detectives Curtice and Moore and Ontario PD officers were waiting. The team scrambled to TGI Friday's, where Ponce was serving beer to a number of FSO undercover detectives (who made sure to order one more round before their bartender was taken into custody).

So that he might encourage Ponce's cooperation later, Souza thought it best that he not personally arrest the suspect. He remained outside when Oppliger, Lieutenant Wiley, and Sergeant Bailey entered the TGIF and located the restaurant manager. Wiley explained the situation, asking that the manager tell Ponce he's needed in the kitchen.

When he made his way into the kitchen a few minutes later, a shocked Ponce was taken into custody. He learned he was being charged with three counts of homicide.

Souza was waiting in the backseat when Ponce was placed inside the sheriff's car.

"Hello, Jack."

Ponce, hands cuffed behind his back, started to speak.

"No," Souza said, jabbing a finger in the air. "You are going to sit there and shut up. I'll do the talking. You had your chance a year ago. You could have been the hero. Instead you're looking at three counts of murder. How old are you, twenty-four? Even after years of appeals, you'll be lucky to reach forty. Hell of a note, huh?"

Ponce turned away, gazing at the restaurant as Curtice slid behind the wheel and Caudle jumped into the passenger seat.

On the road, Souza said, "Jack, I wish I could feel sorry for you, but damn it, I can't. How many chances did we give you? Even your old man tried to get you to use your head. But you were so determined to protect a couple of murderers! What is with you? Well, just so you know, we're on our way to the San Bernardino County lockup. Your first time inside, Jack?"

Ponce was trying his best to look bored, but Souza saw fear behind the poker face.

"Jack, I haven't met anyone yet who thought prison was fun. You're gonna be in there with a bunch of perverts and guys who'd slit your throat for a pack of cigarettes. Was a time you could have called us up, spilled what you knew, and we might have cut a deal . . . unless you were in that house when the Ewells were killed. If that's the case, nobody can save your sorry ass.

"If you think we're bluffing, we have plenty of evidence, Jack. We have Dana paying Joel, we have ballistics that proves an AT9 was used, we have . . . well, you'll see soon enough, Jack. You'll see soon enough."

Ponce and Joel were on their way to jail. But where was the alleged ringleader? Where was Dana Ewell?

THREE

An undercover motor home had parked near Dana's house that afternoon. Detectives saw him drive in, then at 5 P.M., drive off again.

The detectives wondered if he'd heard something and was fleeing. But at the time, the arrest warrants had yet to be signed. The undercover personnel called Souza and asked for instructions.

"Let him go," Souza said. "He'll be back."

But Dana never made it home.

Ponce, as Souza had promised, was booked into San Bernardino County Jail for the night. Detectives and Jim Oppliger checked into a nearby hotel and the celebratory beer flowed. By the early morning only Souza and Oppliger were still awake. They soaked in the hotel Jacuzzi, sipping canned beer and planning the prosecution.

Oppliger, after Souza filled in much of the story that couldn't be fit into the massive warrant, told Souza that the more he heard, the better he felt about a successful prosecution.

Hoisting a can of Miller Lite, Souza said, "They're going down."

Oppliger raised his own beer.

"You're goddamned right they are."

* * *

En route to Fresno, with Curtice driving and Caudle riding shotgun, Souza continued to pressure Ponce. At one point Ponce pretended to sleep, but Souza kept on talking until they stopped at a Barstow convenience store.

Curtice and Souza bought a few provisions. When they came out they saw Caudle leaning into the backseat and talking with Ponce. Caudle surreptitiously extended his hand out the car window, waving back his detectives.

Caudle and Ponce went on for another half hour before Caudle stepped out of the car.

"Okay," Caudle told Souza, "we've been talking golf, and I'm making some headway with the kid. How about you take shotgun now and I'll sit in back with Ponce for the rest of the trip?"

"Shit, John," Curtice said. "Ponce must not like you."

"Now that hardly seems possible," Souza said.

Meanwhile an APB had been issued on Dana Ewell. The bulletin advised that Dana was wanted for three counts of homicide, and possibly armed with a nine-millimeter semiautomatic HK pistol.

The HK SP89, purchased by Monica Zent with Dana's credit card, had not been recovered. What if, detectives speculated, the HK had been bought for use in the event a warrant was issued for Dana's arrest?

Ponce was escorted into the FSO for booking. At long last, after a talk with his father, he agreed to talk—but to Caudle and Curtice, not to Souza. Ponce was escorted to the interview room. A few tense hours later, an ecstatic Caudle emerged. He beamed at Souza.

"It was his gun."

Souza jumped to his feet. "He said that?"

"He also said Joel confessed to him. All the details."

Souza was jumping both fists. "All right!"

"That's not all. You're not going to believe what else."

Souza and Undersheriff Swenning sat down and ran the Ponce tape:

"The date is 3-3-95 and the time is 2010 hours. This is Detective Curtice and Sergeant Caudle, reporting on case number 92-15285, a PC 187, here for the purposes of an interview with Ernest Jack Ponce. Ah, Jack, you brought to our attention that you have some information in this, our fifth interview, correct?"

"Yes."

Curtice asked some foundational questions, establishing Ponce's relationship with the Radovcich brothers.

"Now," Curtice said, "Jack, why don't you explain in your, your own words, what information you have and when it first came about?"

"Yeah. Well, Joel? He began to inquire about purchasing a gun, and I said I didn't know where he could find one, but I let him have an old Llama .380 that belonged to my ex-stepfather."

"Did he ever say why he wanted to buy or borrow a gun?"

"No. I wasn't that curious. But when he gave that back he was still trying to get one but didn't, uh, want to go through regular channels."

"Why was he afraid?"

"He was always, you know, kind of shady."

After some discussion of the .380, Joel's pager, and time the two spent together, Ponce said Joel again approached him about buying a gun. The request was more urgent than ever.

"Okay, Jack. When was that?"

"April. Approximately April of '92. Around my birthday, the tenth. I said no. But I was out of money, and the owner of Pete's work was selling me a van."

Ponce told Joel he needed five hundred dollars for the van, and Joel said he needed a Featherlite AT9. They checked out the weapon at a gun show, then Joel gave him "something like" one thousand dollars in hundred-dollar bills, which Jack deposited so he could write a check for the weapon. He said he bought the AT9 and an extra clip, picked it up after the required fifteen-day wait-

ing period, and then delivered it to Joel in Pete Radovcich's garage.

"So you never fired the gun," said Curtice.

"No."

"Okay, what happens then?"

Ponce said Joel began to construct a silencer in Judy
Radovich's garage, using, "a tube . . . black PVC pipe."

"Did he ever fire it?"

"Yeah, he fired it."

"Where?"

"In his garage . . . into a big piece of wood. A stump."

"Did it make any sound?"

"Ah . . . like pop."

It had taken Joel a week or so to perfect his silencer.
Ponce said he was at the Radovcich house "quite a bit,"
during that period, and, in addition to the PVC pipe, he
saw Joel working with tennis balls.

"Did he say why he was making it?"

"No. I just assumed he did it to sell to someone else
for a profit."

"Where, ah, where would he keep the gun?"

"In the garage, top of the garage."

"Hidden pretty well, I guess?"

"Yeah."

"Is it still there now?"

"No."

"Do you know where it is now?"

"I know where parts of it are. Important parts."

"Uh . . . where are they now?"

"The Reseda area. I'll have to show you where. One of
them is—"

"Is it—"

"The barrel."

Silence. Then, "Okay, is, is . . . When you say it's in
that area, is it just lying in the street or—"

"No, it's in the ground."

"It's buried?"

"Yeah."

More silence. "So you buried different parts of the gun in different locations?"

"That's it. That's about it."

"Okay. Let's back up. After you saw him making the silencer, what's the next incident you saw?"

"We, uh . . . I guess we, me and Pete, tried to keep in touch with him, to call him, and then he just shows up with this stuff and says—I believe I was with Pete—he had a bag of stuff. It was the gun pretty much mangled. He'd taken it apart and drilled into it, you know the numbers were drilled out, and then he said 'just get rid of this stuff.' "

Here, Ponce grew quite vague about the location and date and why Joel would make such a request. He backtracked to a time "around the Rodney King riots" when Joel had shown up at Jack's girlfriend's apartment.

"He was worried, said he didn't know what went wrong."

"But he didn't tell you what it was?"

"Yeah, right then and there, um . . . I'm trying to remember. I think it was then, or the next day. It was like, 'some people got hurt.' I believe he said three people."

At that point the tape ended. Souza hurriedly flipped it over.

Curtice's voice again: "Side two. Time is 2042 hours. Jack you heard side 'A' click off?"

"Yes."

"During the time I took it out, did I ask you any questions?"

"No."

"Did I make you any promises?"

"No."

"Did I threaten you in any way?"

"No."

"Okay, you were telling us you were staying at Leticia's apartment near UCLA and Joel stayed there a few days during the riots, and he started telling you some things regarding three people getting hurt. What did he say regarding these three people?"

Ponce sighed heavily. "I don't remember his exact words. I just said, you know, I don't wanna hear it. We were driving around. I was trying to tell him his options."

"Did he ever say to you, that he committed—"

"Ah . . ."

"The murder of three people?"

Ponce stuttered and stalled before admitting, "He said triple homicide, but he didn't . . . at this point he didn't say exactly."

There! Souza thought.

Curtice tried to pin down his witness on dates and times from the day the gun was picked up to when Ponce first heard about the murders from Joel, but the best Ponce could do was "a few weeks or so."

"Okay, Jack. You said you know where the barrel is buried. Do you know where that nine-millimeter handgun is?"

"Ah, no. It seemed like a drainage thing, in Calabasas."

"Would it come out somewhere where you could find it?"

"By now, you'd probably have to go looking for it."

"Okay, after Joel stayed with you at Leticia's, do you know where he went then?"

"Then he stayed at the Half Moon Hotel on Pico for a while."

"And after we spoke with you, did you have contact with Joel?"

"Yeah, we were at Pete's. Um, he ah, at that time, just blew it off, said don't pay attention to them."

"Did he say why this occurred?"

"Yeah, but he said something, uh, a lot of money, like eight million dollars, he would get a fifty-fifty split."

"With who?"

"With Dana Ewell."

"Had you ever met Dana?"

"No, I heard about him. Joel was upset that Dana was

spending so much money on his girlfriend, cutting into his share. Joel said Dana was real calculating, kind of a sleazy guy, and . . . would you like me to give you more details of what happened?"

"Uh-huh."

"About the killing of his parents, his sister . . . I told Joel that if Dana would have that done to them, he wouldn't think twice about you. But Joel said, no, we have this money deal."

"Did Dana ever try to double-cross Joel in any way?"

"No, he trusted Dana. I . . . I'm trying to remember what happened . . ."

"No, go ahead."

"Sometime after the *LA Times* article came out he started telling me things about these three people who were killed."

"Where did he learn all this stuff?"

"Ah, commando kind of books."

"Okay. And had Joel mentioned anything about getting money from Dana?"

"He said if he needs money, he just asks Dana and Dana gives it to him, paying for helicopter school, but Dana's not giving him enough, and he's pissed, especially when Dana spent that money on his girlfriend."

"Was he approached by Dana first?"

"Yeah. At some point, Dana asked him that, and he said, 'sure.' "

"You mean just like that? Did they think Dana was going to get the money right away?"

"Something about age twenty-five or something. Actually, Dana had to prove he had that much money to Joel, you providing the paperwork."

"Did he say where Dana got that paperwork?"

"Is there a safe in the house? Or somewhere. It's put away."

"Did he ever mention Dana's alibi?"

"Said Dana had a great alibi. He was with his girlfriend, maybe her dad. He was gonna sob and everything when he heard the news. And later, Joel said Dana put some message on his pager, a code, run for your life."

Again, Curtice took Ponce through the process of purchasing and modifying the AT9. He followed with questions about Joel's friends and relatives, trying to learn if anyone else had known about Joel's involvement. Ponce insisted he believed Joel had told no one else.

"Okay, Jack. Earlier, you mentioned that Dana was spending so much on Monica. Did he ever mention she knew what was going on?"

"No, but it sounded like she didn't know and didn't care because she was getting all that cash and stuff."

Jack said the only other money he had gotten from Joel was one thousand dollars in cash that Joel had brought into TGI Friday's, money that he "assumed" had come from Dana. He claimed it had been Joel's idea to say his car had been broken into and the AT9 stolen, and Joel recommended a lawyer at some point.

"Okay, Jack. Now I got to ask you, we tried to work out a polygraph for you a year and a half ago. Now, for somebody who just happened to buy the gun and didn't know what it was for, why was it so difficult to get you to talk?"

"Yeah, well. It's . . . I mean up until the point that I gave it to him. But when I found out he killed three people, that's . . . accessory to triple homicide. I just thought, I'm really screwed, and I tried to cover for him, I thought, I fucked up. Sorry."

"Jack, have you ever known Joel to be employed?"

"Ah, I don't think so."

"Any doubt in your mind as to how he's obtaining one-hundred-dollar bills?"

"No, he told me they're from Dana."

"Have you ever met Dana?"

"No."

When questioned again by Curtice, Jack said Dana and Joel had passports and plans to leave the country and go "somewhere in Europe." Curtice asked Jack if he thought

Joel was, or wanted to be, a professional hit man.

"Not that I know of."

"Okay. Were you at the house when the shooting went down?"

"No."

"And everything you told us today is the truth?"

"Yes."

"Have you ever been to Fresno before today?"

"I may have drove through it, but I never stopped."

And then Souza listened as Ponce described the murders. It was something he'd begun to believe he'd never hear. And incredibly, Ponce knew where the AT9 barrel was buried.

FOUR

On the overcast morning of March 4, 1995, Souza, Curtice, and Caudle began an extraordinary day. The detectives, with Jack Duty, Robert Brown, and other technicians in tow, transported Jack Ponce from the Fresno County Jail to the San Fernando Valley area of Southern California.

At 3:45 P.M. Ponce led them to Peter Radovcich's former apartment, and down an alley he'd followed after Peter had run upstairs the night they'd disposed of evidence. Ponce showed investigators where he'd climbed a fence, entered an empty lot adjacent to a municipal tennis court at Lull and Geyser Streets. The investigators brought out metal detectors. The search proceeded at a glacial pace until Curtice grew weary.

Frustrated, Curtice shouted, "Hey, Jack. Come over here!"

Ponce shuffled over to where Curtice waited.

"Goddamn it, Jack, where did you bury it?"

Ponce looked around. He pointed to a spot in the middle of the lot. Curtice manned a shovel, removed about a foot of thick grass and earth, and found, to everyone's relief and amazement, a rusted, drilled gun barrel about eighteen inches long. Duty and his people took over and began photographing and collecting the vital evidence. Souza danced a jig, overjoyed that a propitious wind had finally blown their way. And when he settled down he

281

remembered the claim of the psychic the Ewell brothers had hired, that the gun had been buried.

Over the next day and half, Ponce directed the detectives to a hillside where he and Peter had tossed Joel's Air Jordan shoes (though the terrain proved too steep for effective searching), to storm drains near the intersection of Mulholland and Canyon that he said contained parts of the Browning pistol, and to a trash Dumpster on Del Valle Street.

Ponce said the Paladin books that Joel studied before the murders had been thrown into that same Dumpster. The 1992 evidence disposal operation had been thorough. Investigators failed to find a single piece of evidence on the hillsides or in the storm drains.

But they had the barrel from the murder weapon.

March 4, 1995 marked Dana Ewell's last day as a free man.

Giddy investigators were planning a victory party for that evening, but before they could tuck into their steaks at the Van Nuys Sizzler, Lieutenant Ron Wiley paged Caudle.

Wiley said he'd contacted John Zent and asked the FBI agent for Dana's whereabouts. Zent told Wiley he didn't know where Dana was, or Monica for that matter.

Souza got on the phone and asked Wiley to inform Zent that there was also an APB out on Monica's car, and if her car was spotted by police, Monica would be doing the low crawl of a felony vehicle stop.

Suddenly, Zent got helpful.

Dana's attorney, Richard Berman, had been attending a California Bar Association meeting in Long Beach when Zent reached him with the news that an arrest warrant and APB had been issued for Dana. Berman phoned Dana and advised him to drive to Long Beach. Then Berman called Caudle and said that he and his client would await the arrival of FSO members at the Long Beach Police Headquarters.

To a detective who has spent years running down a suspect, the payoff comes with the arrest. And Souza wouldn't miss it for anything.

Souza, Caudle, and Curtice grabbed a few quick bites of steak, planned what they'd do when they met Dana and Berman, and then scrambled to the Long Beach PD.

Dana and Berman waited at a conference table. Dana said not a word.

Berman said, "Officers, I'd like to discuss a few things before—"

But Caudle, stepping forward, cut him off. "Stand up, Dana."

Berman sputtered as Caudle brushed past him and seized Dana, now on his feet. On cue, Curtice moved between Berman and his client.

"We'll talk later, Counselor," Caudle said. "After we book your client."

Caudle said to his detectives, "Gentlemen? Would you?"

Souza grabbed one of Dana's arms, Curtice the other, and they led Dana down the hall. He'd be held for release to Fresno County sheriff's deputies the next morning.

"So, Dana," Souza said. "Did you ever think this day would come?"

Dana stared straight ahead, chin in the air. His new life had just begun.

Of the APB that had been put out on Dana on Saturday, March 4, in which it was noted that Dana might be armed with a semiautomatic weapon, Richard Berman later complained, "I had told the Sheriff's Department repeatedly throughout this investigation that if they wanted him, all they had to do was call and he would surrender. He was never a fugitive. The second he learned he was wanted, we made arrangements to turn him in."

*   *   *

A sheriff's van picked Dana up in Long Beach the day after his arrest. Later that afternoon, Souza and Curtice sat with Dana in the FSO interview room and filled out an arrest tag. Then they shackled him in leg irons and led him away.

"Hey, Dana," Souza said. "Ernie Burk asked me to tell you he found that gun he was looking for."

Dana seemed puzzled by the allusion to his comment, made years before to Sean Shelby, that "Ernie Burk couldn't find a gun in a gun store." Then realization seemed to sweep across his face.

The detectives escorted Dana out the east exit of the Sheriff's Department and marched him down the long access ramp toward the new County Jail. Print reporters, photographers, and television news crews were waiting. A TV reporter thrust a microphone towards Dana.

"Were you involved in the murder of your family?"

"Absolutely not!"

"Not in any way?"

"Not in any way. This is ridiculous!"

Souza's glare was caught on film by the newspaper photographers.

The detectives led Dana through the jail's sally port (a secured area into which vehicles could drive before discharging prisoners) and handed over their weapons to correctional officers.

As was done with every prisoner, Dana first had to answer questions from the jail nurse. Was he on drugs? Did he have any serious medical problems?

She instructed him to read a dental form, one used to request free dental work while in custody. The detectives waited as Dana looked the form over. He'd been cool, even cocky, and now he grinned.

"Hey, you know what?" Dana said. "I think I'll have my teeth cleaned!"

Shaking his head, Souza unshackled Dana and sent him

through the metal detector. And then, Dana Ewell, voted Most Likely to Succeed at his high school, disappeared behind the steel door.

Souza and Curtice waved after him and strolled out into the sunlight.

A few days later, Curtice received from California Department of Justice examiner Douglas Mansfield a copy of Ponce's polygraph report. The test series consisted of relevant questions interspersed with irrelevant and control questions. The most relevant:

Q. On April 19, 1992, were you physically inside the Ewell residence when the family was shot?
A. No.
Q. Did you shoot any of the Ewell family members?
A. No.
Q. Did you know that Joel was going to use that gun to commit murder prior to April 19, 1992?
A. No.
Q. Did you know that the gun was going to be used in the Ewell murders?
A. No.

After analysis of the charts produced during this examination, it is the opinion of this examiner that PONCE was truthful in his answers in all the relevant questions.

                              Douglas K. Mansfield

Peter Radovcich was arrested on March 8 at Souza's insistence, and over the objections of the DA's Office. According to Ponce, Peter had helped dispose of the murder weapon and other evidence; Souza wasn't about to ignore that.

Peter was located at his job at Sketchly-Mason Plumbing. When Souza showed up with uniformed backup, Peter froze in his tracks.

"Peter," Souza said. "You know why we're here."

Peter sagged.

"I know," Souza told him. "Come on, we're going to Fresno."

Once in custody, Peter needed no encouragement to turn State's evidence against his brother.

Detectives then executed search warrants on the homes of the suspects. First searched was the home of Ponce's mother; detectives found an address book with Joel's pager number and a receipt for the AT9.

A search of 5663 East Park Circle produced six boxes of nine-millimeter ammunition, a police scanner, Joel's passport, and the box to the Heckler and Koch handgun that Monica Zent had bought in 1993.

But where was the gun itself?

When Judy Radovcich's home was searched, investigators found another police scanner and a rack of drill bits. Samples of the shavings found in the bottom of the rack were tested by Luke Haag. Some were nearly identical in metallic content to the barrel from Ponce's AT9, and one was similar to a tiny metal shaving found on the sweatshirt of Glee Ewell.

A representative of International Creative Management, the renowned Beverly Hills talent agency, contacted Souza after the arrests. The ICM representative had seen Dana's name in the papers and said Dana had recently applied for a position with her firm.

A copy of the application, faxed to Souza, included a résumé featuring Dana's impressive academic achievements, and his bogus business experience as covered by regional newspapers.

But it was a quote from Dana's cover letter that struck Souza:

> *To cut to the chase, I thumbed my nose at the traditional American establishment and became a teenage entrepreneur in the process. I have a reputation for doing absolutely anything to get the job done, going well above and beyond the normal call of duty.*
>
> *I am a person who thrives in a dog-eat-dog, survival of the fittest type of environment.*

The missing HK pistol turned up later when an examination of Dana's employment application led Souza and Curtice to a Los Angeles "safe house"—an apartment rented by Dana under an alias—and, in turn, a Fresno storage unit that had been rented by Dana's defense team.

Beside the HK, the storage-unit search produced one more item of interest: a receipt from a Woodland Hills firm called The Privacy Connection.

Investigators learned that Dana had in October 1992 purchased a thousand-dollar device called a Sweep, used in searching for electronic eavesdropping equipment. Souza traced the initial Privacy Connection call made by Dana to Michael Dowling's office phone. Seconds before calling the Privacy Connection, Dana had been on the phone with FBI agent John Zent.

The days and weeks following the arrest were a whirlwind for John Philip Souza.

The phone jangled ceaselessly—calls from citizens, other law-enforcement agencies, well-wishers inside and outside the Sheriff's office, offers from the *Maury Povich Show* and other tabloid television programs, requests for media interviews. Suddenly, Souza was a hero, a celebrity.

The *Weekly World News* trumpeted:

MUTT 'N' JEFF COPS BUST
REAL-LIFE RICHIE RICH!
MILLIONAIRE'S SON HIRED HIT MAN
TO KILL HIS FAMILY, SAY POLICE

The lurid article featured photos of the victims, a brooding Joel Radovcich, and Dana being led to jail by "potbellied Detective John Souza and his string-bean partner Ernie Burk" (though the other detective pictured was Chris Curtice).

It was all a shock to a man who hadn't spoken English until he was five and had, along with his siblings, Tony, Anne, and Barbara, picked cotton to keep the family from starving.

FIVE

THE LEGAL BATTLES (SOME COVERED BY CNN, the *Today Show*, and other national media) that followed the arrests would not be limited to the criminal charges against Dana and Joel.

In the event Dana was found culpable in the murder of his family, one-half his lost inheritance would go to his grandmother, Glee Mitchell, and one-half to Austin Ewell's estate.

Just four days after the arrest warrants had been issued, Michael Dowling, as executor for the Ewell estate, asked the courts to freeze all assets of Dana Ewell. And Dowling asked that Richard Berman repay to the estate the nearly half million dollars that Dana had paid him as a defense retainer.

Dale's brothers followed with a series of complaints they hoped would ensure that Dana could not use his inheritance to buy his way out of trouble.

Dan Ewell filed a pair of complaints in Probate Court; he contended Dana had caused the murders, and asked that Dana be denied access to $140,000 that should have passed to Dana from the James J. Mitchell Trust.

And Russel Georgeson, on behalf of Dan and the uncles, sought a temporary restraining order that would forbid Michael Dowling from distributing inheritance monies to Dana. After all, Dale's brothers explained, their father's will had expressly stated, "I deliberately make no provision for Dana Ewell," and they were honoring the patriarch's wishes.

If successful, all this legal maneuvering would have one chilling effect on Dana's defense: He'd be forced to rely upon the Public Defender's Office to save him from a date with the executioner.

But then, in a move that would further damage a family already traumatized by the murders, Dana's aunt, Betty Whitted, broke ranks with her brothers and announced she would forgo her $680,000 of the inheritance and make it available to Dana for his defense fund.

Joel's family put up the money to retain Woolf's law firm, but the legal wrangling over Dana's inheritance led to numerous delays in the arraignment. On March 24, over the objections of her brothers, Betty Whitted signed over her inheritance rights to Richard Berman.

On March 30, no less than a dozen lawyers—representing the Ewell estate, Dana, Glee Mitchell, Mitchell's relatives, and Dale Ewell's brothers—packed a superior court hearing.

"Dana doesn't want the money for a vacation in Hawaii," Richard Berman thundered. "It's to prove his innocence, to spare himself the gas chamber, which is where his greedy uncles would prefer to see him go so they can go to Hawaii."

The bearded Russel Georgeson pushed his glasses up on his nose, and countered, "Mr. Berman is sadly mistaken in his allegations. Period."

After Judge Stephen Henry ruled that he would grant Betty Whitted's wishes and transfer the money to Dana, Berman rushed up to Souza, and said, "Great job!"

For his part, Souza wasn't sure to what "great job" Berman had been referring, but the attorney's law firm billings would be considerably fatter for the ruling.

Berman's rapture was short-lived.

Dale's brothers won a temporary restraining order in Ohio, preventing Betty Whitted from transferring money from her father's estate until a hearing determined if she would remain as executrix. The next day, with Public Defender Peter Jones representing him, Dana Ewell pleaded innocent at his arraignment.

A few weeks later, Betty Whitted officially revoked her offer to give Dana money for his defense; Berman was off the case for good, and Dana, now completely destitute, would rely upon the public to fund his defense.

Souza's desk was covered with letters and cards that had been written years before by Dana Ewell. Some went back to Dana's high-school days, sent to a girl named Elke. Others had been handed over to police by Dana's grandmother. Souza hoped the varied correspondence would provide some insight into Dana Ewell's emotional makeup.

From an early letter to Elke:

> *How are you! I totally love girls! I mean it! Not that I was ever homo or anything, it's just that I do nothing in Switzerland but sit on this guy's yacht and look at girls in bathing suits through binoculars! . . . Send me a beautiful picture or I'll pretend I'm Ozzie Osbourne and cut off your head with a chainsaw [sic] and then kiss you.*
>
> *Dana Ewell*

From a 1989 letter to Elke:

> *I wanted to write to you because I haven't heard from you in a long time! I can imagine your school year should be terrific—my junior year was the best yet. However, senior year is now becoming extra sweet—I got a new car. No, not a Porsche, but a much more reasonable, my father extols to me, Mercedes 190E—New! . . . I'm going to put a phone in next week—they are rather convenient when you think about it . . .*

I'll be hosting a German exchange student via our high school. It will be a girl—FUN! Actually, all the German babes I saw in Germany were a little too hairy for my standards—maybe, I can Americanize her with my portable Norelco! ...

I would love to go to Beverly Hills High like you—I can imagine the types of people—I think I would fit in well! I hope you are! ...

Maybe we can catch a movie or something—or a Lakers game, I have courtside seats via my Mom's connections with L.A. based attorneys. I had McEnroe's seats last time to be precise ...

I really did think of you when I wrote this letter— your life better be on the up and up or I'll come down there and spank you.

Dana Ewell

And another:

Just something I picked up in Harrod's [sic], England! It's very small and very expensive, very you! ... You look so beautiful, you know. I have, oh shit, totally fallen in love with you! I love you! I promise I will come down to party your ass off within the next 2 months. I hope you like to party the rich way, believe me, it's the only way to go! Oh God I love you! ...

Registration is tomorrow, fuck, better be sober. We'll talk on the phone, don't worry, I Love You!

Dana Ewell

The last one was Dana at his self-promoting best:

I'm sure you didn't mean that all guys do not have feelings when you said that. I certainly do. Guess What? I am up to 1420 on my S.A.T. now. I do not mean to brag, lie, or anything else derogatory; how-ever, I have beaten all the dumb orientals in my school, you know, the orientals that everyone raves about so. HA! When you think of the ideal, affluent businessman, do you think of a short Japanese guy? I don't think so.

Dana Ewell

For grandmother Glee Mitchell's ninetieth birthday, both Monica and Dana had sent greeting cards with personal notes:

Have a wonderful birthday!! 90 years old is quite a feat—and you look great! Hope you are feeling great, too! Make a big wish when you blow out the candles on your birthday cake!!

Love, Monica Zent (Dana's girlfriend)

And from Dana:

How grateful I am to have a grandmother as sweet as you!

But scrawled in pencil along the top border of Dana's card in an uneven hand were the words:

Dear Dana I am sorry to do this but I am sorry I am tired of living—so forgive me please—

The handwriting, Souza thought, looked similar to samples of Glee Mitchell's writing he had on file. Still, with Dana's moving her to Los Angeles, and with the death of Austin Ewell, he wondered . . .

Then he went through all the Ponce interview transcripts, and reread a portion that had stuck in his mind during the first listening—Ponce said Joel had begun to experiment with poisons.

Two new letters, one sent by Ben Ewell, the other by Richard Ewell, arrived in Souza's mail.

The first correspondence, this to Ben from a college roommate of Tiffany's, provided a poignant look into the victim's short life and her quiet impact on those around her:

> She had so much going for her, so many unfulfilled dreams. I loved her and my parents loved her like a daughter. We've agonized over this for 3 ⅔ years and it's time justice is done.
>
> I've not talked or heard from Dana since Dec. '94. I think it would shake him a bit, to see me after all this time . . .
>
> I dream of Tiffany often, and she says she's happy, and it's time to let go. I'm not ready to let go, not until justice for her and her parent's [sic] murderers is done and served.

In the second envelope, Richard enclosed photos of his father's basement as it had looked days after the fatal explosion. He explained that his father had been blown ten to fifteen feet back from a generator, landing on a pile of plastic storage bags. The burning bags had caused Austin's most severe injuries. Richard wrote that he and a neighbor later relighted the water heater that firefighters believed triggered the explosion.

Richard added:

> Interestingly, I do not recall any signs of an explosion on the water heater itself. The safety doors were still in place and I don't remember seeing any burn or smoke smudges around the pilot light door area.

Richard nonetheless concluded the explosion had been an "unfortunate, tragic accident and no foul play was involved," and he thanked the detective for his "tireless efforts."

For his part, Souza felt less certain that it had been merely an accident. He persuaded his superiors that it was worth looking into Austin's death. Ernie Burk was sent to Ohio, where he haunted airstrips that Dana might have used to fly in Joel. He talked to the volunteer firemen who'd responded to the explosion at the Ewell farm. But there was little to go on, and a week later Burk returned to Fresno without substantial new evidence.

Souza, his Fresno duties pressing, could do little at this point. But he told himself that one day he would personally investigate Austin's death, even if it was on his own time.

As months rolled by, the District Attorney's Office realized the biggest obstacle to presenting the case would be its sheer magnitude, the massive amount of documentation, the complexities of firearms and surveillance evidence.

And the paperwork pile continued to grow as Souza and the DA investigators, Pete Chavez and Ray Cereghino, wrote dozens of new search warrants in their quest for a complete picture of Dana's financial exploits.

Boudreau prepared his report on the trace evidence analysis that was conducted in a search for tennis ball residue and fibers:

> At the request of Detective Souza, physical evidence materials collected at the crime scene were examined for the presence of tennis ball materials. The items consisted of adhesive tape lifts (items AV-1 through AV-11) and a piece of carpet, item JD-42. The tape lifts were taken from the

clothing of the victims. The carpet from
the office where GLEE EWELL'S remains
rested.

Apparent tennis ball substances found
were compared against six different types
of tennis balls, and with particles
ejected from a sound-suppressed barrel
fitted with tennis balls.

The tape lift from GLEE EWELL has particles like those from the test targets.
Additionally, the bundle of bright yellow
fibers from the piece of office carpet is
consistent with the felt of the tennis
balls examined.

Only Glee Ewell had been shot at close
range, but the tape lifts from this one
victim was [sic] compelling indeed—tiny
bits of materials used to build a silencer
as outlined in the Paladin book had been
found at the murder scene.

And Boudreau wrote in his "FINAL REPORT OF THE
COMPARISON OF RECOVERED EVIDENCE BUL-
LETS TO TEST-FIRED BULLETS FROM RECOV-
ERED BARREL:"

On March 6, 1995, Criminologist Jack Duty
transferred item JD-55, a firearm barrel
packaged in brown paper bags, to my custody. Barrel was rusted and chamber bore
filled with earth.

Earth and loose rust were removed with
water. The barrel was dried and submerged
in a product called Liquid Wrench. After
several days, the barrel was found to be a
Feather Industries, Model AT9 barrel,
ported by drilling four rows of holes
through the barrel. The bore (interior)

of the barrel was examined with a boro-
scope; burrs of barrel metal were seen
protruding into the bore.

The barrel was attached to an AT9 for
test-firing.

The cleaned barrel was test-fired with
five rounds of Winchester, 9mmP, 115 grain,
Full Metal Jacket ammunition. These
rounds were recovered and examined.

Microscope comparisons of the individ-
ualized markings on the murder and test
bullets lead me to believe that the murder
bullets were fired from the recovered JD-55
barrel.

If there had been any real doubt, Boudreau had all but
eliminated it: the bullets that killed the Ewell family had
been fired through the Jack Ponce barrel.

The likelihood of a conviction of Joel Radovcich, and
perhaps Dana Ewell, didn't seem such a pipe dream anymore.

Meanwhile, the County Risk Management offices received a copy of a legal claim filed against the office by
Dana, who contended, "loss of liberty, loss of reputation,
denial of right to equal protection under the laws, due
process and the right to enjoy what life I had left after the
tragic loss of my family."

Dana charged the Sheriff's Department "have and are
continuing to engage in a course of conduct which is illegal and is intended to destroy me."

The detectives, Dana wrote, lied and slandered him,
conducted an illegal, biased investigation and ridiculed
him, "in every possible way including to be a homosex-
ual."

Dana contended in his typewritten filing that it had all
been a plan to close the case at any cost, as the sheriff
"engaged in a campaign to deny me my inheritance."

He concluded, "All of these actions have and continue to cause me damages and suffering and impair my right to have a fair trial in my hometown and will continue to produce damages and injury. Total amount claimed: $8 million dollars."

Then, apparently as an afterthought, he scrawled in tiny script: which I intend to donate 100% to a charity involved with representing citizens wrongfully accused of crimes. DJE.

Just prior to the preliminary hearing, a new time line put together by investigators and members of the DA's office included events preceding the murders:

Spring/90: Joel and Dana SCU classmates in Ethics (where, investigators learned, Joel had plagiarized a paper before Dana)

Summer/90: Ponce sublets apartment to Joel

Jan/91: Joel arrested for stealing dorm furniture

Feb/91: Dana asks that his college records be sealed

Spring/91: Joel loads up on college units; Joel visits Ewell house (Souza believed that Joel graduated early in order to increase distance between himself and Dana; the visit to the Ewells may have been to learn the layout of the house)

May/91: Joel orders Paladin Press books (the silencer plans)

June/91: Joel asks that his college records be

sealed (why, Souza asked, did both Dana and Joel request confidentiality of their college records? No single answer proved satisfactory)

July/91: Paladin books delivered to Tom Duong and picked up by Joel; Entrepreneur article trumpets Dana's (fictional) business successes

Oct/91: Joel rents pager; deposit later refunded to Dana

Nov/91: San Jose paper carries Dana article

Dec/91: Joel, having accelerated credits, graduates from SCU

Jan/92: Dana produces family net worth statement; begins dating Monica (Souza asks, did he date her solely because her father was an FBI agent?)

Mar/92: Ponce deposits $1000 cash in bank account; purchases AT9; Joel deposits $200 cash in his bank account (Ponce claims money originated with Dana)

Apr 8 92: Ponce picks up AT9, turns it over to Joel

Apr 9 92: Joel purchases equipment, rents acetylene tanks at Home Depot

Apr 13 92: Joel deposits additional $500 in bank account

Apr 16 92: Glee and Tiffany drive to Pajaro

Apr 17 92: Ponce obtains pager, gives number to Joel; Dale flies to Pajaro

Apr 18 92: Zents and Ewells dine at Pajaro

Apr 19 92: Dana and Zents enjoy Easter dinner; Homicide occurs

Reckoning

". . . something fell out of his eye . . ."

ONE

THE PRELIMINARY HEARING WAS A BATTLE-
ground of arcane legal issues.

In defense of Dana Ewell, Peter Jones objected to the
admission into evidence of Ponce's statement that Joel
had killed the Ewells under contract with Dana.

The Ponce testimony wasn't supported by independent
evidence, argued Jones, and more, Joel's confession to
Ponce was not made in the furtherance of a conspiracy,
as required under section 1223 of the Evidence Code.
Jones maintained that this multiple hearsay violated
Dana's right to cross-examine his accuser, since Radovcich would not take the stand.

The court allowed that some of this testimony could
not be used against Dana, but agreed with Oppliger that
the evidence tended to prove a conspiracy between the
defendants. Besides, Oppliger had successfully argued,
Joel's confession to Ponce constituted a "statement against
penal interest," one contrary to his own legal interests,
and was therefore one of the exceptions to the statutes of
admissibility.

Jones also questioned the admissibility of Souza's testimony in the matter of the surveillance on Joel. While
California law stated that Souza, as a peace officer with
more than five years experience, could provide evidence
in a preliminary trial, Jones argued that the overheard conversations should be tossed out on foundational grounds—

there was no basis, he said, since the prosecution couldn't prove who was on the other end of the line with Joel when his calls were overheard.

Again, the court agreed with the prosecution: cloned pager records, in conjunction with detectives' observations of Dana using phones from which Joel had been paged, provided an adequate foundation for the evidence.

Joel's lawyer sought a continuance.

Terrence Woolf told the court he needed additional firearms evidence that had not yet been turned over to him by the prosecution.

He reiterated his claim that, despite the thousands of pages of police documents, financial and telephone records the defense had received, he could not mount an effective defense for Radovcich. The firearms conclusions of Luke Haag had not been turned over to his office, he said, and without Haag's judgments on Boudreau's work—work that constituted the strongest claim against his client—how could he adequately represent his client?

Oppliger considered this tact a ruse; Woolf, after all, had gotten plenty of firearms evidence.

But Woolf's strategy took a savvy turn, one he'd hinted at weeks before. He refused to cross-examine Peter Radovcich on the basis that Peter's testimony revolved around firearms evidence and the defense simply didn't have enough information to comprehensively cross.

Woolf was playing a long shot: if either Peter or Ponce were to become unavailable for testimony during the murder trial, California law allowed the reading of preliminary testimony into the record if the defense had the opportunity to fully cross-examine. And since Woolf had not confronted Joel's accuser, Joel's right to a fair trial would be denied and the preliminary testimony might be deemed inadmissible. Oppliger, to counter this move, asked the Court to take a personal waiver from the defense. Even though the Court refused, Oppliger had accomplished his purpose—the defense had heard the prosecution state the issue in open court, and an appeals court could deem the defense's silence as an implied waiver.

After a week of preliminary maneuverings, the court ruled: Dana Ewell and Joel Radovcich would stand trial for the murders of Dale, Glee, and Tiffany Ewell.

The October 20, 1995, issue of *People Weekly* magazine, Mary Tyler Moore gracing its cover, was snapped up quickly by Fresno area readers.

"Suspect Son" told the story of the murders, investigations, and arrests. The article included a photograph of Souza and Curtice, noting, "the three-year investigation boosted (Souza's) blood pressure—and tested his marriage."

One *Fresno Bee* article particularly saddened Souza:

EWELL FAMILY POSSESSIONS SOLD TO HIGHEST BIDDERS

Curiosity seekers and bargain hunters crowded into a Sunnyside home Monday to pick through drawers and closets once used by three of Fresno's most famous homicide victims.

The saddest merchandise on the auction block was a Barbie doll collection, 20 Barbies and a couple of Kens, that belonged to Dana's sister, Tiffany.

One of the few indications of wealth, and disrupted plans, was an architect's model of a sprawling new home the Ewells were planning to build in north Fresno.

Another *Bee* piece made public the bilking of Glee Mitchell's trust (set up years before by Glee Ewell) by Dana and his girlfriend, Monica Zent. The story featured an ominous photo of Zent with half her face in shadow.

THE MYSTERIOUS MONICA ZENT

Three members of a wealthy Fresno family were murdered in the spring of 1992. Police believe Dana

Ewell arranged to have his parents and sister killed out of greed. A money trail led to three people: two of them face murder charges.

And while the case continues to claim headlines, the third person, Monica Zent—Ewell's girlfriend and alibi—has remained in the shadows.

The article highlighted many of the findings of FSO detectives and District Attorney's investigators:

- that out of the nearly $400,000 of his grandmother's money with which he had been entrusted, only $2,000 remained. (Mitchell was now 93 years old and suffering from Alzheimer's disease.)
- that Dana had over twenty-seven bank accounts, many jointly with Zent.
- and that, besides the money spent on Berman's retainer and Joel's flying lessons, $39,701 of Mitchell's money was paid directly to Zent, and another $17,014 went for her tuition at the University of San Diego School of Law.

Souza was thrilled with the revelations. Though Zent denied any wrongdoing, Souza believed that, at the very least, greed had clouded her judgment. She'd been at Dana's dorm when Curtice named Joel as the killer, she'd accompanied Dana when he phoned Joel that same night. She'd even stayed at the Los Angeles "safe house" with Dana and Joel.

Maybe she just didn't want to believe, thought Souza.

But to him, her part in this was as unforgivable as her father's, whose activities throughout the investigation had disturbed not only Souza and the FSO, but Dana's uncles and eventually the Bureau. (Zent soon resigned from the FBI. Whether this was a planned retirement or there were other factors in Zent's departure from the Bureau remains unclear.)

*   *   *

The inevitable began on December 16, 1997.

The *Fresno Bee* devoted massive coverage to the trial, and local FM station KMPH would broadcast the event live and in its entirety.

For the People: James Oppliger and Jeffrey Hammerschmidt.

Oppliger, fifty, had a full head of salt-and-pepper hair, heavy-lidded eyes, and a Dudley Do-Right chin. The lead prosecutor was an idealistic, hard-cursing baritone, a skier, surfer, and former Malibu lifeguard, a onetime Public Defender who had grown weary of watching guilty clients hit the streets again. He'd been named Prosecutor of the Year for 1997 by the California District Attorneys Association.

Assisting Oppliger was Jeffrey Hammerschmidt, thirty-six. His dark hair unruly and his nose prominent, the lanky Missouri-born Hammerschmidt was stepping into his first homicide case, but as he said, "We have a job to do. There's not a lot of time to be thinking, 'Should I have been put on this case?' "

In defense of Joel Radovcich: Phillip Cherney.

Ponytailed, gray-bearded Cherney, forty-eight, a staunch opponent of the death penalty, was not a public defender. But as Dana Ewell was a client of the Defender's Office, and the interests of Ewell and Radovcich would clearly be in conflict (the Fifth Court of Appeals had denied defense motions for a severance), Cherney was hired by Fresno County to defend Joel. Yet before going into private practice Cherney had spent years in the Defender's Office, often arguing murder cases. When not before a jury, Cherney would likely be golfing, cooking, or reading the words of Mahatma Gandhi.

In defense of Dana Ewell: the intense, mustachioed Peter Jones, wide-eyed Public Defender Michael Castro, and a pro-bono participant, Ernest Kinney.

"We're all frail, fragile, finite and fallible," said Jones, forty-four, an idealist who believed everyone had the right to tell his story in court. Charles Dreiling, Fresno County Public Defender, called Jones, "one of the finest trial lawyers in the state."

Castro, fifty-one, who had spent much of his pretrial time poring over financial records that the prosecution would use to tie his client to Joel Radovcich, had a reputation for being popular with jurors.

As for his attitude toward his work, Castro said, "We're dealing with a person's life. It isn't a game."

Ernest Kinney, fifty-three, stated bluntly, "I think Dana Ewell is absolutely innocent, and I will fight to the death for him."

Another former public defender (in fact he had trained Oppliger years before), Kinney was the boisterous winner of four recent "not guilty" verdicts in Fresno County murder cases. When Ewell was denied inheritance money that would have funded his defense, Kinney rode to Dana's rescue. Rumors surfaced that Kinney and Ewell had a secret contract, with Kinney receiving one million dollars if Ewell walked at trial's end. But the balding, mountainous Kinney insisted no such deal was cut, that his reward would come in the form of a spectacular trial, and when he "sees Dana Ewell free again."

Judge Frank J. Creede, Jr., seventy-five, who had rejected defense requests to move the trial out of Fresno, estimated the trial would run through early March 1998. Should either defendant be convicted, the penalty phase would begin. In the event of a jury deadlock, the District Attorney would most likely seek a second trial.

And if both defendants were acquitted, the most expensive investigation in Fresno history would end ignominiously.

On December 15, two months after prospective jurors were first summoned to court, the last of the twelve jurors and six alternates had been sworn in.

The jury profile:

Juror 1: Male in his fifties; municipal-government employee. A chemistry major in college, the prosecution thought he would be comfortable with the forensic evidence.

Juror 2: A career-oriented mother of two, in her thirties, and a medical assistant.

Juror 3: A female Ph.D., in her forties. A psychologist, and a Republican.

Juror 4: Female, fiftyish. "Well organized." Bookkeeper.

Juror 5: Female, fifty, studying law. Former juror in another murder case. An insurance claims adjuster (who, in Oppliger's opinion, make "great" jurors).

Juror 6: Male Hispanic, fifties. "I hold up my end."

Juror 7: "Workaholic," soft-spoken male in his forties. Phone company administrator.

Juror 8: Female in her forties. "Wife, mother, serious-minded." Travel agent with a strong personality.

Juror 9: Female, former juror on four occasions.

Juror 10: Male, forties. Truck driver. (Nicknamed "Elvis" by the prosecution.)

Juror 11: A male in his mid-thirties. Considers himself, "A very good person."

Juror 12: Male, fifties. Related to police officers. A baker, and importantly to case, a gunsmith.

On the morning of opening arguments, deputies escorted Dana and Joel into the somewhat small, paneled courtroom. Both wore sweaters (referred to in private by Oppliger as Menendez sweaters) but while Dana looked neat and crisp, Joel's sweater hung from his frame and his hair appeared untouched by a comb. Deputies attached ankle chains to both men, and then Souza, the attorneys, their assistants, and the court reporter took their seats.

Souza stared hard at Dana. Dana ignored him.

The clerk sat on the judge's right, the court reporter directly in front of him. Witnesses would appear on the stand to his left. Defendants and legal teams had situated themselves around an L-shaped table. Nearest the jury box sat Oppliger, then came Souza, Hammer, Cherney, Joel, and Cherney's paralegal assistant. Dana, Jones, Castro, Kinney and his assistant faced the jury box.

It was no accident that Dana faced the jury; Souza and Oppliger knew juries, and they knew Dana. They were certain that any emotion exhibited by Dana would be faked. The jury would watch him, and, the prosecution believed, and they would see him for the greedy, amoral monster he was. And, while Judge Creede had prohibited much of the evidence that spoke to Dana's character, insisting instead that motive evidence be presented, Oppliger had learned from past lengthy murder trials that, over time, jurors came to well perceive a defendant's true personality.

How much hearsay would make its way in remained a concern for the prosecution, and there were others: Would Judy Radovcich's testimony evoke great sympathy for her, and in turn for Joel? Would Boudreau's work be too heady, beyond the grasp of some jury members? Would Dana take the stand? He had proven himself intelligent, a world-class liar and con man, and while it remained unlikely he could match the People's knowledge of details of the case, there was always a chance he could charm a jury into letting him walk.

Of course, Dana's attorneys had more than their share of worries, among them: How much would the jury feel pressured by the community to convict? And how far might Dana's defense push Joel without Joel turning on their client? As for Joel's defense, Oppliger told Souza that Cherney's sole aim was to keep Radovcich off Death Row, and he would go about that with integrity, perhaps striving to show that his client could not have masterminded the crime (which would likely help the People's case against Dana).

Kinney himself was a wild card. Oppliger believed Kinney's bombastic approach would wear thin in a lengthy trial, on judge and jury, and the lead prosecutor formulated a strategy to exacerbate the "Kinney effect": Oppliger would on occasion provoke the short-tempered, seventy-five-year-old Judge Creede in morning sessions, and sit back later while Creede took it out on Kinney.

The jury was shown into the courtroom, followed by spectators. The air was alive with expectation, adrenaline, fear.

Souza's testimony, as lead detective on the case, would be sporadic and primarily foundational. He would serve as a tactician for the prosecution, and Oppliger and Hammerschmidt would daily rely upon his vast knowledge of the case.

Though he wasn't scheduled to testify for weeks, Souza's stomach was in knots. Still, he smiled broadly at Dana. Dana managed to raise his chin even higher; still, when the huge Kinney leaned over and made a comment, the nervousness in Dana's laugh belied his cool appearance.

Joel put on a show for no one. He sagged in his seat, staring off at places and things only he could see.

TWO

THE JUDGE'S CHAMBER DOOR OPENED AND JUDGE Frank Creede strode in and took his seat at the bench.

"Good morning, ladies and gentlemen," he said in his somewhat creaky, high-pitched voice. "Please be seated. All right. We'll call the case of the People of the State of California versus Dana James Ewell and Joel Patrick Radovcich, number 5462221."

Creede established that all parties were present and ready to proceed, then went on to instruct the jury as to their duties and responsibilities.

"You must base the decisions you make on the facts and on the law. First, you must determine the facts from the evidence received in the trial and not from any other source. A fact is something proved by evidence or by stipulation. A stipulation is an agreement between attorneys regarding the facts.

"Ah . . . second, you must apply the law that I state to you to the facts as you determine them, and in this way arrive at your verdict."

Creede admonished the jury to not be biased because a defendant was brought to trial, nor because of conjecture, pity, prejudice, mere sentiment, sympathy, passion, or public opinion.

He defined legal terms and said he would explain anything that needed clarifying, and warned them not to discuss the case with anyone. Then, cautioning that opening statements are not evidence, Judge Creede addressed the lead prosecutor.

"Ah ... Mr. Oppliger, do you wish to present your opening statement on behalf of the People?"

"Yes, I do. Thank you, Your Honor. Counsel, ladies and gentlemen, good morning to you all. The last national figures I have seen indicate that more than three hundred times a year a parent is killed by a son or daughter."

Both Kinney and Jones jumped up, objecting on grounds of discovery and relevance.

Judge Creede said, "Is there going to be evidence of that, Mr. Oppliger?"

"I hope so, Your Honor."

Creede sustained the objections and Oppliger continued.

"This case, ladies and gentlemen, does not involve the passion of a crime where a child kills a parent. Such crimes that you have read about, that you know from your normal existence, are different from this one. In this crime, the son is the mastermind, not the triggerman.

"The case against Dana Ewell, therefore, rests in large part on the fact and the proof that Joel Radovcich is the triggerman in the killing of the Ewell family. While some evidence is admissible only against one defendant or the other, most of it will apply to both and is interrelated.

"Execution murder is planned and carried out in secret. Motive in an execution murder is paramount. I will show you, in this case, the triggerman can have no motive of his own. I will show you the killer cannot possess the knowledge or precise timing ... without what I loosely call insider knowledge ...

"Mr. Radovcich cannot commit this act alone. He is incapable of doing so. Mr. Radovcich cannot benefit from this murder in any way. In the end, Mr. Radovcich cannot escape detection without the assistance of Mr. Ewell."

Oppliger underscored that Dana was the sole heir in this triple homicide, and "all murder has a motive. And we will eliminate all motives, save one, and that is financial."

He said Joel could only benefit from "a gifting by an innocent heir or a payoff by his crime partner."

And then Oppliger outlined the crime: A man with no income buys murder and gun books. He is Dana's buddy, but the two cease associating publicly prior to the murders. Easter Sunday, the hired killer knows the family is away, knows how to enter undetected, knows there is a weapon and ammunition in the house, ammunition that can be loaded into his own silenced gun. He lies in wait and kills the women, then the big prize, the father, the man with the money.

"When it's all over, this surgically gloved killer collects his bullet casings, and then in a move that is sinister yet unsophisticated, he stages the crime scene . . . to fool the police into thinking it was a spur-of-the-moment killing by a burglar who used the victim's own gun."

Oppliger insisted crime scenes are staged for a reason, and the poorly executed ruse by Radovcich was "the conspiracy's undoing." He called it an "execution-style, planned-in-advance killing, leaving only one heir."

And later, said the prosecutor, "the killer moves into the Ewells' residence and Dana gives him large sums of money. They begin a series of activities. For lack of a better word, they act like spies."

Oppliger told the jury that Dana and Joel, "use only pay phones . . . communicate by code, avoid togetherness in public. And through all this, the money from Mr. Ewell to Mr. Radovcich keeps on flowing . . . even after Mr. Ewell is informed by the sheriff that they have named Joel Radovcich as their prime suspect."

After introducing Souza and the baby-faced Hammerschmidt ("the brains of the operation"), Oppliger outlined how his case would be presented. Then he began to walk the jury through the crime and its investigation, from the early friendships to the murders, to Joel's confession to Ponce.

*   *   *

Though scheduled to be completed that first day, Oppliger's opening statement went on until shortly before the recess of day two. His final comments: "The evidence will show that the murder was planned, and it was planned to be discovered. The evidence will show that Dana Ewell was a part of the conspiracy . . .

"Dale, Glee, Tiffany, are dead. The motive I will prove in this case is money. My blueprint here seeks to answer, by evidence, this question: Why did the young lady have to die? The executioner was connected to the victims, and that connection spelled out financial gain. To actually become a millionaire, Tiffany, too, had to die, so those two could reap the benefits of the murders of Mr. and Mrs. Ewell."

Ernest Kinney painted quite a different picture.

"The DA spent much time with his opening statement on theory. Later, I'm going to have some facts for you."

Most of these facts involved the "lying" Jack Ponce. Kinney loudly pointed out inconsistencies in Ponce's police statements; inconsistencies, Kinney suggested, that were cleared up later only with help from the DA's Office.

This didn't have to be an inside job, Kinney said. The alarm code (1-2-3-5) he said, was a no-brainer, and if "you want something to look like a burglary, you kick in a window."

Dana didn't run, the large, balding attorney pointed out, pacing the floor. Joel did, after the first incriminating articles in the *Bee*, but not Dana. Dana did what he was advised to do by counsel.

"His father's attorney . . . says, 'Dana, you're a logical suspect.' "

So Dana hires criminal attorney Rick Berman, who Kinney quotes as telling Dana, "Don't talk on those phones. Whether it's tapped or whatever, you go to pay phones."

And what of the large payouts to Joel? The evidence

would show Dana had a promissory note from Joel for monies received.

Dana and his family were very close, thundered Kinney, and the favored son had all the money he needed. But the family had enemies. Kinney mentioned Glee's "CIA days," and "the Philippine Mafia," adding, "Dana knew big-time people didn't like his family. Dana knew if he walked through the door, he could have been killed, too."

Then it was back to Jack Ponce.

Ponce believed there was a safe in the house.

Ponce know the layout of the Ewell house, though, "according to the testimony of Mr. Ponce, he's never been in the house."

There was no tape of Ponce mentioning the diagram of the Ewell home that Joel had drawn in the Malibu sand. Perhaps the prosecution had dreamed up that story, hinted Kinney.

"Dana has no problem with tapes. And law enforcement has those two tapes of Mr. Ewell, and we hope they're played for you."

Oppliger got to his feet. "Well, I'm going to object to his hopes."

The court reminded Kinney that "this phase of the case is what you expect the evidence to show."

Dana, Kinney maintained, was the victim of overly aggressive investigators. "You will hear where Detective Souza, very nice man, but you will have to look at his work here."

Kinney belittled Souza's work on the various affidavits for search and arrest warrants. The defense attorney gestured broadly toward Souza, telling the jury the detective had lied often during the investigation.

Souza wanted to take a swipe at Kinney, but of course he had no choice but to sit, bite his lip, and hope his face wasn't as red as an apple.

Moving on to the phone calls, most of the suspicious calls were "probably made to Jack Ponce."

A grueling time line followed, before Kinney wound down his statement.

"The material that I've just gone over will show . . . the evidence that goes over will basically show, in two minutes, that Mr. Ponce, on October of 1990, with the dorm-room number on the receipt, in the summer of '91, lives with Joel, gives Joel a .380, a .22, puts a silencer on the .22.

"March 23 buys the AT9, various other aspects. Gets the pager on April 17, two days prior to the killing."

Kinney brought up the buried AT9 barrel, and said of Ponce, "He lies and lies and lies until they arrest him for murder, then he pulls the grisly, dirty gun out of the dirt."

But it was Dana whom Kinney focused on as he closed.

"The evidence will show the state of mind of Dana Ewell, and his concerns with an investigation, his concerns with safety and concerns with everything, and his concerns with law enforcement. But it will also show the love and . . . closeness of this family at the time of the killings.

"Dana Ewell always knew, according to the evidence, and he will tell you, he was an innocent man. He was wrongly accused. And he knew it. And when they're accusing Joel, he never believed he was involved, never believed it, didn't want to believe it, didn't believe it, never did believe it."

"I went too goddamned long," said Oppliger of his opening statement.

Souza and Oppliger were poring over notes in the DA's offices. It was nearly 10 P.M.

"Once I got into it, I told myself, 'Hell, it won't be pretty, but I've just got to plow ahead.' "

The men agreed, however, that Kinney's opening statement had also fallen flat. Dana, who by all accounts had welcomed Kinney's help, had been in tears as Kinney wrapped up.

*   *   *

The trial, said bearded Radovcich defender Phillip Cherney in a speech laced with allegory, would be like an ocean voyage, and would tell a tale "of imperfect men on an uncharted sea." Joel Radovcich was "one mariner here who appears like the ancient Greek mariner trying to navigate between Scylla and Charybdis."

Cherney solemnly told the jury that Joel had been raised in a strict and disciplined household, going home only when his father wasn't there. "This spiritual and geographic separation is important."

And Cherney maintained that Joel, "a muscle-bound loner," who was "loyal, like a dog," had no history of violence and an alibi for the day of the crime.

Cherney also invoked the name of Jack Ponce, emphasizing that the police had persuaded Ponce to name Joel as the shooter.

" 'Tell us you bought the gun for Joel,' " Cherney read from police transcripts, " 'and you can eliminate yourself as a suspect. You can be a hero and solve this thing.' "

Cherney warned the jury that Joel's defense team would disagree with some of the prosecution's conclusions in the case.

"Facts are elusive and often two-faced. You have a right to be convinced. If you are not convinced, we have a right to a not-guilty verdict."

THREE

THE PEOPLE CALLED PARAMEDICS AND MEMBERS of the Sheriff's Department to set the scene of the murders. Emergency Medical Technician David Akers, who had been dispatched with a crew from the nearby Department of Forestry station after Darwin Knapp had called 911, told the court that he and Captain James Hart went to Tiffany and, "immediately evaluated her for signs of life and found none whatsoever."

Hart took the stand. He said a third firefighter called out to him as he was examining Tiffany.

"He said, 'Captain, we've got another victim in the hall.' I went to see what he had, and looking past him, I could see the third victim. There are a lot of heart attacks in Sunnyside. You'll find grandpa has a heart attack, grandma finds him, they've been together for fifty years and she has the big one. Two people being dead is really not that unusual. What's unusual is finding the third one."

The paramedics backed out of the scene and radioed the FSO. Responding deputies testified briefly, explaining that they had secured the scene and called for homicide detectives. Knapp then testified, though details were murky. Ewell housekeeper Rose Avita followed.

Anxious, her voice barely audible, she recounted that neighbor Knapp was standing in the Ewells' yard when she drove up with two other women who often assisted in her duties. Knapp asked who she was, then he asked if she had a house key.

"He said Dana called and asked him to go in because he couldn't get hold of his parents."

When she unlocked the door, she "saw a sheet with a stereo on it, and the alarm didn't go off. I thought it was being burglarized."

And, she added, the alarm was always set, unless Glee was home. "I noticed the kitchen door was open. That's when I saw Tiffany." She said Knapp then hurried over to his house and phoned Dana.

Reid testified Friday morning. She said Dana had called her at home the night before the bodies were discovered.

"[Dana] said, 'Do you know where Dale and Glee are?' I told him, 'I'm assuming something happened with your grandmother health-wise and they went up there.' "

But Dana told her he'd spoken with his grandmother, and she didn't know where his parents were.

"When I heard that, I had a very horrid foreboding."

But after she asked Dana to phone a neighbor and call her back if anything was amiss, she heard nothing further, so she'd assumed all was well. Then Tuesday morning, Reid testified, Dale failed to show up for work. She called Dana. He told her it had been too late to call a neighbor the previous evening.

"I got angry," Reid said. "I said timing could be critical. I said, 'I'll go investigate, tell me where the key is hidden and tell me how to turn off the alarm.' " (Oppliger knew that Dana's failure to call in help the night before the discovery of the bodies had turned Reid against Dana.)

During cross, Kinney sought to show that Reid shared the blame with Dana for waiting.

Q: Do you recall telling Detective John
   Souza, 'But because it was too late, we
   decided to wait until the next day'?
A: Never.

Oppliger and Souza were pleased with Reid's performance, especially her quashing the defense's attempt to downplay Dana's delay in calling in authorities. She had an impressive Teutonic formality, her testimony underscored the tragedy of three lives callously snuffed out, and her portrayal of Dale as very human would make it difficult for the defense to attack the victim and blame him for his own death.

FSO Sergeant Joe Flores followed. Flores had interviewed neighbor Knapp that morning, and he quoted Knapp as saying, "How do I tell him his sister is probably dead across the street?"

And later, after calling Dana with the news, Knapp said Dana had cried, "Oh, my God, oh my God!"

When the afternoon break was called, Joel Radovcich sat nearly motionless, his head propped on his arms on the table. Dana consulted with his lawyers as they paged through exhibits.

Mindy Ybarra took the stand after lunch. Jurors were shown dozens of photographs taken at the scene (though no photos of the victims were introduced at this point).

The jury learned that a thirty-seven-thousand-dollar Patek Philippe watch had not been stripped from Glee's wrist, but cassette tapes and coins had been tossed on a bedsheet as though to be stolen. The jurors also were told that Dale Ewell's wallet was empty. He'd died with one nickel in his pocket.

The second week began as it had ended on Friday, with crime-scene coordinator Ybarra describing for the court what Sheriff's Department personnel had found the morning the bodies were discovered. During the first recess, out of the presence of jurors, lawyers from both sides argued over which victim photographs would be allowed into evidence.

Once a deal was struck, Ybarra's testimony continued with the color stills being projected through a large-screen television monitor. Many jurors glanced from the scene photos to the defendants.

Joel stared blandly at the pictures. Dana averted his eyes, though at one point he visibly teared up. (Convinced these were crocodile tears, Oppliger and Souza devised a scheme: for the balance of the trial, whenever evidence was presented that could give Dana a chance to appear saddened, Souza would glare and smirk at the defendant, hoping to tick him off; in Oppliger's opinion, the scheme worked.)

Oppliger asked Ybarra if the scene looked like a genuine burglary.

"It appeared to be staged," she said.

But defense attorneys had other theories. Why were there two sets of footprints in the home, Ernest Kinney wanted to know, one set made by bare feet, the other by someone in shoes?

Souza knew where this would lead: Kinney would attempt to persuade the jury that Joel and Jack Ponce had committed the crimes, and Dana was merely a patsy.

Kinney moved on. In mocking tones, he asked Ybarra, "Isn't it correct that the area (in Tiffany's bathroom) around the skylight is not on a motion detector?"

When Ybarra affirmed that point, Kinney announced dramatically that if someone had come in through a skylight, he could easily have made it to the closet where backup batteries for the alarm were located. After all, he pointed out, an alarm clock in Dana's bedroom was flashing 12:00 when police arrived. Under redirect, Ybarra told the court that the outside breaker box, where power would have been shut off, appeared undisturbed.

Oppliger whispered, "Jurors love Mindy."

Souza agreed that Ybarra's good looks, fine memory, and her professional demeanor comprised a package that jurors, male and female, tended to admire.

Questions of the Ewell alarm's vulnerability continued when representatives of Telco Enterprises, the alarm installation company that had sold and serviced the system, testified.

While there were ways to beat the alarm, admitted the representatives, including taping paper over the motion detectors or turning off the power switch on the alarm panel, there was no way of knowing whether the alarm had been armed before the Ewells left their home Easter weekend.

At the end of the day, Judge Creede announced that court would recess for the holidays and reconvene on January 4, 1998.

The Ewell murder case was moving into its seventh year.

Souza spent much of the extended recess on his houseboat, reading, studying, making notes, and phoning members of the prosecution team. It was the holidays, but Souza and team members found little time for joy or relaxation.

The trial began its second week, and second calendar year, with lawyers arguing legal points in closed-door hearings. Once the jury returned, Jack Duty, now retired from the I-Bureau at FSO, took the stand and described how evidence was collected and marked at the crime scene.

But the prosecutors were red-faced when they attempted to introduce into evidence the box that had contained Dale's nine-millimeter ammunition. When Duty cut open the sealed evidence envelope, the Winchester carton was missing.

Another evidence bag was found to contain envelopes that apparently had not been sealed correctly; the exhibits, dozens of pieces of jewelry, jumbled inside the bag. The press would make hay with this apparent Keystone Kop buffoonery, especially after the televised courtroom mayhem of the O. J. Simpson trial. But Souza believed it was much ado about nothing. Most of the evidence exhibits had been properly labeled and initialed, even if certain envelopes had broken open.

Oppliger continued questioning Duty.

> Q: Based on your background, did you reach a conclusion whether this was a staged burglary?
> A: Possibly. Or, it was an amateur.

Oppliger pressed on, establishing that the kitchen skylight had been dusty and cobwebbed. The skylights in Tiffany's bathroom, which Ernest Kinney had hinted might have been the point of entry for the killer or killers, were sealed with roofing tar, Duty claimed.

And again he volunteered opinion beyond that which the prosecution had sought.

"They did not appear that they had been removed and put back and retarred. It could have happened, but I don't think so."

Ponytailed Radovcich counsel Cherney asked Duty under cross if there could have been more than one person in the house, based upon Duty's testimony that some drawers had been opened carefully, while others had been dumped out on the floor.

"Yes," Duty said. "Or one person trying different things."

Kinney asked the court reporter twice to read aloud Duty's quote that the skylights "could have" been removed and retarred. Duty's testimony for the day concluded with the jury viewing photos of the recovered gun barrel.

The next day jurors saw pathologist Dr. Michael J. Chambliss on the stand the entire day. He authenticated autopsy photos of the three victims, though the jury did not see the pictures. Then he described the deaths (as Souza stared down Dana in an effort to prevent his tearing up).

Said Dr. Chambliss of Tiffany's death, "The bullet hit the brain stem and the vital areas of the brain that control breathing and heart rate. Death is immediate or within seconds."

He said Glee had been shot four times. A bullet entered her right arm, passed into her chest, and lodged in her left shoulder. Another hit her right upper back, exiting her left shoulder. A third was fired into her chest and came out her back. The fourth (though Chambliss added he couldn't be certain in what order the shots were fired) struck Glee below her right eye, passed along the floor of her brain, struck the brain stem, and exited the back of her skull.

Dale, Chambliss said when questioned whether the father could have survived a few moments, might have taken a few labored, aspirating breaths before succumbing to his injuries.

Defense lawyers, not wishing to dwell on the graphic details of the murders, asked few questions of Dr. Chambliss.

Joel Radovcich, thief and accused murderer, "did lots of sweet surprises," according to the testimony of Michelle Diepenbrock.

They had been friends in college, said the tall, dark-haired beauty. He had even asked her to be his girlfriend. She told the court he was mysterious and considerate and "shut down." Souza thought she was genuinely soft-hearted and protective of Joel.

In 1994, she said, he left a one-hundred-dollar bill in her coat pocket.

Hammerschmidt, at thirty-six the youngest attorney trying the case and visibly nervous in his first murder trial, asked, "Did he ever give you money before April of 1992, the time of the murders?"

"Not in cash, but in other ways. He would buy lunch, dinner—"

"Nothing like a hundred-dollar bill or anything that significant?"

"No."

Big Ernest Kinney cross-examined. He brought up Joel's relationship with his family, and she claimed there was, "deep-seated hurt and anger."

"Were you aware of his relationship with his father?"

She'd asked Joel about that, she said, and found Joel and his father "had a lot of irreconcilable differences."

Kinney asked about the time Joel had brought up the subject of the two friends becoming more than just friends.

"He was very nervous and he started to sweat on his forehead. And he just sort of retardedly asked me if I wanted to be his girlfriend and I thought it was very . . . very sweet and endearing, very sincere, but I said no, and he was fine."

When first interviewed by investigators, Jennifer Wallis had been cooperative and plainly dressed, with light brown hair and a bubbly manner. For her court appearance, her hair was jet-black, she wore a fake mole and ample makeup, and she clearly had no intention of going out of her way to help the prosecution.

She said she had met Joel at Santa Clara when she'd partied there as a high-schooler, and she tearfully echoed the favorable opinions of Diepenbrock. Souza and Oppliger winced at the kindly picture the women were painting of Joel. But their appearance had been necessary: Oppliger's questioning established that Joel had not been speaking to any of his female friends when he'd made the overheard comments that reeked of conspiracy and guilt. The implication was clear: Dana was on the other end of the phone.

Patricia Kustron, associate director of housing at the school, remembered two things about Joel Radovcich: his slovenly appearance and his friendship with Dana Ewell.

Prosecutor Hammerschmidt questioned her.

Q: When you would see Joel Radovcich in
   the Casa dining hall, who would he eat
   with?
A: If Joel did not eat with Dana, he did not
   eat with anyone.
Q: Did you ever see any other student in
   the Casa as close to Dana Ewell as Joel
   Radovcich?
A: I can't say I did.

Radovcich attorney Cherney cross-examined Kustron.

Q: (Joel) was raggedy-looking?
A: Yes.
Q: In fact, you thought he was a homeless
   person.
A: He had that appearance.

Kustron stressed the differences between Joel and Dana
in dress and in social skills. Joel had checked in with his
clothes stuffed into a plastic bag, Kustron said, Ewell
wore Ralph Lauren. Yet, she added, the two were insep-
arable soon after moving into the Casa Italiano dorm.

Jack Duty returned to the stand and told the jury that no
fingerprints were found on items apparently moved by the
intruder. Oppliger wanted Duty's meaning clearly understood.

Q: What can cause that?
A: Covered hands.

Under cross-examination by Ewell lawyer Michael Castro, Duty admitted he'd tossed out his crime-scene notes
after his retirement.
"I didn't think I'd need them again."

*   *   *

Andrea Van Der Veer de Bondt also testified. She gave the jury a primer on the difference between blood drips and spatters, and methods used to reconstruct a scene to determine where the victims were when shot. She concluded with testimony about the tape lifts taken from victims' clothing.

After a few days' delay resulting from a juror's illness, Van Der Veer de Bondt returned to the witness stand. Michael Castro spent the morning cross-examining the forensic specialist, raising a second-gunman theory.

What if a second killer had blocked Glee's path to the garage, Castro wanted to know, would it have made sense for her to run into her office?

The criminalist said it would; besides the office, Dana's room was the only other place she could run. Van Der Veer de Bondt also acknowledged that she had recently found blood drops on Glee's pants; the drops had never been blood-typed.

Though this seemed a revelation, attorneys from both sides chose not to pursue it; new blood evidence could prove a nasty surprise to somebody, and no one wished to roll the dice. (It was later established that the blood had gotten on Glee's clothing as a result of cross-contamination in the morgue.)

The prosecution called Branch Meanley of Green Mountain Barrel. Meanley talked about the barrels his company had made for Feather Industries, explaining the rare one-in-twelve twist of the barrel as jurors examined the rifling button used in the manufacture of the AT9.

"The standard (rate of twist) is one-in-ten," he said.

Souza and Oppliger were generally pleased with Meanley's testimony. Despite the arcane subject matter, Meanley's learned, articulate presentation should have impressed even the most impassive juror (especially, Oppliger felt, the chemist and gunsmith).

The day concluded with testimony from Dana's flight

instructor. She said Dana referred her to a friend of his. Dana gave her the Ewell home phone number, telling her to contact someone named Joel at that number.

It was a slow Tuesday morning and Oppliger questioned Feather Industries former president Mervin Chapman (Feather had since gone out of business). Chapman described the AT9 as a "semiautomatic nine-millimeter carbine-style rifle," with a military design and a collapsible stock.

Chapman, as had Green Mountain's Meanley in earlier testimony, described the rare one-in-twelve rifling twist, and went on to say it had been a "competitive selling feature."

Allen Boudreau took the stand briefly, introducing into evidence bullets from the crime scene, and describing how they had been sent to the FBI crime lab for metallic-contaminant analysis.

That elemental composition was then outlined in grueling detail by Special Agent Roger Peele, who had performed the experiments in the FBI's Washington, DC laboratory.

Peele explained to the crowded, stuffy courtroom that in 1994 he'd employed two separate scientific tests on the bullets; one heated the lead in gas plasma, the second made the lead samples radioactive. Both tests allowed Peele to measure the amounts of trace contaminants, such as copper and bismuth, in the lead.

In 1997, Peele added, he completed a third, more advanced test on the recovered bullets. He concluded that the murder bullets were "analytically indistinguishable" from the bullets found in the Ewells' nightstand.

Yet, when Michael Castro asked, "Can you say with certainty that the bullets not in the box came from that box, and not some other box?" Peele admitted he could not.

But what was important, said the FBI agent under redirect, was that the murder bullets and the nightstand bullets matched each other when analyzed in three different ways.

Souza was glad to see Peele step down; he felt the boring topic had just further confused the jury, and a bored and confused jury was seldom friendly to the prosecution.

Things did liven up for a few minutes. Oppliger, who favored perching on the end of his chair when watching testimony, tumbled out of his seat. As soon as it was clear he was unhurt, the jury erupted into laughter. The rest of the courtroom joined in when Souza grabbed Oppliger by the sleeve and said, "Get back up here!" (When Oppliger returned the next day, he found bailiffs had affixed a makeshift "seat belt" to his chair.)

Winchester supervisor Donald Greeling opened up testimony Wednesday morning, explaining the marks made on the bullets by a worn coning punch. Harry Massuco followed, introducing into evidence the receipts from Dale's 1971 purchase of the Browning nine-millimeter and ammunition.

Some of the most damning evidence to date came Wednesday afternoon when James Brannen, president of Mazzie Flying Service in Fresno, told the jury that Joel Radovcich had received $11,000 worth of flying lessons in the summer of 1992, with Dana Ewell paying the bill.

"(Dana) said, 'What's the best we can do if we pay in advance?' "

Brannen said Joel Radovcich received his license later that year, and inquired about getting his commercial certificate. Oppliger asked how much that would cost.

"Over $20,000," Brannen said.

During cross, Ernest Kinney asked, "Do you recall at any time Dana telling you Joel Radovcich had signed a promissory note, dated June 25, the same day as Joel's first lesson?"

Brannen said he'd seen no such note, the prosecution

objected strenuously, even contentiously, and the Court agreed in equally strong terms.

(This line of questioning by Kinney infuriated Oppliger, who considered it pure, premeditated abuse of the legal system, undertaken to con the jury. Oppliger believed that Kinney knew no such evidence existed, and was pursuing this line in order to plant in the juror's minds an idea unsubstantiated by evidence.)

The testimony of Tom Duong, former classmate of Radovcich's and now a US Air Force intelligence officer, seemed to bring the jury to attention, with many leaning forward and taking notes.

Duong, tall and slight, his words precise, recounted quietly how he'd given Joel permission to have a few books mailed to his address. But when Duong opened the box and found manuals for constructing silencers and building bombs, he'd been livid.

The jury was shown the invoices for the books and the second Paladin shipment in the name of Duong's brother.

Hammerschmidt, growing more comfortable as the trial had progressed, his natural courtroom talent emerging, asked Duong about Joel's personality.

```
Q: Didn't you describe to police that Joel
   was one of the most unstable persons
   you knew?
A: I remember saying that, yes.
Q: But you took him to be harmless, cor-
   rect?
A: Yes.
```

Duong's mother also took the stand. She testified that Joel had come to her home in San Jose to pick up a few boxes of personal items. He was with another young man, she said, who drove a Mercedes and wore a suit.

Oppliger asked, "Do you see that man in court today?"

Hop Duong pointed to Dana Ewell.

"I think that's him."

The defense was shocked, as Mrs. Duong had not previously identified Dana from photographs. It was only during the break that she had informed Oppliger that she recognized Dana as the young man she'd seen with Joel.

Souza's first appearance on the stand served to link up the testimony of Tony Duong and Allen Boudreau, who would follow. Oppliger took Souza through the trip to Boulder, and Souza's delivery of copies of the Paladin books to Boudreau.

The first testimony was always the toughest, Souza knew, and he felt it had gone well.

FOUR

ALLEN BOUDREAU WAS ON THAT AFTERNOON and into Friday morning, describing for the jury his early attempts to replicate the stria on the murder bullets and determine if a silencer had been used.

Oppliger asked, "How many times have you been asked to look at crime-scene bullets fired through a silencer?"

Just once since he'd started his forensics career in 1975, Boudreau said. "This case."

Boudreau made it clear that, early in the investigation, he had no idea what model of weapon had been used. He outlined his Tec-9 experiments and the Paladin silencer handbook information, over defense objections that the books were irrelevant. He pinned up on the bulletin board behind him photographs of test bullets and weapons.

But before he could explain further, court was adjourned for the weekend due to another juror illness.

Week four of the Ewell trial. Tuesday, January 20, 1998.

After a closed-door hearing about procedures, the jury heard more from Allen Boudreau, picking up where he'd left off Friday afternoon.

The supervising criminalist said early tests did not produce bullets similar to the murder bullets—until he drilled holes in the barrel per instructions in the Paladin books.

"They bore remarkable similarity in my mind's eye to the evidence bullets."

333

And the bullets could not have been fired from the missing Browning, he said, despite evidence that the murder bullets came from the Ewell nightstand.

"If that ammunition was used and the Browning pistol was not used," he said, "it establishes prior knowledge. That's based on the premise that it makes no sense to go into a house with a loaded gun, unload it, and then reload it with bullets found there."

Michael Castro, Ewell's defender, cross-examined the criminalist. He followed a two-pronged strategy: demonstrate that police work had been sloppy and point an accusing finger at Jack Ponce.

The prosecution's star witness, Castro said, had purchased two ammunition clips when he picked up the AT9. Perhaps he loaded this second magazine with ammo found at the Ewells' and used that clip when he murdered the family.

Castro also asked Boudreau if it was possible the box of ammunition had been in the unlocked Wagoneer. Boudreau said he had no way of knowing where the ammunition was located before the shooting. And Castro did his best to taint the competence of technician Jack Duty and his work at the scene.

Q: If it was your job to make that inspection, you would have taken notes, wouldn't you?

A: Yes.

Q: And you'd have kept those notes and brought them with you to court?

A: Yes.

Much of Souza's job in the courtroom, knowing the particulars of the case as he did, was to feed questions to the prosecution. When he did appear as a witness, it often came without warning. Oppliger would simply elbow Souza at the table, and say, "You're on."

Oppliger had his own worries about Souza's effectiveness on the stand. Not that Oppliger doubted the detective's work or intelligence, both of which were impressive, but Souza's unique use of the English language (Souza's pronunciation of words was often quirky) concerned the veteran prosecutor. Would the jury think Souza an eccentric, and simply tune him out, or would the detective's sincerity and compassion win them over?

Testimony came from officials of two Los Angeles–area flight schools that Joel had attended in 1993 and 1994. Radovcich spent over eight thousand dollars at the schools, the jury was told, this in addition to the nearly twelve thousand dollars he'd spent in 1992 on helicopter lessons—most of it paid in one-hundred dollar bills.

The president of the pager company that had provided service to Joel in 1991 and 1992 also testified. He told of mailing the refund check to Radovcich at Dana Ewell's address.

Another pager company representative, Steve Walker, told the courtroom that on November 24, 1992, Radovcich had paid $247.95 for a pager and one year of service. Walker went on to describe how the company had cloned the pager at the request of FSO homicide detectives, an event that brought Joel Radovcich into their offices.

"Did he mention anything about police or cops?" asked prosecutor Hammerschmidt.

"He asked specifically if the police had been asking about him or in the store," replied Walker.

Nick Radovcich and his son Joel made no eye contact with each other when the tall, conservatively dressed engineer appeared on the stand Wednesday afternoon. He told prosecutors he didn't know whether his son had a job, didn't know much about flying lessons, and believed his son had had no money at all.

Under cross, Ernest Kinney asked, "Did you have a close relationship at that time?"

"No."

"You and your son had a falling-out?"

"There was no event that you could say we had a falling-out. We just ceased to communicate."

Joel's lawyer had no questions for Nick. Outside the courtroom during the break, Cherney explained, "I thought he spoke volumes. He didn't need me pushing buttons for the jury to get a sense of him."

Souza respected Cherney; he found Cherney to be honest and dedicated to his client's interests, though given to poetic imagery that at times might have soared over jurors' heads. But Cherney had the unsavory task of battling nearly everyone involved, including Dana's lawyer, Kinney, who seemed as eager to convict Joel as the prosecution was. It was evident that Cherney found Kinney's tactics unsavory. His temper flared from time to time when Kinney sought to bury Joel under a mountain of innuendo.

And Kinney's booming delivery began to grate on jurors. One passed a note to the judge, asking, "Is it necessary for Mr. Kinney to stand directly in front of the jury box? His voice has a tendency to reach yelling levels and is very irritating to the jurors."

Kinney, too, had his temperamental moments. As the judge was ruling during a closed-door hearing one morning, Kinney muttered, "Fucking asshole," after Oppliger had giggled. Hammerschmidt leaned forward in his seat.

"What did you say?"

The seventy-five-year-old judge, Frank Creede, appeared oblivious to the exchange and continued on. The court reporter's gaze went back and forth between the judge and attorneys.

"Asshole," Kinney said.

"No, you said, 'fucking asshole.'"

Whereupon the reporter threw her hands in the air and

said she could only follow one speaker at a time. (The record would show the profane sidebar comments.)

And then it was Souza's turn again. Oppliger wanted the jury to know why Souza thought the burglary scene was staged.

"There was the precision shooting of the victims," Souza told the silent courtroom, "and the fact that there was obviously a separation in time from the mother and daughter getting home and Mr. Ewell getting home.

"I think the biggest thing that told me this was not a burglary was the policing of the shell casings. You have to ask yourself why a person would do that? Why would you pick up brass fired from a gun you just stole?"

Jim Oppliger asked the detective for his conclusions.

"This was a make-believe burglary, or someone wanted us to believe it was a burglary. And those people were killed for a reason."

Souza was back on the stand the next day, and the subject of Oppliger's questions was the alleged hit man in the crime:

Q: Did you have any particular interest in him?
A: No, other than he was a friend of Dana's.

Souza told the court about that first phone call to Joel, and Oppliger asked for details.

Q: What did he say?
A: Again, he asked why we wanted to talk to him. At which point he made the comment, "Are you going to arrest me?"

(This curious, some would say stupid, question from Joel was the source of considerable speculation among participants and analysts. Earlier, Oppliger had told Souza he'd read a primer for hired killers called *Hit Man*, which Oppliger became convinced Joel had studied. In *Hit Man*, the reader/would-be hired killer is instructed to deal with investigators by immediately determining if he is to be arrested.)

Oppliger walked Souza through the interview with Joel.

> Q: Did you inquire a second time about the
>   closeness of his relationship with Mr.
>   Ewell?
> A: He stated it wasn't a boyfriend-
>   girlfriend kind of thing.

Souza said Joel claimed during the interview that he hadn't heard about the murders until the detective called.

> Q: Did that conflict with the answer he
>   gave you (the day before)?
> A: Yes it did.

Souza's appearance was followed by testimony from the floral-shop owner, who said Joel signed for a plant delivered to Dana's house. The jury was shown a receipt that had been initialed, "J. R."

Souza thought, Should have initialed it KILLA J. R.

The day's final prosecution witness was an investigator for health-insurance provider Blue Shield. Francine Verdier told the court Dana and Joel had policies with her company, and the bills for both were mailed to 5663 E. Park Circle Drive.

While seemingly subtle, this testimony was in fact powerful in its implication: the Blue Shield billing provided a direct—not circumstantial—financial link between Dana and Joel.

Estate attorney Michael Dowling explained the particulars of the Ewell will. Dana received nearly half a million dollars shortly after his family was killed, Dowling said, though the balance of funds was to be paid out over a period of years. In addition, Dana assumed control of his grandmother's three-hundred-seventy-five thousand dollar trust account.

Another witness testifying on money matters was Kyle Stephenson, an accountant hired by the DA's Office to audit Dana's financials. Stephenson told the court that a total of $124,153 in cash was unaccounted for. (It was vital the prosecution establish that Dana had had the funds available to make payments, directly or indirectly, to Joel as alleged.)

The prosecution used an ELMO slide system to project financial records onto a large screen, but it soon became clear that the presentation lacked cohesiveness (mostly resulting from the complexity of the evidence and the logistics of juggling appropriate witnesses). Oppliger considered this portion of the trial an unfortunate necessity, and was glad to get it behind him (the financials could not be put off until closing arguments, when a succinct, captivating presentation was called for).

Opening up week six, a former Santa Clara University resident director, who had lived in the dorm with Dana and Joel, testified that Ewell had claimed to make "two to three million dollars" when he'd sold his Piper airplane dealership.

Dana bragged he'd bought the ailing dealership and turned it around, making a fortune, David DiBono told Jeff Hammerschmidt.

> Q: Did he tell you what his father did?
> A: He told me he was a vice president of a major stock brokerage.
> Q: Did he say the name?
> A: Shearson Lehman.

All this spoke to a number of Dana's traits that the prosecution felt the jury must recognize: his obsession with riches, his ability to con and manipulate, and, already living his dream of being a multimillionaire, his desire that it not end.

DiBono explained that part of his job at Casa Italiano was to learn who was friends with whom, and he often spotted Dana and Joel together in the lunchroom, or in Dana's room. As for Joel's attitude and habits, Joel "had his clothes all over the floor," and had been involved in several incidents at the dorm.

> Q: One of them was when he spit an apple in the hallway?
> A: Uh, yes.
> Q: And another incident was when he took some salad out of the bowl with his hands and smelled it and put it back in the bowl?
> A: Yes.

Then Boudreau was back. He provided foundational information for the upcoming testimony of criminalist Luke Haag. Haag himself appeared briefly before court recessed for the day, and Oppliger established Haag's credentials as an expert.

"I'm involved in the first official investigation into the death of Meriwether Lewis of Lewis and Clark," the polished Haag responded to Oppliger's inquiry about famous cases in which he had consulted. "When the body is exhumed (I) will conduct the firearms portion of the investigation (into the mysterious death of the famous explorer and secretary to Thomas Jefferson)."

The next morning, before Haag resumed testimony, Ernest Kinney offered two stipulations. First, Kinney offered to stipulate to the expertise of Haag and, "in the separate trial of Dana Ewell, we would also stipulate that the Ponce gun barrel is the murder weapon of Tiffany and Glee Ewell."

This was a return to a theme proffered in Kinney's opening argument: Ponce bought the gun that Joel used to kill the Ewells, and, by inference, Ponce and Joel had committed the crime.

In Oppliger's view this tactic was designed to: help Kinney establish his own credibility; argue that Dana did not question the truth here, only the falsehoods; and undercut Cherney's probable challenge of Boudreau's conclusion that the evidence (murder) bullets had been fired through the recovered Jack Ponce barrel.

Cherney, shaking with anger, told the court that such a stipulation would implicate Joel Radovcich. The judge instructed the lawyers that the issue would be taken up out of the presence of jurors.

This cleared the way for the resumption of Haag's testimony, during which he concluded that:

- the six murder bullets came from the same gun.
- the barrel of the murder weapon was ported.
- the steel-wool fragments found near Glee's body contained gunshot residue.
- the murder bullets probably came from the box of bullets found in the Ewell nightstand.

In a bizarre incident, a deputy hurried into court and whispered into Hammerschmidt's ear. Hammerschmidt asked the court for a moment, and told Souza to follow the deputy.

Souza was led into, of all places, the men's bathroom, where the deputy pointed out a note he had discovered. It read:

I believe Monica Zent coerced your client. For a good time call her at Saban Entertainment, 10960 Wilshire Blvd Los Angeles, CA.

Saban was Zent's current employer.

The note was unsigned. Souza had no clue as to its authorship, and none was ever found. Sometime later, a deputy found another note scrawled on the posted courtroom schedule:

Monica Zent did it!

FIVE

TESTIMONY GIVEN ON THURSDAY, FEBRUARY 5, further served to link the lives and destinies of Dana Ewell and Joel Radovcich, and stipulations between attorneys established dozens of financial ties between the two. Cashier's checks drawn in the pseudonym "Dan James" or the fictional LTW Trucking, bearing the signature of Dana, were used to pay Radovcich's health insurance. Both men's signatures appeared on the back of a refund check from Mazzie Flying Service. Radovcich bills had been sent to Dana's Los Angeles PO Box. And all financial transactions ceased after their arrests.

Oppliger believed this presentation forged further indisputable links between the defendants. But most important, this covert close contact took place well after Joel had been named as the primary suspect in the deaths of Dana's family—a strange association at best.

The prosecutor called witnesses to establish that Dana had rented the Broadcast Center "safe house" apartment in LA. A defense team private investigator then testified that he'd moved Dana's belongings from Broadcast Center to a Fresno storage unit after Dana's arrest. Souza and the prosecution considered this action a crude attempt to hide evidence from the prosecution.

(When uncovered, investigators found a sign on the unit that read: THIS IS ATTORNEY-CLIENT PRIVILEGED MATE-

RIAL IN CONTROL OF NUTTALL BERMAN ATTORNEYS. It may not be seized or searched, even with a search warrant, without the participation of a special master appointed by the court. Nuttall Berman will cooperate with any special master appointed.

Oppliger laughed off what he called a "blatant ruse" by Berman and pasted the sign up in his office, attaching an addendum that read:

THE CONTENTS WERE SEARCHED AND THEN SEIZED ON MARCH 22, 1997. One could draw a number of inferences:

1. If Berman's language had been more precise, i.e., "May not be searched and then seized," perhaps the warning would have been heeded?
2. We don't read too good . . .
3. We love you, Rick! This notice was an inspiration and identified the property that we were interested in.
4. All we wanted was this really neat souvenir.

FSO Detective Mark Chapman was up next, explaining that he had served a search warrant on the storage unit and delivered the property to Souza (which included Monica Zent's HK 9-millimeter pistol).

Before the day's session concluded, Oppliger called FSO forensic technician Mary Joseph to the stand. Joseph said she'd processed for fingerprints a gun-cleaning kit found among Dana's stored items.

"Did you find any [prints]?" said Oppliger.

"Yes, more than one," Joseph said.

And one, she said, matched Radovcich's right index finger.

On Monday, February 9, the trial opened with Shelby Grad on the stand. He was called to shore up the image of Dana as a money-obsessed con man.

Now a *Los Angeles Times* reporter, he had been an

intern with the *San Jose Mercury News* when Dana persuaded him to do a story profiling his financial wizardry. Dana called himself, Grad said, the "Cal Worthington of airplanes," a reference to a California businessman who had used cheesy television spots to build one of the world's largest auto dealerships.

"We wouldn't have printed it unless we believed it to be true," Grad said, acknowledging that the story turned out to be bunk.

The first surveillance undertaken by detectives from the Narcotics Unit was the subject of much of the testimony of February 10.

Oppliger, anticipating the possibility of jury confusion and boredom as they sat through hours of dry surveillance testimony, decided to schedule the narcotics detectives in teams. If a team had tailed Joel on a particular day, members of that team would appear one after the other to re-create the events as they'd happened.

Mostly, this approach was a success. While the jury seemed to fade when testimony dragged, members would perk up upon hearing the occasional eye-popping detail.

Allen DeCamp said he'd followed the defendants to the United Security Bank on Shaw Avenue. Surveillance photos of the pair were displayed.

"They came out a short time later, Mr. Ewell carrying a briefcase. He put it in the backseat of the Mercedes and they drive off."

"Was there a period as they left the bank when they both appeared to be smiling?" Oppliger asked DeCamp.

"Yes sir," DeCamp said.

Kinney cross-examined DeCamp, establishing that DeCamp did not know what was inside the briefcase. Toby Rein was up next, describing the countersurveillance driving techniques employed by Dana during this period, the week of June 25, 1992.

The day was cut short by the illness of a juror, a chemist with heart problems who had already undergone an angioplasty treatment during the trial.

The jury was taken on the road for a tour of the crime scene, accompanied by the judge, trial attorneys, and a court reporter.

One juror asked about the alarm. "On the alarm box or inside the alarm box, is there a trigger that when you open the door would set off the alarm?"

Though jurors' questions would be answered later in the week, it was clear they were attempting to test defense contentions that intruders had entered in a manner other than that theorized by detectives. (The prosecution, as the defense knew, had intended to propose that Dana gave Joel a key to the Ewell home, but the difficulty of firmly establishing this, especially in light of Ponce's claim that Joel had not had a key, led the prosecution to abandon their theory. The defense, for their part, hoped to show that Sheriff's Department personnel had not checked every possible entrance.)

Other juror questions:

Was the breaker box locked at the time?

Were photos taken of the breaker box?

Were windows wired into the alarm? (Jurors were seen to examine windows, as if checking for cobwebs described by Ybarra.)

Was the door leading from the garage to the house locked?

Could all exterior doors be opened with one key?

One request was refused by the judge at Souza's urging. A juror asked if he could climb up on the roof to examine the skylights. Souza told the judge that the roof was wet from recent rains; it would certainly be dangerous to go climbing around.

Besides, the juror who had asked was the very same chemist who had been experiencing heart trouble of late.

* * *

The ailing chemist was replaced on February 18 by an alternate juror in his thirties, a "hard worker and Sunday school teacher" whose sister worked with the FBI.

Allen Boudreau was recalled after follow-up testimony by surveilling narcotics detectives. He said the rifling grooves in the barrels of the AT9 and Browning differed slightly, and told the jury this was determined by lining up tracings made from photographs of bullets fired from both guns.

During the lunch break, Oppliger wished aloud to Souza that Boudreau's testimony had been condensed, especially details of the scientist's early firearms research, much of which was now academic in light of the discovery of the Ponce barrel.

Still, Oppliger allowed, an intelligent juror watching Boudreau on the stand would come to appreciate Boudreau's first-rate intelligence and abilities; the criminalist's work on the case had been objective, innovative, even brilliant.

After weeks of mostly technical discussions in the courtroom, the jury saw outbursts of emotion from lawyers, witnesses, the judge, and Dana Ewell himself.

Dana's uncle Dan Ewell, making no effort to disguise his contempt for Dana, described events of the night after the bodies were discovered, when burial plans were discussed among family members. He said a funeral-home representative had asked whether there was a will that might contain burial instructions.

Oppliger asked, "Did anyone speak up with apparent knowledge of existence of a will?"

"No one was familiar with one," Dan said.

But Dana and the brothers had clashed openly when Dana insisted all three bodies be cremated. The uncles argued that their big brother would receive a traditional burial.

When Dan testified that his nephew threw a fit after

learning he wouldn't immediately inherit the family fortune, Dana called out in a stage whisper, "Liar!"

Ben Ewell took the stand and said he had contacted Dowling for a copy of the will. When the family later got together for the reading, Special Agent John Zent invited himself in.

"John Zent started into the room, and Dana said, 'No, I think you should stay outside.' "

The three brothers sat down with Dana. Ben, an attorney, noted there were no burial instructions in the will.

"Then Dana said, 'Well, what about the money?' "

When told he'd get half when he was thirty and half at thirty-five, Dana reacted harshly.

"He seemed startled. He sort of lunged, lurched forward, brought his fist down and said, 'Why did my father do that?' "

Kinney crossed, forcefully asking Ben if any of the brothers had threatened their sister, pressuring her not to help Dana.

"No, I love my sister," Ben said. "I'd never threaten her. We don't agree on everything. We don't agree on this. She got taken in."

As the cross-examination continued into the late afternoon, Ben Ewell and Ernest Kinney grew more combative, testing the judge's patience on areas previously ruled inadmissible. When the two engaged in a virtual shouting match, Judge Creede, too, blew up, pounding the bench with his fist.

"Listen! I don't know if the sheriff has a [cell] across the street, but if they do, we just might be utilizing it!"

At which point the questioning wound down quickly, and Creede dismissed everyone early.

The next week resumed a day late and without the presence of Ernest Kinney, ailing with a flu, and defender

Peter Jones, whose father had suffered a pair of heart attacks over the weekend.

The day's first witness was a Pacific Bell employee, explaining the function of a Dialed Number Recorder. Souza was up next. He introduced a list of phone numbers logged from the cloned Radovcich pager. The prosecution also pointed out an April 9, 1992, Canoga Park pay-phone call, made one day after Joel received the AT9, to another pay phone at the Santa Clara Wendy's restaurant.

Jennifer McDonald also took the stand. A classmate of Joel's, she claimed she'd once had romantic feelings for him. Oppliger established that she had often spoken by phone with Joel during 1992 and 1993—but he'd never, she insisted, called her at the Santa Clara Wendy's.

Cherney asked about her personal relationship with Joel. He wanted to know, did Joel like to be touched?

"No," McDonald told Cherney. "He said he couldn't really feel it."

The surveillance of Radovcich was the topic of an entire day of court testimony. FSO narcotics detectives said Joel took his helicopter lessons, ate at Taco Bell, and drove, "Extremely fast. Very fast."

Detective John Avila, questioned by Cherney, talked about the time he followed Joel to the edge of the Malibu cliffs. Cherney asked what was below the edge of the cliffs.

```
A: Just rocks and water.
Q: You became concerned for Mr. Radovcich
   at that point?
A: Yes sir.
Q: How long did he stand on the edge of the
   cliff?
A: Five or ten minutes at most.
Q: Did you form an opinion?
```

```
A: I felt he may [sic] commit suicide and
   jump over the edge of the cliff.
```

Detective Pursell recounted Joel's call, "Bring your parents and your sister. Give me the keys and we'll have a party at your house."

The courtroom seemed to inhale collectively.

Detectives continued their testimony about Joel's movements in mid-1993, and for the first time Judy Radovcich appeared in the courtroom to watch her son's trial.

Detective Robert Moore told of spotting Joel in downtown Fresno traffic, and the hastily gathered surveillance team following Joel to 5663 East Park Circle, then to the 7-Eleven and the meeting with Dana.

"What did Mr. Ewell say?" Jim Oppliger asked Chris Curtice during testimony on Wednesday, March 4.

"That he didn't believe this was the appropriate time or place."

To an unusually attentive courtroom, Curtice continued with his story of the night he and Ernie Burk had paid Dana a visit at his dorm. Oppliger asked how Dana reacted to the statement that detectives suspected Joel Radovcich had killed the Ewells.

Curtice said, "He went from being aggressive, his chest out, to basically hunched over. He looked kind of shocked."

And the jury heard how, a short while after the dormitory confrontation, Dana drove off, Monica at his side, and employed counter-surveillance techniques to lose the detectives. Curtice testified that when he located the Mercedes again, Dana was leaving a phone booth from which someone had paged Joel Radovcich.

Souza watched the jury carefully as Oppliger questioned Michael Poindexter. Poindexter spoke effectively of Dana's greed (both surprising and pleasing Oppliger that he had apparently come to recognize the dark side of Dana).

What, the prosecutor wanted to know, had he seen in the Ewell house weeks after the murders? Poindexter said there was still blood on the walls. And brain matter.

Most of the jury—all of the women jurors—turned slowly toward Dana, and Souza felt the monster's mask had been ripped completely away.

By March 9, 1998, almost six years after the murders and three months into the trial, prosecutors had called a total of ninety-two witnesses to the stand. Still to come were Jack Ponce and Peter Radovcich, who prosecutors said would appear near the conclusion of the People's case.

One question remained—would Dana Ewell testify on his own behalf?

Over the next week and a half, the jury heard hours of testimony that prosecutors hoped would firmly establish the communicative ties between Joel and Dana—communication the People believed was blatantly conspiratorial and damning to the defendants.

Most damning, perhaps, was Detective Haroldson's account of the May 19, 1993, call, which he'd recorded with a hidden transmitter. Not only did phone records and surveillance notes indicate that Dana and Joel were talking at that time, but the jury heard Joel say on tape, "I think they have the phones tapped."

And then the jury heard Joel call Dana by name.

On March 16, after days of testimony about Joel's flying-lesson expenses, Peter Radovcich's ex-wife made an appearance on the stand. Blond and undemonstrative, Danielle Bargerstock was asked about the Easter weekend of 1992. She claimed to recall few details of either that Saturday night or Sunday morning.

Knowing Peter had stated in police interviews that Joel had been in Los Angeles on Sunday morning, Oppliger asked Bargerstock, "Do you have any recollection if Joel

Radovcich was there when you got home in the morning?"

"I don't recall."

And, Bargerstock testified, while she remembered seeing Peter on the night "when the earthquake happened"—the night Peter and Ponce claim they'd disposed of Joel's guns, books, and clothes—she had no recollection of having seen Ponce.

(Despite her failure to recall dates, the prosecution would weave her statements with Ponce's and Peter Radovcich's using a technique called "event dating"; that is, using events such as the earthquake and LA riots to attach actual dates to events described.)

Souza was up next. Kinney wanted to know what had happened to the second box of ammunition purchased in 1971 by Dale Ewell. He asked Souza whether investigators had searched the storage shed for that second box of cartridges. Souza said he hadn't.

How about the Jeep, Kinney said. Did Souza know if the second box had been left in the unlocked Jeep?

"No," Souza said.

Oppliger was less than thrilled with Souza's response. Had Souza taken a moment to explain that searching the Jeep had been the responsibility of technicians, rather than simply answering "no," he might have blunted Kinney's obfuscation tactics.

Kinney apparently hoped jurors would doubt the killings had been an inside job, as the prosecution had contended. If the killer loaded his gun with bullets found outside the home, and then followed the women inside, he could have been a complete stranger.

Moving on, Souza recounted how he had left a message on Peter Radovcich's answering machine claiming Dana had hired someone to kill Joel. Under cross, Ernest Kinney hinted that Souza's actions had put Dana's life on the line.

"You knew the killings were done with a high-powered weapon?" he shouted.

"I knew they were done with a nine-millimeter weapon," Souza said.

Kinney asked whether Souza had considered the consequences to Dana when leaving the message.

"The purpose of me leaving that message was that I felt Joel had information I was trying to solicit."

Radovcich's lawyer followed up on this line of questioning.

Q: It's not uncommon for police officers to create a situation in order to further an investigation?

A: It's not uncommon, no.

Q: It's not uncommon to attempt to get a reaction by fabricating or lying about certain information?

A: That's correct.

Oppliger winced. He wished Souza had clarified that this was sometimes done, and why, and Oppliger wondered if other cops listening to the radio were at that moment using Souza's name in vain.

Boudreau also resumed his testimony. He detailed his early firearm experiments, the recovery of the buried barrel, and the nature of the scratches that are formed on bullets when fired through a ported barrel. And then it was time for an appearance by the first of the People's key witnesses.

On the stand over the course of three days, Peter Radovcich told the Court about helping his younger brother build and test silencers, and of the time a few days after the murders when Joel showed up in a state of panic. Looking very much like Joel, but with thinning hair cut into a spiky flattop, Peter also testified that he and Ponce had destroyed evidence given them by his brother.

But it was under cross on Monday, March 23, that Ernest Kinney brought out what it was that had Joel in such a state.

Q: He told you he'd gotten a message?
A: Correct.
Q: How long before?
A: He didn't say.
Q: You don't know if it was two hours before, four hours before, or eight hours before?
A: No.
Q: What did he say?
A: He said he got a message and he needs to get out of town.

Judge Frank Creede appeared astonished that Kinney had brought in this evidence—potentially highly damaging to his client—after it had been ruled inadmissible.

Oppliger was thrilled. He believed that what had come to be called the "panic page" reasonably established Dana's position as Joel's accomplice, as the page had come shortly after Dana was informed by John Zent that an arrest was imminent. Oppliger asked that similar statements from Jack Ponce be considered by the jury against both defendants, but Creede continued to limit the hearsay evidence.

Cherney, seeing that Dana had waived previous objections to this testimony (and possibly seeing his chance to strike back at the Ewell team for their early attempts to sacrifice his client) pushed Peter for the remainder of the hearsay testimony.

"What were (Joel's) exact words?"

"That he got a code on his pager," Peter said.

Then the mustachioed Jones, his prior rulings in a shambles, asked the judge for a hearing out of the jury's presence. When the jury returned half an hour later, they were admonished by Judge Creede that the evidence concerning messages on Joel's pager could only be considered in the case against Joel, and not used against Dana.

Richard Ewell, the last of Austin Ewell's sons to take the stand, corroborated his brothers' accounts that Dana had been shocked and upset upon learning he would not immediately inherit the family millions. At the completion of Richard's testimony, the time had come for Ernest Jack Ponce to make his appearance as the prosecution's star witness. The date was Friday, March 27, 1998.

Lawyers for both sides had already questioned Ponce's sister, Sabrina Bates, and brother-in-law, Jack Bates. Both insisted Ponce had been with them and other family members on Easter Sunday, 1992. Oppliger showed the jury a photo of the Bates family, standing in their kitchen with Jack, and Sabrina said the photo had in fact been taken on Easter.

Ernest Kinney had tried to corner her. Was she positive that photo was taken Easter Sunday?

"I'm pretty positive, yes. I'm positive."

"Well," Kinney said. "It was pretty positive, now it's positive?"

"I'm positive."

SIX

THE COURTROOM FILLED TO CAPACITY FOR THE afternoon session, with much of Fresno anticipating fireworks during Ponce's testimony. Richard and Dan Ewell were in attendance, as was Judy Radovcich.

Jack Ponce coolly took the stand. Oppliger broke the silence, walking Ponce through his early association with the Radovcich brothers. It had begun in high school. Then, somehow, they fell out of touch until 1991, the year Ponce sublet his apartment to Joel. That was the year, Ponce said, that he and Joel became partners in crime.

Oppliger, as a matter of strategy—to show he wasn't hiding the ball, and to blunt the potential damage the defense could later do with this testimony—pressed for details.

> Q: During that summer, did you and Mr. Radovcich steal a motorcycle?
>
> A: Yes, we did.
>
> Q: Describe that for me.
>
> A: I had purchased a—it wasn't a salvaged, but it was crashed—motorcycle. I wanted to be able to fix it up.
>
> Q: Did you do anything else wrong that summer?
>
> A: Yes. We stole another motorcycle with

356

the idea of making a profit on it, but
that didn't happen.
Q: Did you do anything else that summer?
A: Yes, we did. Joel crashed his Honda and
needed a part for it. I stood outside
while he stole one, then we went to a garage and took the part he needed.

Oppliger progressed to asking Ponce about the first gun
he had furnished to Joel, a .22 caliber Beretta.

Q: Why did you give it to Joel?
A: He was learning how to make silencers
for weapons. He needed a weapon with a
barrel that protruded, and the Beretta
has a protruding barrel.

Joel built a silencer, Ponce said, one that had to be held
to the Beretta's muzzle, and it worked.

Ponce later gave Joel a Llama .380 handgun, so that
Joel could continue his experiments on silencers. After
that, Joel said he required a gun with an extended barrel
that could be removed.

The jury learned about the van Ponce wanted to buy,
and Joel's urgent need for an AT9 in March of '92, and
they learned how Ponce bought the gun with money provided by Joel.

Oppliger asked Ponce what he had thought Joel would
do with the weapon.

"I didn't know. I thought he was going to sell it."

As days of testimony progressed, Ponce related the
story of his growing involvement with Joel and the crime
in 1992.

First, he supplied the weapon. Then he helped dispose
of the gun and other evidence, and finally Joel confessed
on the beaches of Malibu.

Q: On the beach that day in Malibu, did Joel Radovcich tell you what he had done with the AT9 that you had purchased for him?

A: Yes, he did.

Q: What, if anything, did he say he did with it?

A: He shot three people with it.

Q: Did Joel Radovcich state the names of the victims that had been shot?

A: At that time, no.

Ponce stated that he knew, soon after the confession, the name was Ewell, from Fresno.

Q: Did Mr. Radovcich tell you whether or not he knew the family would be gone on this particular occasion?

A: He said he knew they'd be away at the time when he arrived.

Q: Did Mr. Radovcich tell you whether or not he knew that they would be coming back?

A: He knew roughly the time when they would be coming back home.

Q: Did Mr. Radovcich tell you whether or not he made any preparations prior to the homicide?

A: He said he shaved his body of all . . . taken all the hair off his body.

After the lunch recess, Oppliger came back to the discussion between Ponce and Joel at Malibu beach.

Q: Did he mention anything about an alarm system?

A: No, he did not.

Q: Did he mention anything about any windows that he was cognizant of?

A: He knew there was a window going—leading into the garage that didn't have an alarm on it.

Q: Did he specifically state whether he used that or not?

A: No, he did not.

Q: Did he state whether or not he arrived before the family?

A: He said he got there before the family arrived there.

Q: Did he, in the course of this conversation, did he mention how he got the AT9 into the house?

A: He loaded it into his backpack.

Q: Did he say what, if anything, he did with the gun once he got it into the Ewell house?

A: He took it out and assembled it.

Q: Did he say where he assembled it?

A: Uh . . . no. He only said where he disassembled it.

Q: Did he say whether or not, besides the gun, he brought anything else with him?

A: He stated he brought some plastic sheets to lie on.

Then, said Ponce, Joel slipped on latex gloves and prowled the "lush digs" that was the Ewell home.

Q: And who did he tell you arrived first?

A: The mother and daughter arrived first, he said.

Q: Did he tell you what happened when the daughter arrived?

A: Yes, he did. He said she walked by the

room that he was waiting in and he shot
her.

Q: Did he say where on her person he shot
her?

A: He said he shot her in the, the . . .
in the head.

Q: Did he say on which side?

A: In the back.

Q: Did he tell you what happened to the
daughter after he shot her?

A: He said she fell straight down.

Q: What room did he say he waited in?

A: The laundry room.

Q: Did Mr. Radovcich . . . what did he
say about the mother at the time that
the shooting of the daughter occurred?

A: He said she must not have heard it because she kept on talking.

(When Oppliger had mentioned this tragic human detail
in his opening, several jurors cried.)

Q: What did Mr. Ewell—strike that. What
did Mr. Joel Radovcich state with respect to what he did in terms of the
mother?

A: Uh, he said he went and shot her and that
possibly she was the only person who
saw him.

Q: Did he state to you during the conversation how many shots were involved
with the mother?

A: Uh, he stated multiple times, and that
he had to reload the clip—or put in a new
clip after that.

Ponce said Joel put on another pair of gloves—and later
feared he had left one glove behind—then waited for the
father to come home. Oppliger asked Ponce to use an
easel and marker to draw the scene as Joel had described
it to him. Then Oppliger moved on to the death of Dale
Ewell.

Q: Describe the scene at the point where
   the father was shot, as related to you
   by Joel Radovcich.
A: The father was shot in the throat area,
   I think, and something had come out his
   eye. And Joel was, was . . . actually,
   the thing he was looking for, I think
   about a glove, or I think that maybe
   . . . What I suggest is maybe someone
   was alive, so he—

Kinney asked that the answer be read back to the court,
and the judge obliged. Oppliger instructed Ponce to back
up in his testimony—did Joel describe the location where
the father was shot?

A: Joel stepped out of the room after he
   entered the front door.
Q: Did Mr. Radovcich state what type of
   place the father was in when the shoot-
   ing occurred?
A: I believe it was in a hallway.
Q: After—strike that. Did Joel Radovcich
   tell you how long he had to wait before
   the father returned?
A: No, he did not.
Q: Did Joel tell you what, if anything,
   Joel Radovcich did to the victims after
   the shootings?
A: He tried to check their pulse.

Q: Did he say by what method he attempted to check their pulse?

A: He used his forefingers with the gloves on and tried to dig them into their forearm to get a pulse.

Q: And did you make any statements with respect to the efficiency of that method?

A: I said it probably wouldn't have worked very well.

Ponce went on to demonstrate the method he'd explained to Joel, touching two fingers to the inside of his wrist. Oppliger asked if Joel removed anything from the residence after the killings.

A: He said he took a cover weapon and some money.

Q: Did he tell you why he took a weapon?

A: Yes, because he'd learned that a cover weapon was something that you take to throw off people as to what gun was actually used.

Q: Moving back—pardon me for doing this—did Mr. Radovcich tell you whether or not he heard any noises associated with the father after the time of the killing?

A: He heard a gurgling sound.

Q: You mentioned that he had stated he had taken some money?

A: That's correct.

Q: Do you recollect how much money he told you he took?

A: I believe it was the $1,500 he had at the hotel, the only reason I know is because he had it out when he was telling me how much money he had for rooms.

[This was a reference to the Half Moon Hotel in Los Angeles, where Joel had stayed on April 23, 1992, using a stolen ID provided by Ponce, after Joel claimed he received a page to "get out of town." Souza later found the registration receipt and matched the handwriting to Joel's.]

Q: Did he say where, specifically, he got this money?

A: No, he did not.

Q: Did he say whether or not he had expected to find money at the Ewell residence?

A: He did not.

Joel, Ponce testified, then disassembled the AT9 on the office desk and put it in his backpack.

Q: Did he tell you whether or not any portion of the gun had . . . had malfunctioned during the event?

A: Yes. He said that was the shell catcher.

Q: Did Mr. Radovcich tell you when he left the Ewell residence?

A: He had to leave when it was dark outside. That's what he said.

Q: At some point during this discussion, did you castigate Joel Radovcich for using the gun that you had supplied him?

A: Yes, I did.

Q: And what, if anything, did he say?

A: He said he was sorry.

Q: After he said "I'm sorry," did he say anything else.

A: He said, "If there is a God, I'm fucked."

Q: Did Joel Radovcich tell you why he had
   committed these murders?
A: Yes, he said to split $8 million.

(The pretrial rulings on this hearsay statement had been
mixed, even contradictory. But Oppliger, determined that
this vital statement come out in open court, had warned
his witness that he would need him to produce a copy of
the preliminary transcript at that point. The question was
asked exactly as had been asked at the prelim, and after
determining that Ponce still remembered the details,
Ponce was to answer in the exact same manner. Oppliger
rushed through this portion of the testimony.)

Oppliger asked Ponce to read his statement made to
police.

Q: Does that refresh your memory?
A: Yes it does.
Q: Okay, I'll reask the question. Did Joel
   tell you why he committed these mur-
   ders?
A: To split the inheritance.
Q: Did he tell you how much the inheri-
   tance would be?
A: Eight million dollars.
Q: Did Joel Radovcich tell you when he ex-
   pected to be able to collect any money?
A: He expected to collect when Dana turned
   twenty-five years old.

SEVEN

SURPRISINGLY, NONE OF THE DEFENSE ATTOR-
neys objected to this controversial hearsay. It was Judge
Frank Creede who spoke up.

"Wait a minute, I've ruled on that. It's inadmissible,
and the jury is to disregard it."

"No," Oppliger said, "you didn't."

He and Hammerschmidt were prepared for this, armed
with a copy of a transcript of the Court's ruling, though
they made a show of appearing to search their papers for
the appropriate section.

"That's the Court's ruling now. And [the testimony] is
to be disregarded, ladies and gentlemen. I'm not implying
that counsel did anything wrong, but it's to be disregarded
for rulings that I've previously made."

Creede called for a break in testimony, and went on to
explain to the jury that he'd made an ambiguous ruling,
and the prosecution could not be faulted for asking the
questions of Ponce that they did. Oppliger and Souza exchanged tight smiles—score one for the prosecution.

Oppliger then attempted to tiptoe through questions of
the inheritance; after all, the jury had already heard
Dana's name, instructions to disregard notwithstanding.

Finally, the judge would allow Ponce to state only
when Joel himself had expected to profit by the killings
(approximately three years after the crime). Nonetheless,
the damage was done—Ponce's account of the manner of

Dana's inheritance matched closely details provided in previous testimony by estate attorney Dowling.

Oppliger later moved Ponce's testimony along to the days and months after the crime, from Joel ordering the lockpick to the arrival of detectives on Ponce's doorstep, and finally the arrests, and the deal cut with prosecutors.

Q: In terms of the contract, what is your understanding of your obligations under the contract that you have with the People of the State of California?

A: My understanding is that as long as I am truthful in my testimony and—I guess being truthful would be part of not being involved in the murders—then the charges would be dismissed.

Q: What is your understanding of what could occur to you if you were to lie about the circumstances of the AT9 [purchase] or the statements that you made in your testimony?

A: To my understanding, the only way I can be injured or charged is if I do lie about any of those circumstances.

Then, for a short while on Friday afternoon, and continuing into the next week, it was the defense's turn with Ponce. An aggressive Kinney confronted Ponce about the many lies he had told to detectives.

"I was lying to them, yes," Ponce admitted.

Kinney identified inconsistencies between Ponce's account and Peter Radovcich's account of the night they destroyed evidence. But Ponce seldom wavered, keeping his cool and on occasion correcting the much larger, much louder attorney.

Kinney cornered Ponce about his Friday testimony,

when Ponce had claimed something had fallen out of Dale's eye when Dale was shot.

Q: Mr. Ponce, did you see something come
   out of Mr. Ewell's eye?
A: No.
Q: Did you pick up a bullet that came out
   of his eye because it was from a different weapon?
A: No.

Another day on the stand, and Jack Ponce continued to withstand Ernest Kinney's assault. Kinney alluded to the statement of a neighbor (Edwin Hewitt) regarding voices heard outside the Ewell home on the night before the slaughter.

"You have a soft voice, Mr. Ponce. Were you speaking in a soft voice outside the Ewell house at two or three in the morning the night before the murders?"

Ponce said, "I've never been to the Ewell house."

Before he finished with Ponce, Ernest Kinney made certain the jury heard that Ponce had been well cared for by the prosecution before the trial. For their part, the prosecution welcomed the display of a close association between themselves and Ponce; Oppliger felt the jury would conclude that the People's team did not consider Ponce a murderer, for if they had, prosecutors would have taken a hands-off attitude toward the witness.

Kinney asked about a golf game between Oppliger and Ponce.

A: I think it was nine holes.
Q: Was a total fee of $10,500 spent on you
   in that five-month period?

A: I don't know how much was spent. I know
   I was given a place to stay with a sher-
   iff's officer.
Q: Did you go golfing with the detectives?
A: I did that, yes.
Q: Did they buy you a twenty-dollar golf
   shirt?
A: I believe so.

Kinney asked about Ponce's future plans.

Q: Yesterday, did the District Attorney's
   Office fly you back to LA for a law class
   last night?
A: I had a final obligation last night.
Q: When you get out of law school, do you
   want to become a district attorney?
A: No. I want to stay as far away from crim-
   inal law as possible.

Cherney, in defense of Joel, seemed intent upon por-
traying Ponce as a ringleader. "It was your idea to steal
a motorcycle, is that true?"

Ponce admitted it was true. And Cherney broke new
ground, as it were, with Ponce, when the witness admitted
that he had once taken Joel to the field where the gun
barrel was buried.

He and Joel had been unable to locate it, Ponce told
Cherney. Cherney probed, seeking to illustrate that Ponce
well understood the importance of the buried barrel.

Q: You knew when you were talking to police officers that the barrel could be
   used in firearms identification?
A: That's correct.
Q: You knew when you told officers where
   the barrel was this was an important
   part in the investigation?

A: An identifying part, yes.

Q: But you didn't tell the officers that
   you and Joel had looked for the barrel
   before?

A: It didn't come up.

Q: And you didn't bring it up?

A: No, I did not.

On Joel's reaction to the murders, Cherney asked, "Did
he tell you how he felt?"

A: He said he got really cold. He got the
   shakes and shivers.

Q: He wasn't gloating, was he?

A: No, he wasn't gloating.

Q: And he didn't threaten you?

A: No, he didn't threaten me.

Q: He didn't betray your trust in you during this entire investigation, did he?

A: No, he didn't.

Q: What he said was, "I'm sorry, Jack"?

A: He said that repeatedly.

On April Fool's Day, proceedings concluded with the
words of Dana Ewell, captured by FSO recorders on two
consecutive days of interviews following the discovery of
the victims.

His calm monotone filled the courtroom as he described
the days before, and after, the murders. Recollections of
his father, mother, and sister were punctuated by snickering and criticisms of neighbors and Western Piper employees.

On tape, Ernie Burk asked if his parents had any enemies who might want them dead.

"Who would want them dead? My mother was very
politically minded, on the State Bar Board of Governors.
She had a lot of political power. My sister was the most

harmless creature in the world. I don't think she's ever offended anybody."

On Souza's last trip to the stand, Oppliger questioned him about possible leaks to the media. Souza maintained there was a gag order, and few details had been released by the FSO.

Kinney took a final turn with Souza, asking why, if there was a gag order, a March 1993 article in the *Bee* had contained so many details of the murders.

Judge Creede broke in, asking Kinney how long this would take.

"They brought it up, Your Honor," Kinney said, gesturing toward the prosecutors.

"They did bring it up," Creede said, "and I wonder why."

Creede knew that the introduction of the 1993 newspaper account was important to Dana's defense; Ponce had testified earlier that Peter Radovcich had read portions of the story aloud. Kinney wanted planted in the jury's minds the premise that Ponce had not learned about the case through Joel's confession, but through the *Bee* article.

The People's case against Dana James Ewell and Joel Patrick Radovcich ended with a whimper.

An alarm technician was recalled to comment further on the security system. The funeral-home representative, present during the reading of the Ewell will, appeared. Then an assistant to estate attorney Michael Dowling testified that she'd received a typed copy of the family financial statement from Dana, but she'd found no copies of the will in the Ewell home after the killings.

The judge then ordered the jury to return at 1:30 P.M. Monday, April 6, to hear defense presentations.

A neighbor of Peter Radovcich's, Yoland Wright, was the first defense witness. Wright said she'd seen Joel at her apartment complex a day before the murders. A pair of Ewell neighbors followed, describing the Sunnyside neighborhood. One added that she'd heard sounds like someone, "hitting a light piece of metal with excessive force."

Next, the defense called private investigator Craig Winstead. Winstead stated he climbed onto the roof of the Ewell house in 1995 and easily lifted the skylights above Tiffany's bathroom.

The jury saw photos of Winstead holding open a skylight.

Kinney finished the day by calling Ernie Burk. The defense wanted to know what Ben Ewell had told the detectives about the reading of the will.

Q: During that entire hour-long interview, did he ever once say Dana Ewell reacted with anger at the reading of the will?

A: No, he did not.

Q: Did he tell you Dana slammed his fist down?

A: No sir.

Q: Did he ever tell you any unusual comments Dana made at the reading of the will?

A: No sir.

Dana's defense did what they could to let jurors know that the prosecution's theories were not the only possible explanations for events in question. A Sunnyside resident said he saw a man in a tan pickup just before dusk on Easter; a former Fresno P.D. detective criticized some of the department's scene work; a roofer who hadn't tested the Ewell skylights and said "most" skylights, in general, were not screwed down.

Michael Castro offered evidence to show that Joel,

while Dana was in Mexico, had received a page originating in San Francisco.

Bob Pursell was called, and gave his account of events on the morning the bodies were found.

(After the arrests, Pursell had realized his dream; he'd purchased Western Piper Sales from the Ewell estate. And during the postarrest investigation, the District Attorney's Office verified something Dana had suspected and brought to Souza's attention. DA investigators wrote in a 1996 report:

```
Mr. Pursell stated when he was confronted
by the Estate Attorney that he had falsi-
fied the letter, dated April 12 and bearing
the typewritten signature of Dale Ewell.
He stated Mr. Ewell was very hard on him as
an employee and he did not like that at
all.)
```

Souza watched Pursell, remembering the letter and the times Pursell had vilified Dale in the press.

Calling out, "Hi, Dana," on his way to the stand, John Zent testified about his time with the Ewell family. He was asked about the grocery and drugstore receipts dated April 19, 1992; Zent insisted it was his idea, not Dana's, to retrieve the paperwork from his trash, and said the notion had come to him after conversations with his daughter Monica.

Yet to Souza this testimony was troubling. While detectives didn't question Dana's alibi, Zent's account of the receipts and their origination didn't add up.

When Zent had come to the FSO with receipts on April 22, 1992, Lieutenant White recalled that Zent had done so at Dana's request. And DA investigators reported that Zent, in a post-arrest interview, had claimed it was Dana who had told him about the Easter 1992 purchases. Yet in court, the story was different.

On cross-examination by Oppliger, Zent denied he'd told DA investigators that Dana informed him of the purchases and where the receipts could be found.

Oppliger frequently objected to Zent's favorable comments about Dana. Several of those remarks were stricken from the record. Souza, no fan of Zent's, bristled as Zent implied that he himself had run the show during the walkthrough the day after the bodies were found.

Souza listened, wondering how Zent would feel if he had seen the Santa Clara University yearbook found at the "safe house" and turned over to the prosecution. When Souza had thumbed to the page containing Monica Zent's photo he found, to his astonishment, that her eyes had been shot out. Ponce claimed that Joel had been jealous of the amount of money Dana lavished on Monica, and Souza wondered if Joel's arrest hadn't prevented Monica's becoming another homicide victim in the Ewell case.

Oppliger asked for Zent's opinion about the crime scene. "On that occasion, was it apparent to you this was a phony burglary?"

Zent said he'd made that statement after viewing the home.

"What caused you to make that statement?"

"A number of things. At the scene, there wasn't a lot of blood. I asked a detective if Tiffany had been molested or raped, and he said no. Based on that, and what appeared to be very minor property set out on a sheet, led me to believe it was not a legitimate burglary."

When it was over, Zent's testimony seemed to have hurt the defense more than it helped.

Outside during a break, Oppliger nudged Souza. "Watch this." He approached Peter Jones. "Hey, you gonna put Dana on the stand?"

Jones snorted. "Are you kidding? After what you did to Zent?"

It was official—Dana would not testify in his own defense.

Edwin Hewitt repeated the story he'd told investigators: He was dating a Ewell neighbor in 1992, and while awaiting her return had heard noises next door.

"It sounded like somebody loading something into the bed of a truck." Of the voices he heard, Hewitt said, "They were completely different. One was like telling the other what to do."

Kinney asked Hewitt to describe that voice.

"Mild and soft."

"Mild and soft," echoed Kinney.

It was, of course, an allusion to Ponce, but as interview tapes had revealed, the same description might have applied to Dana's voice.

Souza had wracked his brain over Hewitt's account. What if Dana had driven from Pajaro Dunes to Fresno the night before the murders, let Joel into the house, and returned to the beach house early that morning? Souza wished he could prove this had happened—the case against Dana would be watertight—but with only the sodden neighbor's account, the prosecution thought it best simply to ignore it.

And another possibility plagued Souza: What if the van seen on East Park Circle had been the van Ponce purchased from Peter Radovcich's employer?

Ponce had witnesses who put him in Los Angeles on Sunday afternoon. He'd also passed the polygraph. But suspicions remained in the minds of certain FSO investigators.

In the last witness, the courtroom got a sense of the collateral damage done when murder shatters a family. Betty Whitted, sister to Dan, Ben, and Richard, had unsuccessfully attempted to use her share of the estate in the defense of her nephew. The estrangement of siblings was clear

when Kinney pressed Whitted to share her current view
of her brothers.

> Q: Have you formed an opinion as to the
>   honesty or dishonesty of Dan Ewell?
> A: Yes sir, I have.
> Q: What is that opinion?
> A: That he is dishonest.

Her opinion of Ben Ewell was identical. Only her view
of Richard was tempered—somewhat.

"He's honest," Whitted said. "Most of the time."

The defense team rested its case on behalf of Dana
Ewell after only three and a half days of testimony. Cherney asked for a closed-door meeting out of the jury's presence. Five minutes later, the jury was returned.

"On behalf of Mr. Radovcich," Cherney announced,
"we have no additional evidence to offer for the jury's
consideration, and at this time we rest."

EIGHT

THE FINAL WEEK. CLOSING ARGUMENTS WERE EXpected to last until Thursday, perhaps Friday. Then it would all be up to the jury.

If the jury were to find both defendants guilty, the case would move into the penalty phase. If they should deem Joel guilty but hang on Dana's guilt, a retrial of Dana could be greatly in his favor—much of the evidence presented here would be excluded if he stood trial alone.

The prosecuting attorney understood this better than anyone, and in closing Oppliger sought to illuminate for the jury the kind of person he believed Dana to be.

"I submit to you Dana Ewell wanted to be rich like no one else who has come before him, and no one will come again. His love of money was absolutely perverted."

Oppliger displayed the bogus news articles. He reviewed the testimony of witnesses who admitted Dana was obsessed with wealth, and students who'd believed Dana was a self-made man.

"Think about how the other college students treated him because of his false persona. How do you think Dana Ewell felt? He was no longer just some rich man's son."

But that persona would be threatened upon graduation, said Oppliger. And so, with Joel lined up as his stooge, Dana began to hatch his scheme.

"In the beginning, it's reasonable to assume that there was a rather unfocused, general crunching of ideas. But they would soon have, in any plan such as this, developed some central concepts to any successful plan. And remember my . . . the basis of what I'm saying is that the plan, to be worthy of the cost-risk and benefit analysis, needs to be successful."

And that plan required secrecy, said Oppliger, as well as an expectation of risk, protection from discovery for the heir, a separation of conspirators prior to the crime, an element of surprise during the crime, a method for covert communication after the crime.

"What kind of person can have his parents killed? A spoiled, perverted, obsessive man who has tasted the trappings of wealth and doesn't want to give them up."

What about the crime scene, Oppliger asked the jury.

"Strangers do not alter crime scenes. The killer in the Ewell house did. Why? A crime scene is staged to redirect investigators away from the most likely suspect."

And Joel "had no reason to stage the crime scene," and "no connection with either Fresno, Mr. and Mrs. Ewell, Tiffany Ewell, or the Park Circle address."

The second day, Oppliger moved on to attacking defense theories, which he said were moronic. "And nothing in the evidence shows you either of these men are morons.

"There has been no rational explanation for Joel Radovcich's cash. There has been no rational explanation for the secrecy between the two defendants."

Oppliger noted the many postcrime connections between Dana and Joel. "Nothing in itself is a smoking gun. But it's one thing after another. It's like the bright line stria on a bullet. At some point, those matching lines cannot be random."

And he conjured up in jurors' minds the taped interviews with Dana, citing the snickering, the offering of possible suspects.

"I submit to you that the tape recording is a behavioral confession."

Oppliger's final comments to the jury that day:

"The evolution of this case, from April 21, 1992, has

produced an overwhelming case of guilt against these two defendants. A complete and fair evaluation of the evidence in this case, mixed with a God-given common sense that you were born with, conclusively proves that these two men are guilty of the most heinous crime that man can commit, that is, multiple homicide for financial gain. In your hands lies the fate of justice. And justice, ladies and gentlemen, demands that these men answer for these three murders. Thank you."

As expected, Ernest Kinney's closing argument on Dana's behalf focused on the "real killer," Jack Ponce.

At points veering into the bizarre, his voice booming through the courtroom, Kinney told the jury that Ponce was "fueled and heated by the devil." Kinney displayed a poster featuring Ponce's name embellished with a devil's horns and tail.

"Mr. Oppliger referred to Jack Ponce as an unwitting participant. Can you believe that? Do you believe everything Jack Ponce said in this case?"

From the DA, Ponce got "the deal of a lifetime. I wouldn't play golf with Jack Ponce in a million years."

The rotund, stentorian attorney said, "I get going pretty fast in the defense of Dana Ewell, who I believe, based on this evidence, is not guilty."

The Sheriff's Department rushed to judgment about Dana, insisted Kinney. There simply wasn't sufficient evidence to convict him.

Kinney attempted to disassemble the work done by the Sheriff's Department. He questioned the motives and honesty of Dana's uncles, and friends who had testified against Dana.

He dealt with the question of Dana and Joel's association. Dana, he said, "was alone and vulnerable after the killings. A friend came who Dana never in a million years believed was involved with this, and that was Joel Radovcich."

The defendants did contact each other by phone, but

the statements made by Joel that seemed to implicate him were made to Jack Ponce, not Dana. And the money from Dana to Joel was just Dana's way of "helping out a friend."

Kinney said the deaths of three family members was a tragedy.

"Do not compound that tragedy. Do not convict an innocent man."

Cherney's emotional closing was called "eloquent" by some, "flowery" by others. And though Cherney said, "Some people wanted me to attack Dana Ewell, but I'm not going to do it," he spent most of his time calling into question Dana's character and defense.

"Joel Radovcich is the target of Dana Ewell, have no illusions about that. He's not a mastermind, and there's no betrayal in him."

He, as had Oppliger, reminded the jury of what they'd heard in Dana's tapes. "These words are preserved, for good or ill, and will resonate forever."

Cherney rejected Kinney's tactics and version of the crime.

"Dignity and integrity are qualities you have to judge from what you see and hear."

Wrapping up, he said, "Whatever your verdict, we're prepared to accept it."

Jim Oppliger, in the last presentation of the Ewell murder trial, told the jury that the lawyer for Dana Ewell admitted that much of the prosecution's case was true.

"He admitted there was a staging at the crime scene. He admitted the murder was an execution, a hit. He admitted that Dana Ewell arranged for and hired Joel Radovcich's lawyer.

"He admitted the financial allegations proposed by the prosecution. He admitted Dana and Joel communicated covertly, pay phone to pay phone. He admitted their exhaustive efforts to maintain a relationship.

"He admitted for the purpose of Dana Ewell's separate trial that Joel Radovcich was the killer.

"This case cannot so lightly be referred to as a tragedy, 'This tragedy this and this tragedy that.' This case is an outrage!"

And why, Oppliger asked, would an innocent Dana avoid investigators?

"Mr. Ewell should have had an obsessive desire to bring the killers of his family to justice. Instead, he didn't return the detectives' phone calls."

All the evidence, the prosecutor insisted, proved the guilt of Dana Ewell. Dana stared at Oppliger and shook his head.

Speaking directly to the jury, Oppliger said, "You are a team. You represent the collective consciousness of this community."

The final words of the prosecutor:

"I'll ask you this: I'll ask you to do the right thing here, folks. Don't be fooled by propaganda and legal tricks. The evidence here is strong. Very strong. And the cause of justice in this case, with this evidence, is clear . . .

"We used to have a successful businessman, Dale Ewell and his wonderful wife and companion, Glee Ewell, and their daughter Tiffany. Each of those three names are just that today—not faces, but names on a form. And as a close, I'm going to ask you for nothing more than truth in your verdicts and justice in your verdicts. I'm going to ask you, ladies and gentlemen, please sign the right form. Because justice for these triple homicides is going to be in your hands tomorrow. Do the right thing. Bring the killers of that family to justice."

Oppliger moved forward and pointed Joel. "They sit there," he said. Then he pointed to Dana. "And they sit there."

NINE

THE TRIAL, AS SUCH, WAS OVER. BUT MUCH work remained. Lawyers on both sides prepared for the penalty phase, should it come to that. They spoke to reporters about the difficulty of the moment.

"I call it the hardest part of the case," Phillip Cherney said. "It's out of our control and we really don't know what goes on in the jury room."

Ernest Kinney: "It's really terrible, number one, because of all the little things you forgot to do. The things that wake you up at two in the morning."

Peter Jones: "I have mixed emotions. It's a relief in many ways, tension in many ways."

And Jim Oppliger: "I'm sure anxiety is around the corner, but right now I'm sort of filled with—I don't know—call it the joy of finishing.

"My main sense right now is a sense of accomplishment."

The first question the jury asked of Judge Frank Creede, after the first full day of deliberations, was quite simple: Can we consider the courtroom demeanor of the defendants when reaching our decision?

Creede's equally simple response: "No."

The somber jury went back to work.

* * *

Thursday brought more jury questions. Can we take into consideration the fact that some lawyers made statements that were unsupported by evidence?

Creede said the jury was to base its decision solely on evidence, and lawyer statements were not evidence.

May we review transcripts from the preliminary hearing, other than those portions that were read into the record during the trial?

No, said Creede. The rules are different, and some testimony from the preliminary had been excluded from the trial.

We need a printed transcript of the testimony of Peter Radovcich and Jack Ponce!

Creede indicated this would be difficult—a transcript would require heavy editing to delete closed-door hearings and inadmissible statements. He suggested they ask for rereadings of testimony as the need arose.

The need did arise, and on Wednesday, May 6, the jury heard portions of Ponce's testimony. They also reviewed Ponce's phone records from the day of the murders.

Then days passed without questions or requests from the jury; Friday, then Monday, Tuesday. Wednesday. The press reviewed events, speculated on the outcome. The lawyers wrung their hands and wondered. Souza paced. Then, shortly before noon, Thursday, a request came down from the jury room:

Show us the gun.

The duplicate, silencer-equipped AT9, built by the "mad scientist," Allen Boudreau, was rendered unfireable with a plastic zip-tie and carried to the jury by court deputies.

No one but jury members knew why they wanted it.

TEN

INSIDE THE BEIGE CONFINES OF JURY ROOM 5A, twelve jurors knew the banal reason why the AT9 had been sought. In fact, one of the jurors simply wanted to see the damn thing.

Deliberations had begun around a rectangular table, jurors uneasy in their purple chairs. For six months, this tiny room had been their own prison; for much of the time, they'd been locked up, powerless and edgy, as lawyers argued fine points of the law out of their view.

Now, on the first day of deliberations in the most complex murder trial in Fresno history, all the emotions that had been corked up for a half a year roared forth as if from a bottle of warm champagne.

"Were you at the same trial I was?" one juror shouted in exasperation at another's assessment of proceedings, and indeed, it seemed each of the jurors had spent the last half year in entirely different courtrooms.

Despite the close quarters, jurors had been forbidden for the duration from discussing any aspect of the case. Nor had they been able to ask the lawyers or judge any of the myriad questions that had come to mind. So, while they'd seen one another on a daily basis, and even come to think of themselves as a family, it was a rude awakening to find such radically diverse views among members.

The two-hour initial session of deliberations was not

enough to allow each member to speak his mind, but one important decision was reached—to select Mike Elder as jury foreman.

The second day, however, was much the same as the first: bickering, topic-hopping, strong opinions, disagreement even about how to proceed. Then, utilizing an opening statement suggestion of Jim Oppliger's, Elder decided jurors would construct a case time line. Elder gave each an assignment in the time line's construction.

The jury was not sequestered, and many of them took their stress home with them. For some, even sleep was intruded upon. One female juror said she dreamed that she had forgotten to set the alarm at home and "everybody in my family had been killed and I was the only one left."

As the time line, mounted on a wall in the jury room, slowly came together, the jurors agreed on two points: They accepted Boudreau's conclusion that the Jack Ponce weapon had been used to kill the Ewell family; and they did not believe, and so would virtually ignore, Ponce's testimony (Oppliger would later insist that juries often delude themselves that the testimony of "finks" involved in crimes was of little import in their decision).

Foreman Elder learned to separate jurors with conflicting personalities, and they all learned to release pressure by turning the tide on the lawyers who had controlled their every move for so long.

"Now it's their turn to wait and guess what's going on," became a rallying cry in Jury Room 5A.

They discussed Ernest Kinney, whom most jurors had grown weary of as the trial progressed (so much so that they had collectively slammed their notebooks shut in court when Kinney spoke at length), and they decided they wouldn't punish Dana simply because they disliked his counsel.

They joked about the endless appearances of Boudreau, though they believed he was highly intelligent, honest, and competent. They agreed, for the most part, that Peter Radovcich had been an effective prosecution witness, and they felt sorry for him and Judy. They liked and respected Cherney.

And all hoped they could bring in not guilty verdicts against Dana and Joel.

"All of us have kids," Elder said. "It was so important for us that these two guys were not going to be guilty."

But with each day of analysis, argument, crying, the tide turned against the defendants. In one instance, jurors noted that Joel had received a speeding ticket in San Diego on the same day that Dana stayed at the San Diego Hilton. And the event at Santa Clara, when Curtice told Dana that the police believed Joel had murdered his family, proved hard to explain. The time line weighed heavily; one juror stared at it, muttering, "They're guilty," and collapsed and cried.

Finally, on the eighth day, it was time to vote.

ELEVEN

THE DAY OF RECKONING FOR DANA EWELL AND
Joel Radovcich came on May 12, 1998. At 10:00 A.M.,
Judge Creede took a note from the jury.

We've reached a verdict as to one defendant but are
unable to reach a verdict as to the other defendant.

Souza and Oppliger, convinced only Joel had been convicted, were despondent. Would Joel pay the ultimate
price while Dana got away with this "outrage," free to
spend his inherited millions?

Dana, Kinney, Jones, and Castro were upbeat. The conviction of Joel alone would make it nearly impossible to
later convict Ewell. Souza watched Dana grin at Kinney,
and the detective felt his stomach churn. Six years of
work, and most of what the Sheriff's Department and
prosecutors had fought for, were slipping away.

Phillip Cherney was out of the area, and the verdicts
would not be announced until he appeared. The minutes
seemed to drag by. Souza felt emotionally imploded,
overcome by dejection. Another trial would certainly be
held out of town, and Souza wondered if he and his family
could go through it all again.

Then, at 10:30 A.M., the jury asked for a tape player,
puzzling everyone. At 11:00, Cherney arrived and spectators were admitted. Twenty minutes later Judge Creede
appeared. He asked for the jury.

But when the bailiff returned, he whispered in Creede's ear.

"The bailiff informs me," Creede announced, "that the jurors need a few more minutes and that they're still filling out some forms."

What did that mean? Souza and the prosecution team huddled, trying to make sense of the judge's announcement.

Eleven-thirty-six. The jury sent out another note. The court reporter passed copies of the note to attorneys. Oppliger returned to the prosecutor's table and handed the note to Souza.

Can a person not at the scene still be considered armed?

It was a bombshell. Souza was euphoric. Oppliger struggled to subdue a grin, but Dana went rigid, and Kinney's mouth fell open. The question went to one of the enhancements in the charges, under California law: use of a gun in the commission of a homicide.

The jurors filed in to hear Creede's answer.

"Yes," he told them. "Does that answer your question?"

They nodded affirmatives and filed out again. Five minutes later, they returned. Creede asked if they'd reached verdicts on one or both defendants.

"Both, Your Honor," said the jury foreman.

The palpable silence was unbroken as Creede examined the verdict forms. He then returned them to Court Clerk Bea Perez. Perez began to read aloud:

"We the jury find the defendant, Dana Ewell, guilty of the murder of Glee Ewell, as set forth in count one of the complaint. We the jury find the defendant, Dana Ewell, guilty of the murder of Tiffany Ewell, as set forth in count two of the complaint. We the jury find the defendant, Dana Ewell, guilty of the murder of Dale Ewell, as set forth in count three of the complaint. We further find the defendant guilty of all special circumstances: multiple murder, murder for financial gain, and murder by lying in wait."

The clerk read the verdicts against Joel Radovcich.

Guilty. Guilty. Guilty. Like Dana, on all counts, including special circumstances, which could send both men to Death Row.

Two female jurors fought back tears. Dana stared vacantly at the clerk. Jones slung his arm over Dana's shoulders. Joel seemed to be studying the woodgrain in the tabletop in front of him. Mindy Ybarra placed her hands on the shoulders of Dan and Susan Ewell.

For Souza, the years of struggle had finally caught up with him. He wept.

Courtroom observers clapped and cheered, only to be told by Judge Creede, "This is not a place of entertainment."

Then Creede sent the jury home. The penalty phase would begin on May 20. Sheriff's Department personnel lined up to shake hands with Souza and the prosecutors. Souza and Oppliger faced each other, clasped hands, and grinned.

Cherney left immediately. Joel was alone, his chin cradled in his hands. The courtroom began to empty.

Outside, Dan Ewell told reporters, "We've been waiting for six years. Hopefully, we can get started now with the rest of our lives. This won't bring my brother back, but . . . I want to thank the DA's Office and the Sheriff's Department for sticking with it."

Oppliger praised the jury, and defense attorneys said they still had work to do.

Sheriff Magarian said, "I have nothing but the highest praise for Detective John Souza."

Souza faced cameras. "As the verdicts were read, I was thinking about the three deceased persons, the three victims in this case. I got a little emotional."

The press asked Souza how he felt about the defendants.

"If you watched the defendants," he said, "I think it spoke for itself. I looked at Mr. Ewell and I looked at Mr.

Radovcich during the reading of the verdicts and I was not surprised by their reactions."

"What a diligent jury," said former Bar Association president and Ewell family friend, Don Fischbach. And then he summed up events perhaps better than any observer. "It's a sad day for the entire family."

It was a hell of night, Souza would tell friends of the evening after the verdicts came in. (He had learned that the jury, during that tense half hour after they'd requested a tape recorder, had been playing a surveillance tape for the benefit of the lone holdout on Dana's conviction. Once he'd heard the tape of Joel on the phone, he sagged in his seat, and said, "I'm convinced.")

Sharon and the boys waited on the doorstep, applauding, as Souza stepped out of his car.

"Hail the conquering hero," she said.

He laughed. He'd been grinning, alone in the car the whole way home, and now he laughed out loud and he felt lighter, bouncier than he had in a long time.

"Where do you want to go to celebrate?" Michael asked.

"Go? I'm not going anywhere! I'm going to fire up the grill, sear some steaks, maybe have a beer or three or eight."

Sharon pulled him close. "You did it, baby."

TWELVE

ONE WEEK AFTER HANDING DOWN GUILTY VER-
dicts, the jury returned to the courtroom to decide if Dana
and Joel would live or die. The people of Fresno wondered, would the jurors' desire to punish the guilty be
tempered by mercy?

In his opening statement on behalf of Dana, Peter Jones
said, "The prosecution had the burden to prove their guilt
beyond a reasonable doubt, and our responsibility was to
ensure that they did exactly that. We must, and do, accept
your verdict. Now you must decide whether Dana Ewell
will be put to death or spend the rest of his life in a
penitentiary where he will die."

Some in the courtroom seemed surprised when Jones
concluded, "No additional evidence will be presented on
behalf of Mr. Ewell."

As Oppliger explained to Souza, Dana's lawyers had
argued vehemently before the jury that Dana was innocent; to now demolish their own credibility by attempting
to excuse his guilt could move the jury to punish Dana
not only for his crime, but also for his defense.

Oppliger chose to let the jury see and hear how the
murders had affected those still alive—the family members.

"He was my older brother," Dan Ewell told the courtroom, "but more than that, he was my big brother."

The jury heard about life on the Ewell farm in Ohio, a

life of windstorms that blew grit into dinner, a life without indoor plumbing. Dan Ewell said it was Dale who led the way off the farm; when Dale attended Miami University, all the brothers did, too. When Dale settled in California, his younger siblings followed him there.

"He was my idol, my role model," Richard Ewell said. "Much of what I learned, I learned watching him."

And the youngest, Ben, said he mourned for Dale's whole family. "Christmas will never be the same, and Easter obviously will be changed forever."

Of Glee he told the quiet courtroom, "I'll miss all the discussions we had about what was wrong in the world . . . and what she was going to do about it."

Tiffany was on the mind of Dan's wife, Susan.

"I miss the fact that I didn't see her mature," said the quiet blond. "I didn't see her wedding. I didn't see her children."

With the refusal of Dana's attorneys to present a defense in the penalty phase, the life and mind of Joel Radovcich took center stage in the courtroom.

Phillip Cherney had said of Joel in his opening statement, "I have made a choice to bare his life before you."

Joel's college friend, Michelle Gamble, fighting back tears, told the jury she was physically attracted to Joel, but, "It was like going to bed with my brother. He slept on one side, I slept on the other."

Joel's middle-school teacher recalled Joel's gift for drawing disturbing pictures. "(They) portrayed a lot of blood and gore. I've never seen anything so graphic in all the years I taught."

And Joel's oldest brother evoked the image of an oppressive father, an image to which other witnesses would lend credence. Sister Mary Malone once suspected that Joel had been involved in a theft at his Catholic school, but she refused to tell Nick, Sr.

"I wanted to protect Joel from that man," Sister Malone testified.

Joel's mother knew something was wrong with Joel, a child so distant that she had suspected he suffered from autism.

"Didn't Nick describe Joel to you as sick?" Cherney asked Judy Radovcich.

"Yes," she said, and she smiled at Joel, but he turned away.

These apparent emotional defects in Joel were analyzed by defense witness Mindy Rosenberg. The psychologist claimed Joel had been belittled by a domineering father, and the child's development arrested when Nick Radovcich, Sr., beat Joel's puppy to death.

"In Joel's own perception, this was the only living creature he felt safe with," Rosenberg said of the dog, Pearl.

"Joel remembers his feelings before the dog and while the dog was alive. He remembers feeling pain, mostly. But after the death of the dog, the only feeling he remembers is white noise.

"He felt every other family member could hurt him. Joel asked, 'At what point are we the dog?' "

But it was left to another psychologist, Dr. Michael Thackrey of Fresno State University, to classify Joel's disorder.

Joel's symptoms—detachment from relationships, restricted range of emotional expression, enjoyment of solitary activity, little sexual interest, indifference to praise or criticism, among other things—were characteristic of what Thackrey called schizoid personality disorder.

"He told me, 'I know there is something different about me,' " Thackrey told the silent courtroom. Thackrey said the problem had roots both genetic and environmental.

"It operates in the background range until bad things happen," the psychologist said. "That's the way people fracture."

On cross-examination, Oppliger asked, "Is there anything that would prevent him from knowing right from wrong?"

"No," Thackrey said. "It does not imply that."

*   *   *

On the very last day of testimony, jurors caught a glimpse of the damage done to Radovcich's family, and the possibility that Joel had come to understand the impact of his actions.

"I like to send my brother letters in jail," said Joel's sister Susan, nineteen. "They're usually very simple, and I'd like to keep writing those letters to him."

Phillip Cherney asked another Radovcich sister, "If your brother was sentenced to spend the rest of his life in prison, would it mean something to you?"

Anne was teary-eyed. "Yes, it would. It would mean he would still be in my life."

The most startling revelation of the penalty phase came from Joel's priest, Father Chris Ponnet, whom Joel had spoken to without the protection of the confessional and without seeking penance, and who wished to help Joel avoid the death penalty. The short, balding priest shared with the court Joel's thoughts about the murders:

I hope to be an influence on my family and be part of their lives because they care about me. I will see things in a different light for the rest of my life. I will not be short-sighted.

To the victims, their families and mine: I feel real bad and can't say sorry enough; it is a bad situation all around—unbelievably complex; I am sorry for the victims and their families; it is a real difficult situation. I'm sorry for the victims and the pain I caused.

I do not think things through—look at my history. I have no long-term outlook. I do short-term.

It takes me a long time to realize that. I am sure this turned the victims' lives upside down.

Sorry for the impact it's had on everybody's lives. Sorry doesn't seem like enough.

Without getting into the details; I am sorry about the families; I am sorry for my mom, family, and friends; I am sorry for the victims.

(A jailhouse snitch, a cellmate of Joel's, told investigators that Joel had acknowledged his crimes, but, at least when bragging to his buddies, hadn't shown any remorse. "We called him the happy triggerman," the informant claimed, "and he seemed to like it." The cellmate also claimed that Joel had said his brother Peter "got weak and pissed all over himself," and of Ponce, Joel said, "he's a rat, and I've got plans for him when I get out.")

Dana Ewell, Jim Oppliger told the courtroom during closing arguments, gave his family "a hug and a kiss and sent them to die at the hands of a paid executioner."

While Oppliger made no effort to dispute Joel's emotional problems as presented by the defense ("Any man who would pull off this type of crime is going to be abnormal"), he insisted the death penalty was the most appropriate penalty for the two men who had committed this "coldest killing ever."

Oppliger flipped on a slide projector, and let pictures tell the story.

Click.

Glee perched on Dale's lap at a party.

Click.

Tiffany and Glee smiling.

Click.

Tiffany, sprawled dead on the bloody kitchen floor.

Click.

Glee shot full of holes, her arm over her face, keys in her hand.

Click.

And Dale. Letters and newspapers and shattered sunglasses, and a single hole where the bullet that killed him had exited his cheek.

Click.

A surveillance photo of Dana and Joel, waltzing out of a bank together.

"If coldhearted murders such as in this case do not warrant the death penalty," Oppliger asked, "then why have a death penalty at all?"

Peter Jones acknowledged the difficulty in asking for compassion for Dana, "a quality, by your verdict, you decided he is devoid of."

But consider, Jones said, the questionable testimony of Ponce, and the harshness of life in prison.

"There is little mercy in the penalty of life without parole. Hate Dana Ewell if you must, but putting him to death is not the answer here."

As Phillip Cherney, long gray hair pulled back in a ponytail, pleaded for the life of Joel Radovcich, he also pleaded for mercy for Joel's family.

"I say to you if you have feelings for Joel and his family, mercy should be granted. A vote for life in prison does not excuse Joel Radovcich of his crime. It tells him to suffer with his crime every day for the rest of his life."

Cherney read aloud Radovcich's confession and apology as his priest had taken it down. "I know it's only half a cup," he added, "but I pass it to you now."

As jurors dried their tears, Judge Frank Creede began to read ninety-eight separate instructions that would apply to their pending decision.

The jury struggled to agree on the appropriate punishment. On the third day of deliberations, the foreman sent this note to Judge Creede:

> As stated in the court's instructions, the people and the defendant are entitled to the individual opinion of each juror. We have considered the evidence and have each arrived at our own steadfast decision. A unanimous decision is not possible with regards to either defendant. While we do not agree, we respect the decision each of us has made and have deter-

*mined that further discussion would not be produc-
tive.*

The jury, defendants and attorneys were recalled to the
courtroom. Judge Creede polled each juror: Would further
deliberations lead to a verdict? Was there anything the
court could do to help?

A few said further time might help, most said no, one
said, "Not a chance."

Creede asked the jury to keep on trying, but by day's
end, nothing had changed. And nothing had changed by
12:35 P.M., the next day, June 5, when the jury announced
to a crowded courtroom their final voting in the penalty
phase:

In favor of death for Dana Ewell: 11–1
In favor of death for Joel Radovcich: 10–2

Without the required unanimous vote for death, Creede
granted defense motions for a mistrial in the penalty
phase. With that, the attorneys thanked jury members for
their time and dedication. It seemed anticlimactic, but
there it was.

Oppliger told the press he was disappointed with the
mistrial, yet, "Everybody concerned with my office and
the Sheriff's Department is extremely pleased and feeling
victorious."

Souza said, "I feel I did what I had to do, and that was
get a conviction for the people responsible for the Ewell
homicide. This is fine. Either way is fine with me."

For jurors, the penalty phase had been tougher even
than had been the deliberations of guilt. In the first votes,
they had overwhelmingly favored life for Joel and death
for Dana.

"I have a tremendous amount of compassion for Joel
and no compassion for Dana," said one juror.

But a lone juror again held out for Dana. At the same
time, as many jurors pondered the cold brutality of the

crime, they changed their votes to death for Joel. Then, despite heated battles, the vote counts changed no more. Jury foreman Elder sent a final note to Judge Creede, in which he evoked the metaphor and allegory of Phillip Cherney:

> *We have done all that is humanly possible to reach a unanimous verdict but have determined that it is not possible to do so. It is with the sincerest regret that we must accept the reality that our long and arduous journey must end without ever reaching port.*

From the june 30 issue of the *Fresno Bee*:

> Fresno's murder case of the decade, perhaps of the century, ended Friday when prosecutors announced they will not make another attempt to win the death penalty for Dana Ewell and Joel Radovcich.
>
> District Attorney Ed Hunt had relied upon the opinions of the Sheriff's Department, his own office, jurors, and perhaps most important, Ewell relatives, in deciding not to appeal.
>
> "Part of our decision had to do with closure," Jim Oppliger said.
>
> Richard Ewell commented, "It is time for all of us to move on, to end this time of sadness, disconsolation and emotional tension, and this process of uncertainty and strife. It is essential to continue the healing process."

And while Souza didn't press for the execution of Dana and Joel, he did not disagree with the opinion of Sheriff Steve Magarian:

"May Dana Ewell and Joel Radovcich rot in prison for the terrible crime they committed on that beautiful family."

THIRTEEN

"THAT'S IT," SOUZA ANNOUNCED.

He and Sharon and Jim Oppliger and Chris Curtice had gathered on the houseboat topdeck, the vessel anchored out near Mandeville Tip, tucked between a pair of tiny islands. It was a moonless night, the stars plentiful, the tide low, the breeze steady.

Sharon said, "You sure?"

"I've been a cop long enough."

Oppliger tossed Souza a can of beer. "We won't have John Phillip Souza to kick around anymore. But hey, you could do part-time work as a DA investigator."

"We'll see," Souza said.

He cracked open the beer and wiped foam from his knuckles. The aroma of seared catfish and bass wafted over him from the grill. In the distance, he could see the sprawling Point huntclub of the Hilton Hotel family, where every Fourth of July the family launched fireworks from a barge. The horn of a freighter making its way along the channel echoed over the water.

"Right now I want to just sit around and think. Well . . . sit anyway. Just a dumb cop, like Dana said."

"You might be a dumb cop," Oppliger said, "but you're out here in God's country and Dana and Joel are in prison. They'll have plenty of years to do nothing but think."

Souza nodded. "Still," he said, "that's still more than Tiffany got."

The boat deck fell silent, and Souza squeezed his wife's hand and watched for shooting stars.

EPILOGUE

JACK PONCE IS CURRENTLY WORKING AS A CLERK at a Los Angeles law firm, and is expected to graduate from law school in 2000. Members of the Ewell trial jury have pledged to petition to deny Ponce's admittance to the California Bar.

Monica Zent received her law degree from the University of San Diego. After a series of ethics committee hearings to determine her fitness for admission in light of her alleged part in the fleecing of Glee Mitchell's trust account, she was admitted to the California Bar.

Dan Ewell and Ben Ewell remain in Fresno. Richard Ewell returned to the Bay Area, where he resides with his son, Jason, and works as a Web positioning consultant. The brothers, who have had little contact with their sister, Betty, since the trial, have tried to move on while not forgetting the family members they lost. Said Richard, "This tragedy forever changed our spiritual and family beliefs. We strive to honor the memories of Dale, Glee, and Tiffany for the special people they were and for the hearts they touched during their lives."

Betty Ewell Whitted continues to believe in the innocence of her nephew, Dana. FSO detectives believe that a trust set up in her name has distributed monies for Dana's defense, prison commissary fund, and other uses.

"Big Glee" Mitchell died in 1999.

Ernie Burk left the detectives division of the Fresno County Sheriff's Department, returned to patrol work, and has more time to spend with his children.

Fresno County District Attorney Ed Hunt and Chief Criminal Prosecutor Jim Oppliger continue to actively prosecute criminals for the county of Fresno. Oppliger was recently inducted into the prestigious American College of Trial Lawyers. Jeffrey Hammerschmidt retired from the DA's office and joined the law firm of Jory, Peterson, Watkins, and Smith.

"Mad scientist" Allen Boudreau remains at work in the forensic laboratory of the FSO.

Joel Radovcich and Dana Ewell are each serving three consecutive life terms in separate California correctional facilities. They were escorted to prison by John Souza.

Dana continues to maintain his innocence. In letters to his aunt and to Monica Zent's mother, he says he's a new man who has found God. Once released from prison, he insists, he plans to dedicate his life to helping those falsely convicted of crimes. In 1999 he was removed from the Salinas Valley facility after numerous threats on his life, reportedly from prisoners who took umbrage to the nature of his offense, and transferred to Corcoran Prison. Dana shares a six-by-eight-foot cell with a cellmate who was allegedly a hit man for a Mob crime family. Their cell is not far from the ones which secure Charles Manson and Sirhan Sirhan.

Joel was contacted by his lawyer at Souza's urging. Could we talk, Souza asked, just so I might ask a few questions about details we never quite understood? Joel denied Souza's request.

Barring a dramatic legal development, Dana Ewell and Joel Radovcich will die in prison.

Chris Curtice married in 1999, continues to investigate homicides, and recently recorded his second country music CD.

John Phillip Souza retired from the Fresno County Sheriff's Department on October 9, 1998, with a send-off that included hundreds of well-wishers and dozens of state and county officials. He works his farm, is a member of the County Retirement Board, spends time with his wife, Sharon, sons Johnny and Michael, and granddaughter Mikayla. He also works part-time as a DA homicide investigator, is opening a private investigation firm, and occasionally spends a weekend on his houseboat.

The house at 5663 East Park Circle finally sold after eight years on the market.

The body of Dale Ewell was buried at Belmont Memorial Park in Fresno. His daughter was cremated at Dana's request, and the box containing Tiffany's ashes placed on Dale's casket before burial. Glee, too, was cremated. Her remains, sealed in a cardboard box, were picked up by Dana shortly after cremation. The whereabouts of her ashes remain unknown, but Ewell family members believe they were unceremoniously discarded by Dana. The family marker is near a statue of John the Baptist. Two words are etched into the gravestone: TOGETHER FOREVER.

Compelling True Crime Thrillers

PERFECT MURDER, PERFECT TOWN
THE UNCENSORED STORY OF THE JONBENET MURDER AND THE GRAND JURY'S SEARCH FOR THE TRUTH
by Lawrence Schiller
109696-2/ $7.99 US/ $10.99 Can

A CALL FOR JUSTICE
A NEW ENGLAND TOWN'S FIGHT TO KEEP A STONE COLD KILLER IN JAIL
by Denise Lang
78077-1/ $6.50 US/ $8.99 Can

FATAL PHOTOGRAPHS
by Jack R. Nerad
79770-4/ $6.99 US/ $8.99 Can

CLUB FED
A TRUE STORY OF LIFE, LIES, AND CRIME IN THE FEDERAL WITNESS PROTECTION PROGRAM
by George E. Taylor Jr. with Clifford C. Linedecker
79569-8/ $6.99 US/ $8.99 Can

FATAL MATCH
INSIDE THE MIND OF KILLER MILLIONAIRE JOHN DU PONT
by Bill Ordine and Ralph Vigoda
79105-6/ $6.99 US/ $8.99 Can

SECRETS NEVER LIE
THE DEATH OF SARA TOKARS— A SOUTHERN TRAGEDY OF MONEY, MURDER, AND INNOCENCE BETRAYED
by Robin McDonald
77752-5/ $6.99 US/ $8.99 Can

THE GOODFELLA TAPES
by George Anastasia
79637-6/ $5.99 US/ $7.99 Can

The Best in Biographies from Avon Books

JACK AND JACKIE:
Portrait of an American Marriage
by Christopher Andersen
                         73031-6/$6.99 US/$8.99 Can

WALK THIS WAY:
The Autobiography of Aerosmith
by Aerosmith, with Stephen Davis
                         79531-0/ $7.99 US/ $9.99 Can

EINSTEIN: THE LIVES AND TIMES
by Ronald W. Clark
                         01159-X/$7.99 US/$10.50 Can

BLUES ALL AROUND ME: THE
AUTOBIOGRAPHY OF B.B. KING
by B.B. King and David Ritz
                         78781-4/$6.99 US/$8.99 Can

IT'S ALWAYS SOMETHING
by Gilda Radner   71072-2/ $6.99 US/ $8.99 Can

I, TINA *by Tina Turner and Kurt Loder*
                         70097-2/ $6.99 US/ $8.99 Can

....

Available wherever books are sold or please call 1-800-331-3761
to order.   BIO 0200

> INVESTIGATIONS >
> EYEWITNESS ACCOUNTS >
> STRANGE AND UNUSUAL >

**The Field Guide to Bigfoot, Yeti,
and Other Mystery Primates Worldwide**
by Loren Coleman and Patrick Huyghe
Illustrated by Harry Trumbore
80263-5/$12.50 US/$18.50 Can

The Field Guide to Extraterrestrials
by Patrick Huyghe
Illustrated by Harry Trumbore
78128-X/$12.50 US/$16.50 Can

The Field Guide to UFOs
by Dennis Stacy and Patrick Huyghe
Illustrated by Harry Trumbore
80265-1/$13.00 US/$19.95 Can

> *And Coming Soon* >

**The Field Guide to Ghosts
and Other Apparitions Worldwide**
by Hilary Evans and Patrick Huyghe
Illustrated by Harry Trumbore